ARCHETYPES,
IMPRECATORS,
AND
VICTIMS OF FATE

Recent Titles in
Contributions in Afro-American and African Studies

ARCHETYPES, IMPRECATORS, AND VICTIMS OF FATE

Origins and Developments of Satire in Black Drama

FEMI EUBA

Contributions in Afro-American and African Studies, Number 126
Henry Louis Gates, Jr. and John Blassingame, Series Editors

GREENWOOD PRESS

NEW YORK · WESTPORT, CONNECTICUT · LONDON

Library of Congress Cataloging-in-Publication Data

Euba, Femi.
    Archetypes, imprecators, and victims of fate : origins and
developments of satire in Black drama / Femi Euba.
      p. cm. — (Contributions in Afro-American and African
studies, ISSN 0069-9624 ; no. 126)
    Bibliography: p.
    Includes index.
    ISBN 0-313-25557-1 (lib. bdg. : alk. paper)
    1. Drama—Black authors—History and criticism. 2. American
drama—Afro-American authors—History and criticism. 3. Satire—
History and criticism. 4. Esu (Legendary character). 5. Archetypes
in literature. 6. Fate and fatalism in literature. 7. Yoruba
(African people)—Folklore. I. Title. II. Series.
PN1590.B53E93 1989
809.2′896—dc20   89-7542

British Library Cataloguing in Publication Data is available.

Library of Congress Catalog Card Number: 89-7542
ISBN: 0-313-25557-1
ISSN: 0069-9624

First published in 1989

Greenwood Press, Inc.
88 Post Road West, Westport, Connecticut 06881

Printed in the United States of America

The paper used in this book complies with the
Permanent Paper Standard issued by the National
Information Standards Organization (Z39.48-1984).

10 9 8 7 6 5 4 3 2 1

Copyright Acknowledgments

The author and publisher are grateful to the following for granting the use of material:

Excerpts from "Rebels and Sambos: The Search for the Negro's Personality in Slavery," by Kenneth M. Stamp, in *The Journal of Southern History* 37 (August 1971): 391–392. Copyright 1971 by the Southern Historical Association. Reprinted by permission of the Managing Editor.

Excerpts from "Dream on Monkey Mountain" from *Dream on Monkey Mountain and Other Plays* by Derek Walcott. Copyright © 1970 by Derek Walcott. Reprinted by permission of Farrar, Straus and Giroux, Inc.

Excerpts from *Ifa Divination* and *Sixteen Cowries* by William Bascom. Copyright © 1969 and 1980, respectively, by Indiana University Press.

Excerpt from pp. 131–140 of *Selected Plays and Prose of Amiri Baraka/LeRoi Jones*. Copyright © 1979 by Amiri Baraka. Reprinted by permission of William Morrow and Company, Inc.

Excerpts from "Dutchman" and "The Slave" by LeRoi Jones in *Two Plays By LeRoi Jones*. Reprinted by permission of Sterling Lord Literistic, Inc. Copyright © 1964 by LeRoi Jones.

Excerpts from *Black Theater U.S.A.* edited by James V. Hatch. Copyright © 1974 by The Free Press, a Division of Macmillan, Inc. Reprinted by permission of the publisher.

Excerpts from *The Tragedy of King Christophe* by Aime Cesaire. Copyright © Presence Africaine 1963 and 1970. Reprinted by permission of Presence Africaine, and Georges Borchardt, Inc.

Excerpts from "Sizwe Bansi is Dead," in *Sizwe Bansi Is Dead and The Island* by Athol Fugard, John Kani, and Winston Ntshona, Viking-Penguin, 1976. Reprinted by permission of Theatre Communications Group, Inc.

Excerpts from *A Raisin in the Sun* by Lorraine Hansberry, 1966. Reprinted by permission of Random House.

Excerpts from *Ovonramwen Nogbaisi* by Ola Rotimi, 1974. Reprinted by permission of Oxford University Press and Ethiope Publishing Corporation.

Excerpts from *A Play of Giants* by Wole Soyinka, 1984. Reprinted by permission of Brandt & Brandt and Methuen, Inc.

Excerpts from "A Dance of the Forests," in *Collected Plays* by Wole Soyinka, 1973. Reprinted by permission of Oxford University Press.

Excerpts from *Death and the King's Horseman* by Wole Soyinka, 1975. Reprinted by permission of Brandt & Brandt and Methuen, Inc.

Excerpts from *Sortilege* (Black Mystery) by Abdias do Nascimento, 1978. Reprinted by permission of Third World Press.

Excerpts from *Shango de Ima: A Yoruba Mystery Play* by Pepe Carril, 1970. Reprinted by permission of Doubleday.

Excerpts from *Kinjeketile* by E. N. Hussein, 1969. Reprinted by permission of Oxford University Press.

Excerpts from *Monsieur Toussaint* by Edouard Glissant, 1981. Reprinted by permission of Three Continents Press.

Excerpts from *Iyere Ifa: The Deep Chants of Ifa,* translated and edited by Robert Armstrong, et al., 1978. Reprinted by permission of University of Ibadan Press.

For
Alphaeus Sobiyi Euba
and
Winifred Remilekun Euba

Contents

Illustrations

Preface

The idea for this book was gradually conceived through the encouragement and inspirational support that I received from my professor and old friend, Henry Gates, Jr., during my graduate study at Yale University. This almost telepathic support was engendered by a common interest in the obvious force behind the idea, Esu-Elegbara, the West African trickster figure, whose New World cultural affirmation has been the figurative source of Henry Gates' recent book, *The Signifying Monkey*. Telepathy is here appropriately suggested because in Henry Gates I have found some attributes of the trickster god, hence the appellation with which I have sometimes accosted him—the ultimate Afro-American Esu!

Indirectly related to this support was the influence of my mentor and colleague, Wole Soyinka, whose book, *Myth, Literature and the African World,* has been a challenge and a source of determination to me in probing the cultural imperatives of Yoruba metaphysics. Both Henry Gates and I have often argued with him the necessity of accommodating the potential of his patron god, Ogun, within the power house of Esu. More than this, I have often thought that without Mr. Soyinka's shrewd and diplomatic sway as the head of the dramatic arts department at the University of Ife, Nigeria, I would not have been able to take a leave of absence from the university, from 1980 to 1982, to pursue Afro-American studies at Yale.

Several other people have also variously contributed to the realization of this book. Principally, I must thank John Blassingame and Robert Stepto of the Afro-American Studies program at Yale for making the necessary funds possible from Yale for my initial research of Esu in Nigeria; also Robert Farris Thompson, whose enormous interest and inimitable exuberance in the exploration of cross-cultural identifications of blackness in art history have given me extraordinary insight into the fabric of Esu in Africa and the New World. In Nigeria, I wish to express my gratitude to my colleagues at the University of Ife, principally to Oyin Ogunba for his advice and criticism of the early drafts of this work; to Akin Isola, who assisted me in resolving problems with the Yoruba texts; and to Tola Pearce, off whom I constantly bounced my ideas for a reaction from the point of view of her sociological expertise.

My research in Nigeria has been made productive through the cooperation of my informants. Therefore, I would like to thank Oba Joseph Oyediran, the Oniworo of Iworo, Chief Ojomo Josiah Apata, also of Iworo, Babalola Fatoogun, an Ifa priest from Ilobu, Chief Ojeyemi of Ikirun, Babalawo Faloba, of Ile-Ife, Madame Osunponmile of Iragbiji, and several others whom I just incidentally questioned. Furthermore, I would like to thank all the people that have variously assisted in the research or the writing of this work, principally Mrs. Akomolafe, Tunji Ojeyemi, Kemi Eruosanyin, and William Paulson.

Introduction

The search for a definitive concept of "black theatre" has ultimately led to the resources of the Yoruba pantheon of the gods. That the definition of a theatre should be sought in culture and deity is, of course, nothing new. We only need to look at the way the theatre in Western culture can be traced to the mysteries of Dionysus, from which it was possible to derive concepts of tragedy and comedy. Similarly, the origins of European theatre can be said to be located in the church-oriented, God-centered culture of medieval drama. Both these developments, in fact, suggest the ritual beginnings of theatre.

Scholars and practitioners of black theatre also have continued to reach out into the traditional culture in order to locate features of black expression. Plays abound, some of which will be examined later, which attempt to give expression one way or another to the black experience. Critical works that pursue concepts of this experience include Addison Gayle's *The Black Aesthetic,* Errol Hill's collected essays in *The Theatre of Black Americans,* Amiri Baraka's (LeRoi Jones) "The Revolutionary Theatre," Paul Carter Harrison's *The Drama of Nommo,* and Wole Soyinka's *Myth, Literature and the African World.*[1]

Regarding a concept of black theatre such as that I wish to define, Soyinka, for instance, has already set a precedent by locating tragedy in the mysteries of Ogun, the Yoruba god of iron and metallurgy.[2] In Ogun, the creative essence, Soyinka argues, we find the origins of black (Yoruba) tragedy. For he was "the first creative artist (actor), the first suffering deity, first creative energy, first challenger and conqueror of transition"—the transitional gulf between the "chthonic realm" of the gods and the world of humans.[3] However, Soyinka has not specifically explored much beyond his African locality, and it is only by mental extension that his concepts, especially as established in chapter 1 and the appendix, embrace the theatre in the black world.

Although Ogun, according to Soyinka, is the archetype of the tragic artist, I find that the god's attributes and mysteries, theatrically exploratory and effective though they are in richness and depth, are not adequate to unify, or at least attempt to unify, the blacks and their theatrical expression. Such a unification is possible only if we can identify Ogun's myth and worship or similar attributes in all the other black cultures, an endeavor which, though possible, is tedious and perhaps hardly worth the effort.

Rather than that, the attribution I have in mind is one that could engage, or potentially engage, the fate of every black individual as a possible character or artist in a dramatic and theatrical process. Put another way, it is an attribution that could characterize black theatre, African and Afro-American, through certain preoccupations of the artist in the dramatic expression of relationships in black society and the world. Ogun, as a leader of the other gods through the primordial "gulf of transition" in their effort to reunify with humans, their physical counterparts, emerges as a tragic hero, according to Soyinka. At best, as a universal character he has the stuff of which tragic heroes are made. But what characterizes that mettle, which is essentially Yoruba and by extension black, what presupposes his characteristic tragic leadership, is in reality his will. It is a will which is, culturally, a condition of his fate, as will be explained more fully. This will, this fate, it will be argued, is an attribution of another god, Esu-Elegbara, who is therefore more important to Ogun's destructive and creative, indeed tragic, constitution as an artist than has been credited. In this regard, Juana and Deoscoredes Elbein dos Santos' claim that "Elegbara" is sometimes used in Ogun's attribution is noteworthy.[4] As we shall see, it is not the only time Esu has been so instrumental to the fate of Ogun or that of the other gods. This book will attempt to develop a concept in black drama and theatre through the attributes and ritual of Esu-Elegbara, the Yoruba trickster figure, fate god, principle of indeterminacy, lord and controller of mythic time and space and, by derivation, master of peripeteia and satirist.

To establish Esu as I have done and shall subsequently use him, as the fate of every human, demands some justification at the outset. To start with, the Yoruba, from whose culture the god derives, use other names for fate, words that are not necessarily used in connection with Esu. "Ipin," "kadara" and "ayanmo" (ayonmon) seem to be used interchangeably for fate or destiny, and Ori is usually referred to as the god of fate.[5] These concepts are discussed later in relation to Esu. But to complicate the matter further, Esu's evil inclination and trickery as a negative force, even among the Yoruba, seem to be more emphatic and more widely acknowledged than his inclination toward the good, that is, if the latter is admitted at all.[6]

Apart from the fact that this narrow "evil" view has been encouraged by the advent of Christianity, which equated him with the devil, it is easy to see why this should be so. For, as it presumably applies universally, it is human readily to blame our misdeeds on someone else in order to exonerate ourselves and justify our "good" intentions—a justification that probably formulates the doctrine that man is basically good. Thus, Esu-Elegbara is readily seen to be the source of all our evil thoughts and actions, just as the Christian devil is seen. And when the Christian missionaries came, it was easy to convert one into the other. But as we shall see, "evil" is not, in the Yoruba world view, a foreign influencing force of a fallen god or angel, as in Christianity, but something coexistent with good in, and induced by, man.[7] This view, in fact, seemed to have been held in pre-Christian thought, as David Cole observes. Quoting Freud on the ambiguities of good and evil in all divinities, he notes that the devil was "originally one and the same" with the Christian God.[8]

But then evil, as much as good, and like beauty, is subjective. It is partly because of this and partly to acknowledge God's goodness that the Yoruba (Christian Yoruba?) have sayings such as "B'Olorun ba nsere, aa lo nsebi" (literally, "When God is doing good, we often think he is doing evil"). In other words, God's goodness often appears, at first, to be of evil intent; but the outcome eventually reveals it as a blessing in disguise. Even though the expression suggests a possible Christian logic, one cannot fail to see that to apply it in the Yoruba traditional context is to imply the gods' involvement in the good and evil paradox, and that it makes better sense if applied to the god attributed to fate.

For fate, indeed, tends to play humans many tricks, and it seems that it is on account of this trickery that there are many contradictions about fate. On the one hand, there is the problematic, seemingly irreconcilable contradiction between fate and free will, really a contradiction between the will of the gods or God and that of men. It is a contradiction that has produced tragic heroes like Job, Oedipus and Lear. There is also the puzzling question whether fate is fixed or can be changed. On the other hand, in an attempt to come to terms with the calamitous manifestations of fate, some religions would rather attribute accidents, misfortune and even death to demons who attempt to obstruct the process of fate.[9] In Christianity, where man, made in the image of God, is presented as basically good, the responsibility for man's trials and tribulations is given to the devil, the downgraded rebel angel, the outsider against the general scheme and designs of God who, however, controls man's fate. Here, in fact, is one of the discrepancies of the Christian concept of God posed by the problem of evil. For "if God is all-powerful, he must be able to prevent evil. If he is all-good, he must want to prevent evil. But evil exists."[10] The discrepancy poses the question, Who exactly controls fate?

In Yoruba culture, where some of these contradictions apply, it seems on the whole that there is an attempt to resolve them by posing the forces of good and evil as coexistent and complementary, with Esu (or fate) as the controlling unit. This view needs to be argued, as studies generally are not quite clear on the subject, especially when distinctions are made between Esu and the divination principle, Ifa.[11] However, by posing Esu as the devil against the good and evil complementarity we may note that the missionaries and their converts have attempted the impossible. They have considered only the evil part of the complementary unit, which of course renders Esu incomplete. It is like cutting a life force in two. For Esu-Elegbara, as the essence of fate, is an embodiment of good and evil, and it is from this essential unity that the fate of every individual derives. No scholar of Esu, to the best of my knowledge, has fully explored this possibility, and I will later account for it in detail. But the departure, that the god is fate-essence, is noteworthy since it is important to the explication of my concept of satire.

Essays and books on Esu-Elegbara all seem to have a common flaw. They have addressed themselves more to Esu as the Yoruba god of chance, associated with fate, and as a trickster than to his devotees and all those who possess him, by extension the whole of mankind.[12] Consequently, their somewhat limited interpretation cuts away a very important part of the vast resources of Esu. An example, taken at random, will suffice. Highlighting the most common ritual of the god, Robert Thompson, in his book on the rich resources of art in African civilization and the way they have shaped the black cultures of the Americas, says, "Cult officials [of Esu] pour daily offerings of palmoil to maintain Esu's problematic coolness."[13] Thompson, in his characteristically exuberant style, is both literally and metaphorically correct. For palm oil is a cooling and soothing agent (ero), and Esu as a fate god is indeed problematic, what with the tricks and ironies with which he constantly afflicts people. But we must nevertheless not lose sight of the equally true and, indeed, more crucial concern—that is, the devotees' "problematic coolness," which they, or their actions, try to maintain. They have not simply poured their libations on Esu's laterite mound. They have poured them with a desire or favor in view, for which they have verbally or mentally asked. For Esu is no other than our fate—by synecdoche, ourselves. Just as he is inseparable as a complementary unit of good and evil, so is he inseparable from man. And man, as we shall see, "descends," like the gods, into the world (rowaye) with his Esu, that is, with his complementary unit of good and evil, the balance of which he strives constantly to maintain through sacrifices and rituals. Because Esu is thus inseparable, man needs him every minute of the day in all endeavors, and he (Esu) is accordingly invoked consciously by a physical act of libation or by a mental thought or prayer. Again, this problematic factor of the devotee, and therefore the ritual focus on him, is an important departure.

The Esu-human relationship, once established, opens up the vast dramatic components to which this book is committed. For instance, Esu, of all the Yoruba gods, provides the clearest response and the most positive answer to the extended debate among Africanists about whether ritual can be called drama. This is so for the simple reason that Esu stands at the focal point of all rituals and is therefore the most important factor of ritual.[14] This fact is sometimes either taken for granted or never openly acknowledged, or belittled by a misconception of the function of Esu as the messenger of god and man. What fails to be established, however, is that Esu is no mean messenger. For, unlike an ordinary message bearer, he does not have to run any errand under the force of impoverished necessity, but does so on his own terms, an act that sometimes appears wickedly self-centered. To insist on calling him a mere messenger, by calling up support from some of his praise-poems, is to literalize the ironies that Esu himself calls up. But the ironical fact is that, even though he does not ask for much in terms of sacrifices, the god must be adequately propitiated, or the "message" will not get delivered, nor will what is desired be made efficacious. And then in the unpredictable, unfathomable press of circumstances, there is always a possibility that this "delivery" or efficacy, or its opposite, will happen anyway whether he is adequately propitiated or not. Apparently he alone ultimately knows or decides which demands are appropriate and consistent with man's fate, hence the problematic nature of the god. This seems to be a more significant way to conceive him—in Pemberton's words, as "a past master in the trickery of deception."[15]

This messengerial process will in due course be translated in terms of fate. But probing further than this basic traditional sense of Esu, we will find that, at any rate, all rituals are, one way or another, matters of fate or destiny, as the case may be. (There seems to be a distinction between fate and destiny, "fate" being that which is endowed in heaven, and "destiny" being the way that endowment is actually resolved on earth).[16] We wish for a particular need or desire to be made phenomenally efficacious, either for the good and well-being of the community or for the continuity of our personal lives; we wish against all sorts of accidents, unnatural death, ill-health and so on, all of which relate to our fate, and for which Esu is held responsible. Thus, the act of ritual, or of ritualizing a need so as to be efficacious, makes us potential devotees of Esu, and what we wish, in effect, is a change or a maintenance of certain aspects of our fate. Humans are basically so optimistic about their fate, or what they think that fate is or ought to be, that to resign themselves to it is not their first priority. Thus, they constantly attempt to find ways and means to alter or maintain their state of being, consciously or otherwise. It is this optimism that potentially makes every individual a tragic figure.

Indeed, according to Yoruba ontology, these earthly rituals of fate are connected, directly or indirectly, with the first and main ritual of our existence. For the act of "descending" into the world or of being born, a need desired, is prenatally ritualized by a gatekeeper or Onibode, the representative of the Supreme Deity. Each initiate comes to kneel before him to choose his fate, which Onibode then sanctions.[17] This idea is clearly dramatized by Nigeria's leading traditional dramatist, Hubert Ogunde, in his play *Ayanmo*. The question we may ask is, Who exactly is this Onibode sanctioning chosen fates? If it is not Esu himself, is the character not influenced one way or another by the power of the god—since we may go by the examples of Ogun and of the other gods thus influenced? Interestingly, Esu, in some stories, has been referred to as Onibode.[18] He is also praised as Adurogbona (guardian of the gate). These appellations are in fact attributes that probably syncretized him, in the New World, with the Catholic Saint Peter, the keeper of the keys at heaven's gate.[19]

In view of this ritual function, I have proposed Esu, in dramatic terms, not only as the mover of action in the drama of life, but also as master of peripeteia. Indeed, with Esu-Elegbara, we have encroached upon theatre with the least effort. In ritual, as in drama, a conflict is invariably raised. Put another way, ritual, whether physically or mentally, consciously or otherwise performed, presupposes a problematic state of mind which desires either a solution through a change or a maintenance of a certain condition or state of affairs. The ritual is therefore a confrontation or a struggle with fate, which requires a sacrifice. Without a conflict, there is no need for a sacrifice; and sacrifice is the focal point of the drama. Esu, as the sign of fate, is the master of peripeteia and the effector of the denouement.

Besides the plot of the drama, there are the actors. In any ritual, and therefore in the drama, there has to be at least one participant, the character or actor whose fate is in question. But since Esu does not necessarily need a formal and elaborate ceremonial approach by his votaries, or does not necessarily need a chief priest to invoke the god's heroic deed for a community of devotees, the identity of the actor, especially with all the connotations of the word as an imitator, is not as simple as it appears. I shall explain this a little at this point.

The ritual of Esu at the heart of this book, and one that clearly proposes a concept of fate, is the simple daily libations on the red laterite altar of Esu, called "yangi," commonly found at the threshold of a house, at crossroads or at the approach to a market. We can, for instance, consider a devotee who wishes to make his offering to Esu at the beginning of the day. He goes to "yangi," pours libation and prays for a successful turn of events, for a day which is profitable and free of accidents, of hitches and, most significantly, of death. The process of making these requests efficacious involves not only Esu but also other gods or characters; it all depends on what the ritual entails, and which god is attributed or related to the wish desired. For instance, if any apparatus made of iron, like a hoe, a sewing machine, or an automobile, has to be used, Ogun must be approached. There may also be a need to have or to prevent rain, in which case Sango ought to be approached. And for "coolness" and control of temper at moments of exasperation, the presence of the serene and tranquil god, Obatala, may be needed. As a consequence of any of these needs, Esu literally is meant to act as a mediator in favor of his suppliant, or to assuage and win the confidence of the respective powers. In this respect, since he is acting on behalf of the devotee, he is the main actor, the mover of the action which the devotee has simply initiated by his libation and wishes.

But then, in reality, the devotee's supplication is, if we may stretch our imagination a little, an invocation to his own fate through the fate-essence. Without going into the ramifications of the fate process at the moment, we can say that it is an invocation for making certain that his fate or destiny would follow its normal ordained course within the general scheme of things, and also that it would maintain its balance of the complementary units of good and evil.

This perspective shifts or modifies the identity of the actor. For if the invocation of the votary is made to his own fate (to his Esu) in a world of survival, then he is the physical actor, the fate vehicle whose metaphysical entity has acted on behalf of its physical form. But we can even go further to hold that he is an actor in the theatrical sense of the word, since he (the devotee) has invoked, at a theatrical remove, or at an artistic distance, his own fate (the role to be played that day in the world of survival). Invoking this role, this fate, by his offering, he subsequently internalizes it and, like a theatre actor, gains control of it—or so he thinks in terms of the guarantee of the offering. This aspect, as it involves character, will and personality, and eventually satire, will become clear in due course. But as we have identified the drama and the actor, it will be necessary also, to complete the theatrical process, to identify the audience in relation to Esu.

Who, indeed, is the audience? Esu, having been made an offering, must consider the case for his devotee, whether for good or ill. In other words, the devotee must make a case for his own fate. This also will become more clearly seen in relation to character and will. But since, as we have established, several gods might be involved or have to be consulted in the process, depending on the territories or boundaries the devotee might have to travel over on the fateful day, then these deities are the audience whose approval must be sought.[20] They are the metaphysical audience who must be satisfied, and whose "magic" or therapy, through Esu, the devotee requires in the efficacy of the ritual sacrifice or in the denouement of the drama. But there is, in fact, a physical audience. This is the respective devotees of the metaphysical audience, with whom the actor-devotee must interrelate during the course of his eventful (fateful) day. For the efficacy of his wishes depends on the way he interrelates or interacts with them, inducing a type of audience participation. It is important to note that the therapy—the catharsis—has come via the metaphysical audience that has been satisfied, and without whose encouragement and satisfaction the actor does not have control of his character and therefore of his fate. The catharsis has come to the actor, from the metaphysical, and then on to the physical audience who feels the therapy through interaction. As we shall see, the efficacy of this ritual drama, in terms of the satiric process is, as in tragedy, both destructive and restorative.

The foregoing is intended to serve a double purpose. It is a brief introduction to my position in the ongoing argument about whether ritual can be called drama or theatre. In my view, as regards Esu-Elegbara, there can be no argument, since he is the dramatic controller of the most important aspect of ritual and drama, the sacrifice. Soyinka's insight that ritual is the "drama of the gods" further exemplifies this perspective. We can also note the theatrical analogy, made by David Cole, with the ritual experience of the actor-shaman in a trance state.[21] For without sacrifice, there can be no response from the gods— from Cole's "illud tempus" or Soyinka's "chthonic realm." Without a crisis or a focal point of the action, there can be no resolution, and therefore no drama. Without a catharsis, which requires an audience, there can be no theatre.

More important, as an extension of this purpose, this introduction raises a justification for the first part of this book—an exploration of the essence and image of humans in the black world of survival, thereby locating conditions pertinent to their drama. As we shall see, these conditions are necessary to establish the main objective of the book, which is to develop a possible concept of drama in black theatre from the point of view of Esu-Elegbara. If it is clear that the fate god has possibilities for the dramatic and the theatrical, the question we may ask is, What type of theatre does one envisage with Esu? Actually, I have been suggesting this all along.

I stumbled on the god's potential quite by accident a few years back while writing a paper on the mask as a cultural force that has generated dramatic expression and recreativeness in man.[22] In an attempt to transpose the traditional mode and significance of the mask to its recreativeness in the physical features of modern man, I finally turned to myth and the gods for aid.

Following the story of Obatala, the Yoruba god of creation, who while in a palm wine stupor once began molding deformed instead of perfect human beings, I began to question the act of Obatala's drunkenness itself. I tried to match, visually and realistically, the actual potency of the wine with the enormity of the crime committed. Granted that the action is phenomenally magnified and mythically unrealistic, being of a divine nature, nevertheless by the same admission I was forced to think that the wine was no ordinary wine, but one which was manufactured by and which foamed up the energies of another god, a god capable of such a manipulative and peripetic act. It was then I concluded that only Esu-Elegbara, the seemingly mischievous trickster god, was capable of such a turn. Abandoning at once the idea of the god's often misinterpreted mischief, I established the fact that his act was more a way of challenging Obatala's creative genius, a means of making the creation god more aware of his personality and creative potential. This is so especially since, according to the myth, deformed creatures from that time on are considered sacred emanations of Obatala's artistry, an aesthetic factor. I have, since my encounter, identified the deformed images as satiric gestures of Esu, who therefore will be proposed as a master satirist. This would seem to be a departure from the usual conception of him.

In fact, glaring evidences regarding these satiric tendencies abound and are waiting to be explored. Some of them have been mentioned by a few scholars, but in general terms and only in passing. For instance, Joan Wescott, in spite of her questionable analysis of Esu, hits the nail on the head when she says, "He [Esu] is also a satirist who dramatizes the dangers which face men and the follies to which they are prone and as such he serves as a red light warning."[23] But certainly no one has centralized or highlighted Esu's satiric tendency as important and as a characteristic that could help shed some light on a number of issues, whether traditional or modern, physical or mental. For Esu is not only a traditional concept, he is, as implied above, very much with us, and perhaps more usefully so in modern society. As we shall see, we cannot but feel his presence in a world where motor accidents, greed, inhumanity, ruthlessness, deception, and such externalized pressures are persistently prompting the physical and mental states of man to a frenzied awareness, and all of which make satire seem like a very useful weapon to describe the order of the day. Along with these and other dramatic features, I wish to explore Esu-Elegbara as a theatre concept. For he is the controller not only of mythic time and space, but also of the physical world as a stage where (to modify Shakespeare's expression slightly) all men with their various fates are his mere actors.

Therefore, the concept of theatre expressed by Esu, which I propose to call the "Drama of Epidemic," is both ritual and satiric. The concept, I wish to establish, is pertinent to and persistent in black expression. This implies that satire is prevalent in black drama, that this satire derives from cultural influences and that it appropriately describes the black condition of survival, an experience which has preoccupied black theatre practitioners. It, in fact, implies Esu-Elegbara as an archetype of satire and satirist in black drama.

The link between ritual and satire is, of course, not peculiar to Esu. R. C. Elliott, in *The Power of Satire,* has quite successfully traced that link, historically and theoretically, to the Greek, Roman and Irish satirists.[24] This link, we gather, is a function of the poet in the heroic and mythically bound societies, and Archilochus, the Greek poet of the seventh century B.C., is presented as the archetypal figure in the satiric tradition.[25] While not wishing to refute Elliott's conclusions about Archilochus, I would like to take an inspirational cue from him and propose Esu-Elegbara as an archetypal satiric figure in the black tradition. In this regard, a comparison with Archilochus, in the absence of an already established black African or black American figure, is inevitable. But then this is useful, not only to make a case for Esu, but also to place the god on a broader and more universal spectrum, one in which the Greek poet Archilochus or any other Western satiric archetypes may find Esu informative as a divinity of fate embodying the complementary forces of good and evil. Quoting Johan Huizinga that all "antique poetry is at one and the same time ritual, entertainment, artistry, riddle-making, doctrine, persuasion, sorcery, soothsaying, prophesy and competition," Elliott concludes: "In this cultural situation, the poet can hardly be said to compose verses . . . he transmits them. He is inspired, 'breathed into,' by the god."[26] By this observation, Archilochus the satirist-poet would qualify as a devotee of a god like Esu. Archilochus, in fact, was a priest of Demeter, goddess of cultivation, and he often invoked gods like Apollo to aid the efficacy of his satire. What need be argued later, but again with Elliott as a guide, is how fate and the good and evil complementarity both apply to, and are consistent with, the satiric mode.

The attempt to conceptualize the link between ritual and theatre, which Esu's Drama of Epidemic assumes, is also not new. In his Yoruba experience, Soyinka tries to capture, through the rituals of Ogun, the numinous abyss of transition that confronts, convulses and reintegrates the tragic spirit.[27] This he also explores in his plays, for example in *Death and the King's Horseman.* In Western theatrical perspective, motivated by the classical, the Asian and possibly the African, the link has been variously conceived by Friedrich Nietzsche and Antonin Artaud.[28] They both, in general, relate to a "protophenomenon," like an epidemic or a plague, by which the actor intoxicates, affects, or transforms the audience in a dramatic dyadic of participating votaries of the spiritual essence, that is, the officiating god-patron, the director of efficacity. With Nietzsche, satyrs invoke their patron god, Dionysus, for the spectators; with Artaud this vision is transmitted through a delirium which is communicable like a plague or an epidemic.

Considering Esu, I am concerned less with the communicant-community, actor-audience participation, although this cannot be avoided, than with the "epidemic" factor itself, the intoxication that manifests ritual expression in life and in drama—with Esu as the fate agent and fate itself, the intoxicant and the intoxication, the satirist and satire. The medical word "epidemic" in fact has satiric association. In the Renaissance, it was widely used along with other medical terms to describe the efficacious power of satire as both destructive and restorative.[29] This book will examine the "epidemic" power of Esu that not only satirizes but also prompts the mind to take cognizance of its willed fate or destiny in a world of uncertainties. Firmly establishing its concept of satire, the book will also examine factors and victims of Esu's satiric power, first in the dramatic situations in the black world, then in formal drama. Because of its intimations of ritual and fate, satire, I hope to suggest, is traditionally and historically an inevitable factor of black survival and its expression in drama.

The other clarification that needs to be made at this point concerns the votary. Ultimately, the question must be raised about the seemingly generalized span of the cultural milieu identified with Esu. To be sure, he originates from the Yoruba culture which, by extension, would include only a fractional although significant part of the African ancestry in the Americas, which includes Brazil, Cuba, Haiti, Trinidad and some parts of North America. Apart from the fact that there is possibly an Esu figure in every traditional and heroic culture where there is also a fatalistic view of life similar to that of the Yoruba; apart from the cults of Esu or Legba across West Africa and the New World; apart from the fact that there may be trickster figures in other cultures, like the Zande culture, whose potentials are still waiting to be explored; apart from the fact that there are forces associated with fate, like Nommo of the Bantu metaphysics, that may qualify as satiric archetypes; apart from all these considerations, I have preferred to use the word "black" to include the blacks in Africa and the Americas for other reasons.[30] Historically, they all have been conditioned by similar experiences in terms of slavery, racism, colonization and missionary evangelism. Living through one or all of these contacts with European civilization has had its many fated and fatal effects on blacks and their culture. For instance, one of the common effects of the impact of European civilization upon African civilization is the conditioning of black religion by Christianity, which, for various reasons, identified the devil in traditional worship. This, in effect, implicates not only traditional religion but also, significantly for my purposes, the character, personality, and fate of the black person. For traditional religion is inseparable from its culture. By identifying the devil in African religions, the colonizers regarded black culture as hostile and devil-conditioned. Consequently, blacks were characterized as devil, satan, savage, cannibal, slave, and so on.[31] This image of the black has been exploited not only in Africa by the missionaries, but also, perhaps more emphatically, by the white culture into which the black slaves were taken in the Americas.[32] And the case of the oppression of blacks in South Africa is still very much with us.

Since Esu-Elegbara is one such cultural figure that seemingly has undergone a Christian transformation or rebirth, which identified him with the medieval devil, I have taken liberties in letting him speak for the endurance and solidarity of the black in the face of such misconceptions.

The survival of the black has taken many forms. It has, for instance, taken the form of resistance to foreign influence. It has taken the form of submission or assimilation. And where and when foreign influence gained ground, survival, later, has taken the form of agitation for freedom from slavery or from foreign domination. But it has also taken the form of struggle against the "evils" of black rule, such as neocolonialism. There is also the subtle means of survival—the implications of which are not often considered fully—in the form of rather deceptive compliance with or acceptance of foreign power and acculturation. I am referring to the inevitable but rather deceptive syncretism of black and foreign culture and religion in Africa and the Americas.[33]

Although Esu, it can be argued, speaks for all these forms of survival, it is this last form, the deceptive compliance of syncretism, which probably is the most consistent with his attributes, and also the most explorative. For, in spite of the fact that the missionaries branded him as the devil, and by so doing have won many converts, they have not really succeeded in luring his people away from him, judging by the many Christians who still seek him, albeit indirectly, through the Ifa oracle or Voodoo. Indeed, sentiments toward traditional religion from Christian converts have not really changed since Frobenius' observation:

Wherever a missionary has set his foot, the folks today talk of the Devil, Edju. Yet, go into the compounds, talk to them kindly and they will tell you: Ah, yes! Edju played many tricks . . . but Edju is not evil. He brought us the best of all there is; he gave us the Ifa oracle.[34]

The manipulation of the Christian belief with traditional processes, prevalent in the syncretic religious sects like the Aladura in Nigeria, would seem to support this. We could also consider the case of the slaves in the New World who continued to worship the "divine trickster" in the Protestant and Catholic sects.[35] In order to comply with the wishes of their Christian masters they represented Esu, for instance, as Saint Peter. But the ironic fact is that, for the slave, the focal object of worship was not the physical Christian saint but the mental presence of the African god. And there is even the case of the survival of the Black Church in North America, which seemingly assimilated the Christian doctrine completely but only to establish its own brand of worship with obvious African influences. Syncretism, therefore, was a ruse for the survival of the black slave, and it is consistent with the ironies and satiric subtleties of Esu which, as already stated, are usually misconceived or offhandedly regarded as simply pranks.

As a consequence of these "elegbarine" ironies of the worshipper and the worshipped, the present work tries to reexamine the role of Sambo in North American slavery in relation to the role of Esu in the black world. More important, the black writer's creative potential, as a devotee of Esu, is examined through his or her dramatic expression in relation to the ritual and satiric concept of the god. But such a consideration can be possible only after a firm analysis of Esu's fateful and fatal implications and manifestations, and the impact of these on his people as victims of fate and satire.

The satiric concept of Esu-Elegbara relates, first and foremost, to the theatre of the black. However, theatre really should hold no cultural boundaries. Therefore, it is my hope that this work will also be a contribution to the inexhaustible theories on theatre, specifically concepts on the role of ritual and satire in culture and drama. For the drama of Esu-Elegbara is nothing more than a drama that is committed to expose a social disease and by so doing affect the sensibilities of the afflicted society or culture, in this case the black culture. For Esu, as much as a satirist, is more than just a fate-manipulating intermediary of sacrifices between gods and men. On the other hand, this "epidemic" concept of theatre, according to Antonin Artaud, is not limited to any one kind of theatre. He says, "In a true theatre a play disturbs the senses' repose, frees the repressed unconscious, incites a kind of virtual revolt . . . and imposes on the assembled collectivity an attitude that is both difficult and heroic."[36] This archetypal function of the theatre through drama I shall try to express, and hope to make clearer, with Esu-Elegbara who, to my mind, has unlimited resources for the theatre of the black as well as theatre as a whole.

NOTES

1. Addison Gayle, ed., *The Black Aesthetic* (New York: Doubleday, 1971); Errol Hill, ed., *The Theatre of Black Americans,* 2 vols. (Englewood Cliffs, N.J.: Prentice-Hall, 1980); Amiri Baraka [LeRoi Jones], "The Revolutionary Theatre," in *Selected Plays and Prose of Amiri Baraka/LeRoi Jones* (New York: William Morrow, 1979), 130–133. Originally printed in Amiri Baraka, *Home, Social Essays* (New York: William Morrow, 1966), 210–215; Paul Carter Harrison, *The Drama of Nommo* (New York: Grove Press, 1972); Wole Soyinka, *Myth, Literature and the African World* (Cambridge, England: Cambridge University Press, 1976).

2. Soyinka, *Myth, Literature,* 140–160.

3. Ibid., 6.

4. See Juana E. and Deoscoredes M. dos Santos, *Esu Bara Laroye* (Ibadan, Nigeria: Institute of African Studies, University of Ibadan, 1971), 28.

5. See R. C. Abraham, *Dictionary of Modern Yoruba* (London: University of London Press, 1958), 86, 357, 555; also Wande Abimbola, *Ifa: An Exposition of Ifa Literary Corpus* (Ibadan, Nigeria: Oxford University Press, 1976), 113. On Ori as fate god, see Abraham, *Dictionary of Modern Yoruba,* 480–481; Abimbula, *Ifa,* 113–116.

6. See S. Johnson, *The History of the Yorubas* (London: Routledge and Kegan Paul, 1921), 22; D. O. Epega, *The Basis of Yoruba Religion* (Lagos, Nigeria: Ijamido Printers, 1932), 26; G. J. A. Ojo, *Yoruba Culture: A Geographical Analysis* (Ile-Ife, Nigeria: University of Ife Press; London: University of London Press, 1966), 179.

7. See Morton-Williams' observation on this from an Ogboni cult thought in "The Yoruba Ogboni in Oyo," *Africa* 30, no. 4 (1960): 373.

8. David Cole, *The Theatrical Event* (Middletown, Conn.: Wesleyan University Press, 1975), 65–66.

9. For various concepts of fate, see S.G.F. Brandon, ed., *A Dictionary of Comparative Religion* (New York: Charles Scribner's Sons, 1970), 280–281. For views on the changeable aspects of fate in Yoruba culture, see W. R. Bascom, "Social Status, Wealth and Individual Differences Among the Yoruba," *American Anthropologist* 53 (1971): 490–505; W. R. Bascom, "Yoruba Concepts of Soul," in *Men and Cultures,* ed. A. F. C. Wallace (Pittsburgh: University of Pennsylvania Press, 1960), 401–410.

10. See "Evil, The Problem of," in *Encyclopedia of Philosophy,* 8 vols., ed. Paul Edwards (New York: The Free Press, 1967), 3:136–139.

11. See, for example, Abimbola, *Ifa,* 9, 36–37, 142–145.

12. Studies on Esu include Ayodele Ogundipe, *Esu Elegbara, the Yoruba God of Chance and Uncertainty,* 2 vols. (Ann Arbor: UMI, 1978); John Pemberton, "Eshu-Elegba: The Yoruba Trickster God," *African Arts* 9 (1975), 21–27, 66–70, 90–91; Robert D. Pelton, *The Trickster in West Africa: A Study of Mythic Irony and Sacred Delight* (Los Angeles: University of California Press, 1980); Pierre Verger, *Notes sur le culte des Orisa et Vodun a Bahie de tous les Saints, au Bresil et a l'ancienne Cote des Esclaves en Afrique, Memoires de L'Institut Français d'Afrique Noire* 51 (Dakar: IFAN, 1957); Joan Wescott, "The Sculpture and Myths of Eshu-Elegba, the Yoruba Trickster," *Africa* 32, no. 4 (1962): 336–353.

13. Robert F. Thompson, *Flash of the Spirit: African and Afro-American Art and Philosophy* (New York: Random House, 1983), 21.

14. For the various Ifa verses that relate the efficacious outcome of sacrifices to Esu, see W. R. Bascom, *Ifa Divination: Communication Between Gods and Men in Africa* (Bloomington: Indiana University Press, 1969), e.g., verses 1–10 and 11, 14-1, 131-1, 244-1 and 244-2, etc.; W. R. Bascom, *Sixteen Cowries: Yoruba Divination from Africa to the New World* (Bloomington: Indiana University Press, 1980), verses A5, A15, A37, C18, H8, etc.; Abimbola, *Ifa,* 142–145.

15. Pemberton, "Eshu-Elegba," 25.

16. See Brandon, *Dictionary of Comparative Religion,* 281.

17. See Bolaji Idowu, *Olodumare: God in Yoruba Belief* (London: Longmans, Green, 1962), 174.

18. See Ogundipe, *Esu Elegbara,* 2:20, 2:34, lines 89–92.

19. See James Haskins, *Witchcraft, Mysticism and Magic in the Black World* (New York: Doubleday, 1974), 50.

20. Compare shaman-hungan process: Cole, *Theatrical Event,* chaps. 2, 3.

21. Ibid.

22. Femi Euba, "Of Masks and Men," unpublished paper for seminar on "The

Interrelationship of the Arts in Nigeria,'' University of Lagos, Centre for Cultural Studies, 1978.

23. Wescott, "Sculpture and Myths,'' 345.

24. Robert C. Elliott, *The Power of Satire: Magic, Ritual, Art* (Princeton, N.J.: Princeton University Press, 1960).

25. Ibid., 3–12.

26. Ibid., 10.

27. Soyinka, *Myth, Literature,* 140–160, esp. 149–150.

28. F. Nietzsche, "The Birth of Tragedy,'' in *The Philosophy of Nietzsche,* trans. C. P. Fadiman (New York: Random House, 1927), 951–1088; A. Artaud, *The Theatre and Its Double,* trans. M. C. Richard (New York: Grove Press, 1958).

29. See Mary C. Randolph, "The Medical Concept in English Renaissance Satiric Theory: Its Possible Relationships and Implications,'' *Studies in Philology* 38, no. 2 (1941): 125–157.

30. On the Zande trickster, see E. E. Evans-Pritchard, *The Zande Trickster* (Oxford: Clarendon Press, 1967); also Andre Singer and Brian V. Street, eds., *Zande Themes: Essays Presented to Sir Edward Evans-Pritchard* (Totowa, N.J.: Rowman and Littlefield, 1972), chap. 5. For aesthetic interpretation of Nommo, see Harrison, *Drama of Nommo.*

31. For a survey of the attitude of Europeans to black slaves, see A. J. Barker, *The African Link: British Attitudes to the Slaves in the Era of the Atlantic Slave Trade, 1550–1807* (Totowa, N.J.: Frank Cass, 1978); also Katherine George, "The Civilized West Looks at Primitive Africa, 1400–1800,'' in *The Concept of the Primitive,* ed. A. Montagu (New York: Free Press, 1968), 175–193.

32. See George, "The Civilized West Looks at Primitive Africa,'' Barker, *The African Link.* Also John Blassingame, *The Slave Community,* rev. and enl. ed. (New York: Oxford University Press, 1979); W. R. Bascom, "Eighteenth Century Slaves as Advertised by Their Masters,'' *Journal of Negro History* 1 (1916): 165–216; Eugene D. Genovese, *Roll, Jordan, Roll: The World the Slaves Made* (New York: Pantheon Books, 1974).

33. On deceptive syncretism, see Haskins, *Witchcraft, Mysticism and Magic;* Geoffrey Parrinder, *Religion in an African City* (Westport, Conn.: Negro Universities Press, 1972); Roger Bastide, *The African Religions of Brazil,* trans. H. Sebba (Baltimore: Johns Hopkins University Press, 1978); George E. Simpson, *Black Religions in the New World* (New York: Columbia University Press, 1978).

34. Leo Frobenuis, *The Voice of Africa,* 2 vols. (London: Hutchinson and Co., 1913), 2:229.

35. See Haskins, *Witchcraft, Mysticism and Magic,* 50–55; Robert Tallant, *Voodoo in New Orleans* (New York: Macmillan-Collier Books, 1962), 49–50; Maya Deren, *Divine Horsemen: Voodoo Gods of Haiti* (New York: Dell, 1970).

36. Artaud, *Theatre and Its Double,* 28.

I

ORIGINS

1

Concepts of Fate

When David Worcester describes satire as "The Proteus of Literature,"[1] the image evoked suggests not only the many guises in form assumed by the genre, which in fact are almost all the other literary forms, but also that often elusive power of satire that compels and sustains its impact. This is analogous to the efficacious power of ritual which, as Elliott has elaborately argued, is both magical and artistic. It is the power that has also given this book its main thrust in the consideration of Esu-Elegbara's potential. My objective will be to come to terms with satire as an expression and ritual power of the Yoruba divine trickster and god of fate. As implied in the introduction, to say this is of course to assume immediately that satire involves the fate of the individual. Therefore, before getting into Esu's satiric vein, it seems imperative to first establish the deity, in all his capacities, not only as one whose design is to control the fate of mankind, but also as fate itself, that is, the essence. In doing this, I shall rely heavily on theories and narratives of Esu collected by other scholars and found in the Ifa literary corpus; also on interviews with the devotees of Esu, from whom I learnt a great deal about their relationship with their god and about aspects of his fast-dying-out festival. I must, however, reiterate that the ritual of worship that is fundamental to this analysis and concept of satire, one that most vividly projects perspectives of fate in relation to his devotees— indeed to mankind—is the simple act of libation on Esu's laterite symbol, "yangi." This is the commonest but most important ritual for Esu, whether as a daily supplication with the coolant palm oil, or as a special worship at festivals with the sacrificial blood of a dog (aja), of a pig (elede) or of a he-goat (oruko).

In identifying Esu-Elegbara as fate god or fate-essence, it would seem a pointless endeavor to try to locate his place of origin, as has been suggested severally not only by scholars of Esu but by his devotees, who inform the scholars. For instance, M. Baudin, an early Africanist inquirer writing in the late nineteenth century and noted, more recently, by the Brazilian-Yoruba scholar, Pierre Verger, identifies a village in Badagry, Woro (Iworo), as the place where Esu and his worship originated.[2] A. B. Ellis, another early ethnographer, however, places Esu's original dwelling on the top of a mountain near Igbeti and close to the River Niger.[3] Among other places suggested more recently by researchers and their informants are Ofa-Ile (Idowu), Ife-Wara and Ketu.[4] All these locations are within the Yoruba community in the western part of Nigeria.

Along with this quest for origin there has naturally been one for parentage. The curiosity accorded both ideas is by no means unjustified; but reasons for such endeavors and confusion of locations can easily be proposed. Because of the nature of oral tradition, in its verbal progression from generation to generation, there seems to have been an irreconcilable confusion of the historical and the mythical. This is quite apart from the tendency, inherent in tradition, to have various versions of the same mythic theme, for instance, variations on the theme of creation. In this regard, historical figures may have been identified with mythical evocations of the deities—although, conversely, it is possible to have a historical figure deified.[5] In a similar vein, again by way of oral tradition, significant representatives or devotees of gods may have not only acquired their god's characteristics and performed his feats but also assumed or "become" their god, having been confused with and identified as the original god somehow along the developing process of oral tradition. These two tendencies may indeed account for the various origins, birthplaces and parentage acquired by the same god among devotees.

Following this theory, I suggest that the various praise-names and stories that have identified various places of origin for Esu (Woro, Igbeti, Ketu) may have been the result of fusion, in oral tradition, of accumulated praises and identity of various Esu figures (kings, priests, etc.) over the years. However, although this accumulated tradition of narratives may have blurred the real origin and parentage, it has nevertheless more likely crystallized and made more concrete the character and persona of the original Esu. But then there is support in his literature anyway for the existence of many Esus, since he seems to have the power to propagate himself. For instance, Juana and Deoscoredes dos Santos records a symbolic myth of this power in which Esu is hacked into many laterite components of "yangi" which then become his representatives,[6] hence the various forms of Esu, such as Esu-orita (of the crossroads), Esu-ona (of the way), Esu-oja (of the market), etc. The question one may ask, therefore, is, Who or what is the original Esu? Who or what is he that, like any other god, devotees have identified with him and have sometimes become the god, assuming his praises, his worship, his cult?

The objective of establishing Esu as god of fate and fate-essence has not, on the whole, favored any historical or euhemeristic construct, which can only make nonsense of place origins. Rather, I have sought for insights from mythical origins which have been handed down as symbolic expressions of mythmakers. For fate is nothing human, nothing palpable or visible, like water, iron or lightning, elements by which some of the other gods are known. And, as implied, human representatives of gods were a later development—which included the historical crowning as kings and deification of personages like Ogun and Sango, gods of iron and thunder, respectively. If we regard myth as an imaginative and poetic expression of natural or religious phenomena, Esu as fate and as a mythical expression existed before Esu of Woro, of Ife-Wara, or of Ketu. When one of my informants describes him as an "alijonu," a spirit, which appears and moves like an "efuufu," a light misty wind,[7] the implication of a mysterious power or force is nearer my concept than the Alaketu of Ketu—an appellation which gives him a human identity as the first king of Ketu and as ancestor of the Egba kings.[8]

But mythical origins also have their setbacks. We can assume that Esu, whoever or whatever he is, "descended" with the rest of the gods. Supposedly they descended, like rain (rowaye), at the time they did, from the sky-world (Ode Isalorun) to the earth-world (Ode Isalaye).[9] But exactly in what form Esu descended, in that dramatic mission to strike the earth-world into existence, is difficult to say. In fact, the form and descent of the other gods are also questionable. One myth, along with its variations, relates the descent of the gods in a quest to reunite with humans, a mission from which Ogun emerged as the brave leader who cleared the path through the hostile chaos that confronted them.[10] This myth assumes a sky-world and an earth-world already in existence. It would also seem to assume a prior consciousness of certain personages, or the mythopoeic processing of them, as gods. But we cannot be too analytic as regards the logicality of myths.

However, another myth, perhaps more common than the previous, attempts a more systematic approach at creation. Although it too assumes the prior existence of the gods in the sky-world, the earth-world was, on the other hand, nothing but an expanse of water. Also, in its more common versions, Obatala, or Oduduwa,[11] is the only god mentioned directly as being involved in the initial creation process, although the presence of other gods can be argued, especially that of Esu, since he concerns us here.

Indeed, neither of the two myths mentions the name Esu, and it is only by an indirect analysis that we are able to establish his mythical identity. But the argument is by no means obvious or easy. Regarding this identity, it seems we must bear in mind some uncommon but traditionally held views about Esu concerning the creation process, although these views have been left virtually unexplained.

First is the idea that Esu not only came with the rest of the gods, but also that each god, when he came down, did so with his Esu, as one of my informants reflected.[12] If this is so, then second is the idea that Esu must have descended with Obatala or Oduduwa when he came down on the creation mission—an Esu known in Ifa as Esu Obasin.[13] And third is the more commonly held view that Esu is some sort of messenger of both gods and men.

Also, we may note among his devotees the belief that Esu, of all the gods, is the first to exist, created by the High God, Oludumare. These views are all related, directly or indirectly, to the subject of fate, and with these in mind, I shall proceed to examine the creation myths specified above, beginning with the Obatala myth because it seems to precede the other in a logical narrative sequence, although not necessarily so mythologically; also because an analysis of it can easily explain the other in terms of one of the projected ideas on Esu.

The central action of the Obatala myth, in the most common version of it, attributes the creation of the living-world to Obatala—here distinction is made between the "earth-world" before the creation and the "living-world" after the creation of land. Obatala descended from the sky-world with all the creation implements: an iron chain with which he descended or gave a base to earth, a mound of soil in a container, and a fowl. With these he began the creation process. He put the mound (mountain?) of soil on the surface of the watery expanse and asked the fowl to spread it in many directions.[14]

However, some other records of this version introduce another element in the descent: the chameleon.[15] On the surface, this character seems particularly intrusive. Neither the myth nor its creative interpretation has, it appears, directly explained how exactly we are to conceive the figure, or what symbolic value and function we are to derive from it—that is, other than just being another animal which must eventually cohabit with man in the beginning of the world. But man, unless Obatala represents both man and god, was not yet on the creation scene, which makes the animal representations all the more significant. For if we are to regard myth as a symbolic distillation of a much larger process or deeper meaning, and its represented elements and personages as symbols of thought, based on the present reality of the mythmaker,[16] we cannot be content with waving off the chameleon as an exotic or extravagant reflection of the mythmaker. Rather, we can presume that the chameleon, as well as the cock, has been chosen or conceived, not necessarily consciously, with a particular function and value in mind. And in fact, with a stretch of the imagination as fertile as that of the mythmaker, we will find, looking at some of the available versions, and with a backing of cultural realities, that there are clues that could explain this function and value.

In one version, recorded by G. A. Ojo, the chameleon was sent down as an explorer-forerunner, "to find out whether it was safe to walk the liquid surface below."[17] In another version, recorded by William Bascom, the chameleon actually came down with Odua (Oduduwa) "to create the earth on the primeval waters" and subsequently took the otherwise fatal task upon itself—"threw the earth (soil) on the water and placed the five-toed fowl on it."[18] In yet another version, in a story recorded by Ayodele Ogundipe, the chameleon was sent and returned to give a critique of Obatala's performance. The report, or the appraisal, does not favor the god, for it objectively reveals some "human" weakness in Obatala's character—on reaching the place of mission, he became susceptible to palm wine and got drunk, consequently leaving the mission unaccomplished, which Oduduwa finished for him.[19]

Interestingly, it is in this third version that Esu seems directly involved in the creation process. In the tale, it was he that had brought about (effected) the awareness of the unaccomplished mission and, therefore, Obatala's weakness. It was he who produced the wine for what seems a subjective reason—as retaliation on Obatala's boastful nature for having been chosen by the Supreme Deity to perform the all-important task of creation. This will be explored further after probing the identity of the chameleon.

According to Bascom's narrative (the second version), it is unclear who actually gave the command to spread the earth. But if, according to the story, the chameleon apparently knew what to do by placing the soil on the water and putting the hornbill on it, it seems redundant that Odua should give the order, unless this order was under the foresightful, directing impulse of the chameleon. For *it* had not only come, previously, to explore and assess the situation on earth, according to Ojo's version, but also, in a version recorded by Idowu, sanctioned the accomplishment of operations as the overseer for Olodumare, the Supreme Deity.[20]

What becomes increasingly clear as most important in all the versions noted here is that the fate of the habitation of gods, and subsequently humans and animals in the living-world, was critically observed and resolved by a chameleon. In other words, the efficacy of the mission rested with the chameleon. With this idea, we can now consider further the direct involvement of Esu in the third version—the story recorded by A. Ogundipe. In this version, the chameleon serves primarily as a sort of critic, and its relationship with Esu is particularly suspicious. Obatala boasts of being chosen for the mission to create the earth. Esu wishes to teach him a lesson or to make him aware of the fallible, undesirable trait in his character, that is, his vanity. When Obatala does not return, the chameleon is sent to inquire and to report back about the success or failure of his mission. The chameleon finds out this failure to return is due to Obatala's drunken misdemeanor, and he reports accordingly. Esu is sent to confirm this. The question one may well ask is this: Who sanctioned the quest of the chameleon in the first place? If Esu, who masterminded the trap for Obatala, knew that the chameleon was not going to be helpful in the ploy, would he have favored the inquiring mission of the chameleon? Would he not, trickster that he is, have counteracted the mission somehow? Esu surely must know that the animal is capable of giving a faithful account of his strategy. Or are Esu and the chameleon one and the same? Is the chameleon an instrument or a transformation of Esu? We shall have to take the chameleon's "art" and its cultural interpretations into consideration.

It must remain a mythic mystery and marvel that the slow-legged though prideful chameleon should be the forerunner that traversed the sky-world and the earth-world on a surveying mission. In terms of pride, perhaps, it was a more than adequate match for Obatala's vainglory. Bolaji Idowu suggests that it was chosen "on the merit of [the] extraordinary carefulness and delicacy with which it moves about and [the] still [more] extraordinary way in which it can take in [that is, assess] any situation immediately."[21] More mysterious and marvelous is that *it* actually willed the action of scattering earth on the liquid surface, an act which seems to have been magically and artfully accomplished in the twinkling of an eye. But the "art" as against the seeming physical insignificance is a counterposing irony that one constantly meets as characteristic of Esu, let alone the also similar messengerial role; as Idowu notes, the chameleon is regarded as the messenger of Olodumare.[22] The irony of the chameleon's physical slowness, as against the supernaturally unfathomable spitfire agility and timeless speed with which its willed creation of the living-world was accomplished, in fact recalls the ironies of Esu's physical and mysterious size:

> Esu sleeps in the house
> But the house is too small for him;
> Esu sleeps on the front yard
> But the yard is too constricting for him;
> Esu sleeps in the palm-nut shell
> Now he has enough room to stretch at large.[23]

And it would hardly seem accidental when one of my informants attributed Esu's skin color to that of the chameleon *(Alawo agemo)* which links their art of camouflage.

It is indeed an important fact to bear in mind, this power of deception over human and animal vision. For, like the process of fate, to grasp or identify the features of the chameleon in the process of its camouflaging phenomenon is subject to chance. It is a phenomenon that has since made the animal an "ojiji firifiri,"[24] a shadowy creature, now visible, now invisible. It is also a phenomenon that gives it privileges of power, tolerated by Olodumare, over humans as well as gods, as suggested by the Yoruba saying, "Aba ti alagemo ba tida, oun ni orisa oke ngba" (The High God accepts whatever proposal the chameleon fancies to make).[25] Because of this, one could call him an indulged child of Olodumare.

In this respect, its significance in the creation myth becomes clearer. It is an essential, elusive power, endowed by the High God, that willed Obatala, and without which Obatala seems powerless. And if we take Idowu seriously, if only for a moment, and regard the chameleon as "the messenger of Olodumare or the messenger of Orisa-nla,"[26] then we can note that the messenger whose lord and master accepts the proposals the messenger fancies to make is no mean messenger—this is also a virtue of Esu, as we shall see. But considering the creation phenomenon further, it also makes sense that Esu should be the one to point out the facts and mechanics of "power," by showing up Obatala's weakness through the palm wine test, through the chameleon, and through his (Esu's) equally mysterious art—as recorded in Ogundipe's story. In other words, the power describes Obatala's character, his creative individuality, and yet his fate conditioned by that character and individuality. And as we shall see, it will not be the first time Esu describes Obatala's fate, nor is Obatala alone; Ogun's, Sango's, in fact every god's fate is thus described.

The chameleon phenomenon as a symbolic power of fate receives its fullest recognition in a cult that projects it as an "essential" dynamic—in the Agemo cult of the Ijebu townships of Ogun State in Nigeria.[27] It is a power that, according to Oyin Ogunba, represents the inscrutable High God of the Ijebu Yorubas, a force that "has the right of the road. The uninitiated cannot risk looking at the divine radiance of the almighty."[28] But the possible identification of Agemo with, or as a symbol of, fate goes further than the shared quality of being elusive. Its very color deception, its magical power, suggests the unpredictability of fate—it "assumes any color he pleases and, by implication, any temper he pleases."[29] Ojo also notes that this reptile is said to dictate whatever color it wants at a particular time. "Therefore it was used as an ingredient in making the medicine for a wish or a curse, because God would accept the demands made by the user just as he always accepted the color-change of the chameleon."[30] This elusiveness and unpredictability, which is a demonstration of the chameleon's power, often manifests for his votaries a test of strength and will or, in other words, a testing of each other's fate in terms of power struggle and survival.[31]

The link of the chameleon with fate is therefore conceivable through the elusive, unpredictable and fatal power which it possesses, and which makes it seem to assume the inscrutable "radiance of the Almighty," the Supreme Deity. As a mythological symbol, it completes, in the creation myths, the essential elements in the creation process: Obatala, the pioneer personage or god (the actor) to whom the responsibility is given to create the living-world; the structural materials, iron—which Obatala also used to descend—and earth (soil); the fowl, the mechanism which helps to do the work; and, perhaps most important, the chameleon, the power necessary to activate the props. It is the power that decides or controls the success or failure of the mission, the power whose pronouncement or directive, or "word," through Obatala, is law. This is the will and fate of Obatala—the motivation, the commanding will, the creative potential of Obatala.

The chameleon is therefore the symbolic factor of the fate of Obatala on which the creation of the living-world rests. It is possible to see more clearly now why Esu, also a fate power from whom, supposedly, various fates emanate, should be connected with Obatala's alcoholic weakness, found out and reported by the chameleon, as in the tale recorded by Ogundipe. However, this fateful and fatal power and its link with Esu has not been formerly explained, other than by what has so far been proposed—that Esu, as fate god, must have been involved in the creation process, which decided the fate of the liquid surface of the primordial world. The question arises, Is the chameleon therefore a symbol of Esu?

There is no praise-name or story, or any known reference, that directly links the chameleon with the fate god. Neither does the Agemo cult associate its High God with Esu or his devotees, although it is possible, and most likely, that Esu is reckoned with one way or another, since it is generally acknowledged that nothing is done without him. But if the Agemo cult, or any traditionalist for that matter, should resist any possible link, we can at least attempt to propose an aesthetic link in the interest of the concept this book proposes. But we must reiterate that it is possible that the same power is worshipped under different names in different localities within the same ethnic group. A case in point is the Agemo, "once the supreme deity, the high god" in Ijebuland. The implication here is a power that parallels that of Olodumare, who is generally considered the Supreme Deity. However, this chameleon power still further implicates the power of Esu. As will be suggested, it is possible to alternate the power of Olodumare or Olorun with that of Obatala, Esu, or any of the principal gods, depending on the cultic emphasis. Therefore, by making parallels and similarities in references, an indirect association may be made, an association that is meant to suggest, imaginatively and metaphorically, rather than to assert.

I have already made one link between the color of Esu's skin and the camouflaging power of the chameleon. As noted, there are many references in the Esu corpus, whether praise-names or stories, that suggest his elusive and deceptive nature, which also suggest his magical feat. There are common references like "He who can will his height short and tall, who can manipulate himself tall or short," as well as ironic references like "Having thrown a stone yesterday / He kills a bird today," or its reverse, "Having thrown a stone today / he kills a bird yesterday."[32] In fact, this magical aspect has misled many scholars who see him as mainly a trickster and therefore find parallels between him and the Greek god Hermes.[33] But the difference is clear, for Esu is more than a trickster, more than Hermes, a "cattle-thief," and his mere "tricks."

What makes the link worth attempting at all is an observation on the creation myth made by one of my informants. He said, unprodded and without equivocation, that Oduduwa descended, on his mission, bringing with him a cock, a container of sand, and an Esu.[34] The remark, made by an Elesu, a devotee of Esu, is undoubtedly a cultic concept of creation. But with regard to the views I have been considering, the insight is quite revealing, and one that singlehandedly and imaginatively puts the creation process into perspective. Since each god is supposed to have descended with his own Esu, one would imagine that the Esu that came with Oduduwa was his own, that is, his fate. By substituting one for the other, the chameleon in the descent is, I shall hold, a symbol of Esu, of fate. Also, the insight puts into clearer perspective the role of the chameleon as the commanding power of the creation process. For Esu, as will be explained later, is not only endowed with the most powerful Ase—the commanding power of the gods, or the power of the "Word"—he also controls it. More than just a "charm of command," as Abimbola suggests, Ase is the vital force of efficacy, the evocative power to bring something into effect. Esu is not only the "keeper of Ase" but also its "divine enforcer," the dispenser of the fateful, fatal power contained in his "Ado-iran" "the calabash which contains the power which propagates itself."[35]

The Agemo cult also seems to describe this power, for their god is vested with the power of the word, as projected by the Agemo priests, whose curses apparently never fail.[36] It is a belief that relates back to the traditional concept of the chameleon, the privileged "messenger" of Olodumare who accepts whatever he wishes. But an appellation of Esu, no doubt part of a praise-poem, gives us a parallel concept. He is called "Logemo orun," which Idowu translates "Indulgent Child of Heaven."[37] As the expression stands, with no clues to its background, it may slip by unnoticed, or one may wonder why "logemo" should be an "indulgent child." However, when one conceives the word as some alternative, ethnic form of "alagemo" (o-logemo), the interpretation (perhaps "indulged" is a better word) becomes meaningful. And, more important, the link between Esu and the chameleon is made irrevocably manifest. In fact, some of Esu's praises would seem to reinforce the link with cursing, for example, "Child of the unmitigated curse / Child of the communal curse."[38]

But there are other parallels that could be made between the two fate powers. Dwelling on the Agemo cult, we find that their god, like Esu, is, as represented by his priests in the human world, "the Lord of the market" (Oloja) and "a frontiersman, a bulwark barrier against foreign aggression."[39] As well as being the guardian of the road, Esu is the "master of the market."[40]

The linking of the two gods is therefore pertinent. It is conceivable through the elusive, unpredictable, fateful and fatal power which "descends" with god and man into the living-world and seems to direct and control the individual's activity. It is a link which is captured at once by the applicable imagery—Esu's chameleon skin color. For the influence of the dynamic on the individual is like a habit worn, the character of which describes the individual's peculiar character and therefore molds his personality. In fact, the metaphor expresses a Yoruba concept of fate which has to do with character and personality.[41] This controlling or driving power of character, the will, is the power of fate, the power of Esu.

Consequently, perhaps, the warning to be of good character often comes with the implication of the type of fate or destiny one possesses:

> Iwa nikan lo soro o
> Iwa nikan lo soro
> Ori kan ki 'buru l'otu Ife,
> Iwa nikan l'o soro.

> It is character alone that is difficult
> Character alone needs to be considered
> There is no head (destiny) that becomes
> corrupted in the town of Ife,
> Character alone is what is accountable.[42]

This warning, in fact, strikes a chord, and therefore is consistent with a ritual warning, expressed by Esu devotees and the Ifa priest, to take cognizance of Esu—"E ma fi t'Esu se e." For

> Eeeee, t'Esu Odara
> (It is the matter of Esu Odara)
> Lo soro o
> (Which is difficult)
> T'Esu Odara lo soro
> (It is the matter of Esu Odara which is
> difficult)
> Bakere o'jadi o
> (A Councillor—that he is—does not eat *adi*)
> A ra a Lode
> (Citizen of Ilode)
> Aye ree o
> (This is life!)
> T'Esu Odara lo soro.
> (It is the matter of Esu Odara which is
> difficult).[43]

To understand this link of "iwa" and Esu is to reiterate Esu as the embodiment of good and evil, which are complementary tendencies in a character. The need to bring these two tendencies under control and into balance, thereby averting possible fatal consequences, leads to the evocation of Esu through sacrifice. It is a conscious or unconscious effort at a reevaluation of character and a reaffirmation of self within the boundaries of tradition.

The annual festival of Esu, which occurs late in the year as the dry season sets in, is an occasion for such reevaluation and reaffirmation. With song and dance, the devotees implore their god to tender his blessings:

> Esu o, Esu mi, Esu mi
> Esu o, Esu mi, Esu mi
> Esu dakun ma binu Esu mi
> Esu mi, Esu mi, Esu mi
> Aye tawa ni tire ni
> Aya tawa ni tire ni
> Esu mi, Esu mi, Esu mi
> Esu dakun ma bumi, Esu mi
> Ile tawa ko tire ni . . . etc.
>
> (Esu my god, oh my god
> Don't be angry, my god
> The world we have is yours
> The wives we have are yours
> Esu my god, oh my god
> Don't abuse me, my god

The house we have is yours . . . etc.
(Sung by informant Fatoogun)

The blessings they wish are, in fact, all human needs which their god is capable of giving—all necessities for the continuity of existence, of tradition; all necessities for a balanced self and health.[44] It is perfectly logical that Esu's festival should happen at this time, since the drought is an important condition of fate, a reminder of the end-product of each individual fate, the fatality of death. The drought imposes an awareness of the need to survive, the need to accomplish a full span of fate. My informant supplies the relevant picture of Esu's response to the devotees' supplication: He sits, invisible, at his "yangi" shrine of worship (ojubo) and as the devotees ask for blessings and favors, amid song and dance, he slaps the back of his head and coughs up the desired wish enclosed in his "Ado-asure," his powerful calabash container of efficacious and balanced (wholesome) blessings. He opens the container and launches it toward the suppliant.

The gods then, beginning with Obatala, have come down with their Esus (their chameleons), their fate. It is these that have each described their particular character and personality, with which they have been able to try out and explore the living-world. With the various attributive feats with which they have been associated and identified, they have subsequently fated the culture of their descendant humans, who, by implication, have also come down with their Esus, given and worn like a habit—for each Esu, as stated, is an emblem of character. Going by the traditional concept of the procreation process, we can begin to create the picture of the giver and the given.

As the Yoruba tradition seems to have it, the soul, or to be more precise, since there are multiple souls, the ancestral guardian soul (Ori), having been supplied with body and breath, kneels to choose and be given his destiny or fate.[45] But while what is given is, to a certain extent, unquestionable, the identity of the giver is often unclear and is open to many interpretations. In fact, it will be necessary to put this in perspective in order to throw light on some discrepancies regarding the "given." For instance, the attribution of the endowment of fate, as well as that of the body and breath, is generally given to Olorun, or Olodumare, the Supreme Deity. But at other times Orisanla (Obatala), it appears, endows it—that is when he is assumed as Olorun, as in *Sixteen Cowries,* where he is the ruling divinity.[46] Yet at other times, Orunmila the oracle god, who is also concerned with the individual's fate as the "eleri-ipin" (witness to fate), is, logically, given the task. The justification, suggested by the appellation, is that Orunmila is present when "ori" (head) is chosen by the individual in heaven. He is thus regarded as a mouthpiece for Ori, as one who interprets the individual's fate.[47] Yet there is also an Onibode (gatekeeper) to whom Idowu refers, and in front of whom Ori kneels to get his fate sanctioned, that is, the fate which has been endowed by Olodumare.[48] However, in a culture that is based on hierarchy, and the system of which is based on division of labor, one would expect to see in its pantheon a reflection of its organization. Hence the confusion can be resolved by a clear understanding of who does what.

Without a doubt we must regard Olorun or Olodumare as the controller of everything, from whom all ideas of creation and existence have been generated, and who is represented by all the orisa (gods); and in that sense he can be reached through them. As a generator of all ideas of creation, he has naturally generated the subject under discussion here—fate or destiny. To this extent, it is certainly not wrong to attribute the endowment of fate to Olorun, the "God of Destiny," as William Bascom rightly suggests.[49] But just as he has created everything, he has also assigned certain powers to the orisa or divinities to have dominion over specific functions. This view in fact has led many interpreters into thinking that he is remote and functionless.[50]

I shall not make a defense for Olodumare as an ever-present being in the minds of the Yoruba, but only add what is an important dimension to the division of labor generated by the Supreme Deity. This is the fact that even though all orisa or deities have assigned functions, they should be regarded as part of Olodumare to the extent that he could be taken for granted as the source of any of these functions. In other words, Olorun or Olodumare is the aggregate or combination of all the orisa, and each function is in reality performed by a specific part of him, which is an orisa. This is easily illustrated by dividing a circle, which is Olorun, into many segments, which are the orisa. Functionally, these orisa are agents or intermediaries, as they are commonly called, but in reality each and every one of them is an Olorun, since he or she is part of the whole. In this sense, Orisanla is an Olorun, Orunmila is an Olorun, Esu is an Olorun, and so on. Conversely, Olorun is each of those orisa. This perspective should resolve the seeming confusion that often occurs in Ifa verses or praise-poems when a deity like Orisanla is addressed as Olorun. It also resolves any argument whether or not Orisanla (translated as "The Great Deity") is in fact the Olodumare. With this view in mind, we can proceed to determine which function belongs to whom on the question of fate or destiny.

Really, the divinities under question as regards fate, apart from Olorun, are Orunmila, Esu, and perhaps Orisanla (that is, when he is posed as Olorun), and it might be best to consider each in relation to the one to whom fate is given, that is, the human individual—Enia (womankind). The counterpart of Enia in the sky-world, to whom she is a "slave," as one Ifa verse would have it,[51] is the ancestral guardian soul (Ori). It is this "soul" who comes up to receive her fate (ipin), having been given body (ara) and breath (emi).

Exactly what Ori is, being the ancestral guardian soul, is a bit unclear, especially going by its suggested appellations—"eleda," "iponri," "ipin"—all of which are also names used for, or in connection with, fate.[52] And it would appear that some see *it* in terms of the human head, which is chosen at the house of the maker—a character called Ajala.[53] All this poses some puzzling questions on the concept of Ori.

I have chosen not to follow the Ajala myth, regarding it as a red herring that only complicates the concept further. But even then, does it mean that Ori is a fate entity which comes to receive body and breath? In which case, are soul and fate the same thing? If so, how can fate kneel to receive fate? If Ori is the metaphysical counterpart of man in the sky-world, we can accept the allegorical personification implied in the kneeling; but it will be difficult to conceive the fact that fate kneels down to receive fate, unless some ironic implication, or an Esu transformation, is intended.

Again, we cannot be too critical about the logicality of myth, but there is a possible clue to the seeming confusion in terms of semantics. "Ipin" is the word for fate. "Iponri," really a compound of "ipin" and "ori" (ipin-ori), translates as the fate of head or the fated lot. Is it not possible that when the ancestral guardian soul kneels down with body and breath "he" is still "ori" and when endowed with fate "he" becomes "iponri"? In this sense, one can go along with Idowu to suggest that because of this connection between "ori" and "ipin," fate or destiny has been loosely ascribed to "Ori," which makes "ipin" and "Ori" synonymous in popular speech.[54] Also, in this respect, one may see, fleetingly, the distinction once made by a colleague of mine who thinks that "ipin" is fate endowed, and "iponri" is destiny—what is actually lived in the living-world. But, more important, through the synonym, "ori" has since developed as a deity for fate. I shall come back to this presently, after making further observations on the division of labor.

The ancestral guardian soul (and one could imagine it as an entity of the human form) receives body, breath (energy) and fate. In the absence of any confusion regarding the giving of breath, we will go along with the traditional belief and propose Olodumare as the giver. But this is consonant with my theory. For breath (emi) is one of the multiple souls along with the shadow (ojiji) and "ori," the most important soul worshipped as a deity and, in that sense, part and parcel of Olodumare. And since there is really no need to wish to suggest that a soul (emi) is given to another soul (ori), may it not be, therefore, that all three souls are one entity, and that it is this entity, or life force, in the aspect of Ori, which turns up to receive body and then fate?

With regard to the body (ara), the question of its endowment is hardly disputed since Obatala (Orisanla) traditionally functions as a god of creation who molds the body into the human form. This activity may be interpreted as the endowment of a characteristic physical form to a spiritual entity (a combination of "ori," "emi" and "ojiji"). Or, perhaps more aesthetically, it is the striking of the metaphysical into its physical manifestation. It is in this physical sense that we may conceive Idowu's "Person" who turns up at the "gates" between heaven and earth, encountered by Onibode. However, as the story goes, Obatala, the body sculptor, got so drunk with palm wine one day that he lost control of his creative fingers, which molded, instead of perfect human forms, deformities like cripples, hunchbacks, blind persons, and so on.[55] This idea will later be developed.

We are now left with fate (ipin), the main concern of this chapter, and to arrive at who endows it is not as difficult as it seems. There is no need to involve Obatala anymore, as he already has a function. Also, we can agree, to begin with, that both Orunmila or Ifa and Esu are involved, one way or another, with the endowment of fate. As William Bascom put it, together with Olorun they form an "important trinity" in granting and assisting "men to achieve the destiny which is assigned each individual before the ancestral soul is reborn."[56] Several stories also suggest this close association of Orunmila and Esu as one of friendship. For instance, there is a story in which Esu, among the other gods, emerges as the only one that has stood the test to establishing himself as the true and honest sympathizer of Orunmila's feigned death.[57] There is even a story that tries to resolve their respective functions in terms of who is the more powerful—an unsuccessful attempt which in the end compromises their differences and reconciles them as inseparable friends.[58]

But we can eliminate Orunmila as a fate giver by seeing him solely in terms of his art of divination. There is a general agreement on this function whether by the Ifa divination system or the Sixteen Cowries method, both of which derive from him—even though some views have it that Esu taught Orunmila the art.[59] In this regard, backed by his functional human representation in Yoruba culture by Ifa priests, he is not the one that endows fate, but one who has knowledge of one's fate by virtue of his being a witness to its endowment (eleri ipin); therefore he is the source of one's own knowledge of it, or one's guide toward achieving one's destiny.[60]

With Esu as a possible fate giver, we shall have to go beyond conceiving him as a messenger, a function by which he is commonly, and sometimes offhandedly, identified. Stories abound in myth narratives and Ifa verses in which Esu is involved with somebody's fate, either by altering its process prosperously or adversely, depending on the sacrifice, or by simply jolting people into the awareness of it. Some of these will be considered in detail for their satirical value. However, it must be noted here that even where Esu appears to be no more than a messenger of sacrifices, we should bear in mind that he is first and foremost a mediator, without whom nothing can be effected, as cautioned by the often quoted Ifa verse:

> The world is broken into pieces;
> The world is split wide open,
> The world is broken without anybody to mend it;
> The world is split open without anybody to sew it.
> [They] Cast Ifa for the six elders
> Who were coming down from Ile Ife.
> They were asked to take care of Mole.
> They were told they would do well
> If they made sacrifice.
> If the sacrifice of Eshu is not made,
> It will not be acceptable (in the sky-world).[61]

The "world" in this passage represents the totality of human endeavors in the living-world, to which fate commits man, and over which Esu—"Mole" (Child of Earth; really, Owner of the World)—has control. Or, as Babalola Fatoogun explained, "Esu has to be reckoned with in any propitiation since he alone knows who among the gods needs to be propitiated for one reason or another, and he alone knows where to find them and how to coerce them." This is implicit in the saying, "If Esu does not exist, who would relate to those who eat sacrifices?"[62] His devotees understand the full significance of their god and therefore always give him his due respect. At his festival, where all the orisa are present or represented, the camaraderic tones of the drumming and chanting, at the approach to his shrine of worship, recognize his indispensability and primal status:

> Ani eje Bara o wole
> Ani eje Bara o wole
> Eyin owo kumo ti Laroye, to gbe lowo
> Gan-gan-gan
> Latopa ere kolobo, ere
> Latopa Esu kolobo, Esu . . . etc.

> (Let "Bara" enter
> Let us allow Bara to enter first
> Can't you see the huge cudgel that he holds
> The all-imposing cudgel!
> Lotopa of the enormous powerful hair
> Esu, the mighty one . . . etc.)

What it all amounts to is that Esu not only has to do with one's fate, otherwise he would not be sought or consulted by Ifa, but he is also capable of directing and enforcing that process of fate, for good or ill. More than a messenger at the beck and call of those who sacrifice and those for whom sacrifices are made, he has to be propitiated as a mediator, or the sacrifice is futile. However, before we can perceive the full implications of Esu as a mediator, it will be necessary first to clarify the identity of the giver of fate and the "given"— that is, fate itself.

"Ori," the metaphysical counterpart of the physical head, or, by synecdoche and as I have tried to establish, of the physical individual, is sometimes worshipped as a deity. When thus regarded, "he" functions as the guide and controller of one's destiny, and there are several Yoruba proverbs and platitudes that suggest this. For instance, the common Yoruba saying "Ori eni ni ngba ni" (It is one's head that saves one), or "Ohun ori wa se / Ko ma ni s'alai se o" (What ori comes to fulfill / It cannot but be fulfilled).[63] Or "Eni t'o gbon / Ori e l'o ni o gbon. / Eeyan ti o gbon, / Ori re l'o ni o go j'usu lo" (He who is wise / Is made wise by his Ori. / He who is not wise / Is made foolish more than a piece of yam by his Ori).[64] In fact, some of these expressions imply that

Ori is the greatest of all orisa, or that no orisa can save one, eventually, as one's Ori.[65]

It makes good sense to link the head, the seat of intellect, will and character, with fate, especially when one relates the physical known with the metaphysical unknown. Making this physical link with the metaphysical, a Yoruba gesture expresses the meaning—the Ifa priest transmits the vibrations on his fingers from the fated patterns on the "iyerosun" mystical-powered surface of the divination board to the head of his client (iyerosun is the powder from the bark of the irosun tree, sprinkled on the divination board; on it the Ifa priest prints his divination marks, which would locate an "odu-ifa" verse for his client). A more common form of blessing-giving gesture is when the individual who offers sacrifice (for instance, libations of drink) transmits, with one or two fingers, the significance of the offering on the ground to his forehead.

I have, however, questioned the incongruity of a deity of fate "kneeling before Olorun" to receive that very fate, but in lieu of this have suggested two possibilities, one distinguishing between fate and destiny, and the other observing Ori in the ironic guises of Esu, who has the capacity to reproduce himself.

Because there are, in fact, many parallels that could be made between Ori and Esu both as fate-essences, it seems unfortunate to see them as separate deities. For instance, Bascom writes, based on his collected verses, that Ori the ancestral guardian soul "takes to heaven the sacrifices which the person makes to his own head."[66] But surely this is also Esu's function. Then, an Ifa verse cited earlier describes Ori as a deity surpassing all other deities.[67] But Esu is also usually described thus.[68] Furthermore, the head or face on the edge of the divination tray, often suggested as representing Esu,[69] may also justify or support this link between the separate deities. For, as one rightly questions, is the head or face a symbol of what is being consulted—that is, the fate of the particular client of Ifa—or the symbol through which one may reach the client's Ori? Also, the strung cowries on the representations of Ori are an important symbol on the cowrie-decked vestment of Esu.[70] But an "oriki" (praise-name) recorded by Ayodele Ogundipe directly makes the link: "Esu! / A too bo bi 'ori.''[71] She translates this as "Esu! / Worthy of worship like fate." But the sentence, with Esu and Ori put in reverse order, gives us the same idea: "Ori! / Worthy of worship like Esu (fate)." In fact, Ori as fate is as elusive and as unpredictable as Esu, since the success or failure of any person at a given moment depends, supposedly, on the type of "Ori or Ipin (destiny) which that person had selected for himself from heaven."[72] And possibly it is to justify this uncertainty of fate that the shifty Ajala is posed, who not only makes heads but can also lead one into taking the wrong head.[73]

Consequently, there is no need to create these essences of fate as two individual entities, and I shall hold my argument by simply reiterating an earlier suggestion, that the seeming division, and therefore confusion, is probably consistent with the Yoruba tendency to relate differently to characteristically similar gods under different cult concepts and emphases. However, may it not be

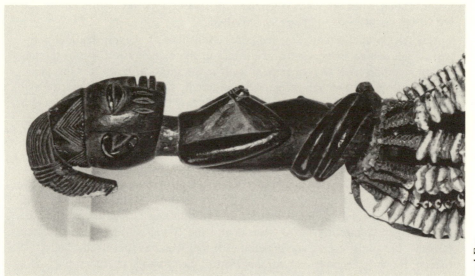

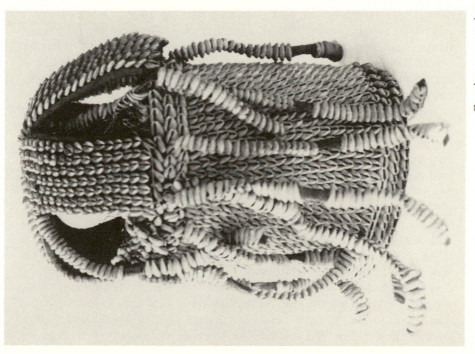

Cowrie representations of Ori and Esu.

that when Esu is consulted by Ifa, and both gods are inseparable friends, may it not be that when Ifa takes cognizance of Esu at a client's consultation, the Ori of the client is also implied as consulted?

Making the intellectually implied connection, then, I suggest that Esu is the god of fate whose essence—the given fate in the metaphysical world, the ancestral guardian soul, Ori—manifests itself in the physical head. It is this physical manifestation that represents the individual, his particular character and personality and, to be sure, the elusive "shadow" that follows him through life. In fact, shadow (ojiji), along with "emi" (breath) and "ori," completes the image of the three multiple souls in one—fate.

But we begin to get a clearer picture of Esu, in terms of the giver and the given in the sky-world, when we consider some of his more common appellations. Called Onibode (tollgate keeper) or, as an informant calls him, Onibodelegi (tollgate keeper of the forest), the picture created of him is, perhaps, one of an imposing figure or force standing at "heaven's gate," at the threshold of the passages connecting the sky-world and the living-world, waiting for the initiates, the souls (each a combination of three) who have received "body."[74] Indeed, Idowu's Onibode and, for that matter, the Onibode in Hubert Ogunde's drama *Ayanmo,* referred to in the introduction, are none other than Esu. There at the threshold he sanctions "the given," that is, the already chosen fate (ipin), emblematized as the all-embracing Ori. And if we agree that Ori and Esu are one and the same essence, what is chosen, or "the given," is an individual part of the essence, hence so-called a personal god. Therefore Esu the essence (himself part of a larger essence, which is Olorun) sanctions, as it were, the chosen part of himself. The sanctioning is necessary because it not only characterizes "the given" but also crystallizes the metaphysical into the physical, and "ipin" becomes "iponri," or, if we like, fate becomes destiny, that is, it formally becomes a representation of what is going to be lived. Put another way, it is this crystallized "character" that will direct the way the individual's fate is actually lived and achieved in the living-world. This view is a more concrete way of looking at the generally believed notion that the ancestral guardian soul tries to protect and to mediate for his earthly counterpart.[75] The initiate Ori has to have his innate fate sanctioned or it cannot get concretized into the physical, nor can the physical pass through the gates. For Esu is also called Olulana, the one who formally opens up the path or passage, after, one might add, a proper ritual. In the living-world is a similar image of him: He stands or sits at his crossroads shrine, at the center of the world, and considers the wishes and intentions of every passerby. His festival is no time for curses, no time for ill feelings, but a time to reevaluate or reorder the fate covenant made the previous year and the year before that, on and on back to that beginning sanctioning in the sky-world before the descent into the living-world. Consequently, after the sacrifice it is time for abundant expressions of thanksgiving and rejoicing through song and dance.

But if the process of Esu, the fate-essence, crystallizing or reproducing himself into a physical presence appears far-fetched, there is a story, in the Odu (Ifa divination verses) called "Osetua" recorded by dos Santos and dos Santos, that suggests just that.[76] In this odu (chapter), usually identified with Esu, we see a relationship with Osun, the river goddess, the great mother (iyanla), the principle of womanhood and fecundity; we see a relationship that seems to suggest a mediator–procreator–self-propagator function of the fate god. As the story goes, the power of the gods (Ase) had been rendered ineffective and worthless by the matriarchal power or the "ase" of Osun, who was always excluded from the male (god) cultus. When the macho-gods finally diagnosed their problem with the right procedure, by conferring with Esu, or, in other words, by consulting their fate on the oracle board with an offered sacrifice, they implored Esu for help. And after much pleading through Esu, Osun finally suggested, again through Esu, a matriarchal concession for the much needed patriarchal dominance. This concession, however, pivoted, in a suspense mystery of womanhood, on whether the fate-fashioned pregnancy of Osun would result in a male or female child. If the latter, the gods were doomed, since it meant continued abortive male power. However, a male product appeared, but with ironic conditions. It was the fate god himself, reincarnated as Osetua ("Asetuwa"—power releases us, or relieves us), whom all the gods must always regard and consult in any respect, activity or function that may apply to their male-chauvinistic lives. The irony establishes and affirms the ritual function of Esu as one endowed with the powerful Ase, the "Ado-iran," "the calabash which contains the power which propagates itself."[77]

And so the initiates come down with sanctioned fates or fated heads, a physical propagation of the metaphysical Ori which is part of the fate-essence. We may also get the image of the ritual of sanctioning or concretizing—Esu at the gates making an impression of the finger (like that which an Ifa priest makes, as described earlier) on the forehead of each initiate, a ritual at which, it is assumed, Orunmila is present. Or it could be the picture of Esu at his festival shrine as he slaps the back of his head to cough up the desired wish, the desired fate, inside the calabash fate-vessel (ado asure). In the living-world, the chosen fate, worn like an emblem, a halo, or a habit (since it describes character and personality), can be virtually described as a shadow, the elusive "ojiji," the camouflaging chameleon sometimes seen, sometimes invisible. It is this fate that each individual explores through life as it interacts with and matches itself against other fates. Or, in another sense, it is the destiny which each individual's character directs its person toward fulfilling.

Conceptually, in Yoruba metaphysics, all beings seem to derive from the same source or essence, but each with a metaphysical counterpart which is constantly in sensory communication with its physical other. These spiritual entities—lesser personal gods, really—are part of greater entities with whom they are also in constant communication as fate mediators for their floundering physical others in the complex world of fateful and fatal encounters and occurrences. These lesser or higher entities, gods or deified ancestors, created in the fertile imagination of mythmakers, have apparently once experienced the living-world, at which time they distinguished their existence with heroic deeds, actions and challenges describing their various fates, but also revealing their strengths and weaknesses. It is these fates that constitute the Odu of Ifa, and it is this body of knowledge that instructs the current human beings who must seek to know from the Ifa priest the prototype of their own fates. Through these fate experiences, the humans try to identify with their patron gods and learn from their human failings, except that, as humans, they are constantly getting incapacitated by the human condition of their particular character, and in fact display flaws similar to those that have trapped and challenged their patron's fate process. In an odu recorded by dos Santos, we are told that the difference between humans and gods is that the gods can see their own Esu (fate) and direct it to whatever purpose they wish.[78] In other words, the gods as spiritual ancestors are able, in their stage of development, to will their own fate to successful ends, no doubt through the wisdom gained from their human experience. Human beings, however, are still undergoing a process of exploration and therefore are incapable of wielding, as it were, their fate in their own hands. However, this view of the Yoruba gods is probably Western-biased and therefore somewhat confusing. It is hardly consistent with the Yoruba myth narratives where the gods commit mistakes and crimes similar to those of human beings and are similarly punished. One way of reconciling these opposing tendencies, perhaps, is to recognize the discrepancies in myths and suggest that some of the narratives may have assumed the gods' human existence in the living-world. However, because of the limitations of man, he must perpetually consult and examine the oracle board throughout life in an effort to establish contact with his patron god and ancestor—he must seek direction to understand their identical essence, their common Esu, or Ori. Or, put another way, the individual perseveres to align, as it were, with his own "shadow."

I have gone to rather roundabout but detailed length to establish Esu-Elegbara as god of fate (the giver) and fate-essence (the given), and what emerges as conclusion, however tentative, is that everybody is, potentially, a devotee of Esu. This conclusion can further be harnessed if we consider the physical and mental awareness of this essence in the living-world, which inevitably brings about a physical, or mental, ritual awareness.

It is also because of the elusive nature of fate that the Yoruba constantly seek the Ifa priest for guidance and to probe the seemingly tricky and unknown areas of their individual fate, or the unclear shades and patterns of their "garment." And, as if we have a tendency to forget, there is that constant reminder to take cognizance of Esu (E ma fi t'Esu see) to avoid unnecessary repercussions. For, as Robert Pelton puts it, "whoever ignores him will experience it [his supreme power] as frantic, wayward sexuality. But whoever pays heed to his directions will know it as the vessel of life renewed."[79] Sexuality, however, must be taken as a metaphor to embrace abundant generality, as I hope Pelton meant it. For there is an almost inexhaustible list of things for which

Esu is responsible, usually identified in his praise-poems or acknowledged at his festival in his devotees' favor list:

> Elfin deity, come home and eat mashed yam (ewo)
> Come quickly and eat the festive mashed yam
> Eat, (that) of money
> Eat (that) of children
> Eat (that) of immortality, Master of wealth
> (That) of the abundance, of good health and long life
> That our lives may be peaceful and calm . . .[80]

Indeed, the Yoruba awareness of Esu, as Robert Thompson rightly observes, is from a "belief that the highest form of morality is sharing and generosity—the strongest talisman to hold against jealousy."[81] The ritual prompted by this consciousness, or recognition of the god, can be undertaken both physically and mentally.

For a conscious devotee of Esu, the physical awareness and ritual are imperative. A mound or boulder of red laterite, which serves as his altar, can commonly be found near or at the threshold of a Yoruba household or compound, but can also be found, significantly, at the crossroads or at the entrance to a market. It is no ordinary ball of laterite, but a compound of small balls of soil and rock, as Babalola Fatoogun intimated. The structure, however, is likely to be missed by the uninitiated eye, except that the buzzing sound of houseflies around it, or perhaps the fact that stray goats or chickens are also feeding on it, may have attracted attention. There is no other altar like this in the Yoruba pantheon. Sango's mortar might be rooted in the ground, and Ogun's mysterious weapon of iron might jut out of the earth, as does his shrine at the Oni's palace at Ile-Ife, where the blacksmith/god supposedly "sank" into the ground ("sink" (wole) is a mystery word often used for the gods, who never die but are "consumed by earth," or become transformed). But in vain we shall seek any god who "essentially" establishes a god-altar triad with earth. Does it evoke the chameleon-involvement of the creation myth, one may wonder?

It is an otherwise normal and insignificant bulge of the earth, but on close contemplative scrutiny, the moist surface, from constant libations of palm oil and blood, evokes a different vision—a miniature mountain with volcanic capacities. Linking the structure, vision and all, with the creation myth, we may realize that we are in the presence of a god in camouflage, the "dissimulator who hides at heaven's gate," as one praise-name reflects.[82] The visual irony is pertinent, since irony is the essence of Esu's manifestations.

This fateful, fatal compound, or ironies imaged by the laterite symbol of his god, the devotee knows only too well. Therefore he must daily acknowledge the god with libations of palm oil, "to maintain Esu's problematic coolness," and with other offerings. But as explained in the introduction, this ritual should be perceived from the devotee's point of view. For each day brings its un-

Esu (Yangi) at the threshold of a house.

known, unforeseen realities, the influence of which on the individual's fate process may be "problematic" in terms of fatality. Consequently sacrifices are constantly made at the altar for knowledge and direction against misfortune, accidents and unnatural deaths, or anything that hampers the natural process of fate, but also for good influences like wealth, child-bearing and general well-being. As explained earlier, what the individual does by sacrifice, in effect, is struggle to maintain some sort of balance or equilibrium within the confines of his fate, between the components of the good and evil complementarity of that fate. The ritual act is as vital and as instinctive as taking care of one's head. And here the symbolism of head as fate is both explicit and implicit. The Yoruba word "ibori" (ibo-ori) relates both to the sacrificial worship of the head at the altar and to the conical, cowrie-dressed symbol of Ori.

The head symbolism, in fact, relates directly to the consideration of the mental, less physical, and less conscious recognition of the god. The expression "Ori mi gba mi o" (May my head protect me!) is a spontaneous exclamation that does not need the physical presence of Esu and can be applied to various situations, desperate or sober. It could be that a certain disaster has befallen the individual, from which he wants to be saved or spared as he surveys a total calamity. But it could be a milder but equally spontaneous reaction in anticipation of a likely ill luck or setback, or even a decision between two possibilities or choices. Whatever the reaction, it is obvious that the expression seeks guidance or protection against a certain difficulty, a difficulty from which it is believed that only Ori, one's ancestral guardian soul or fate-essence, can save one.

There are several Ori references, like the one just expressed, in which the fate god is psychically acknowledged, and usually the acknowledgment is with regard, directly or otherwise, to a protection against something specific. But protection against a certain difficulty often implies a protection against other fates. In a world of interactions among individuals, where fate matches with or reacts against other fates, each with a potential for good and evil, there is an inevitable attraction and radiation of good and bad influences. Indicative of such bad influences is the implication of the expression "olori buruku," literally, a person with a bad head. But more than this, in terms of the good and evil complementarity, it refers to the one whose *bad* fate, brought and sanctioned from the sky-world, lacks the "good" counterpart of the complementarity, so that his personality perpetually radiates evil forces. Hence, when the expression comes in the form of its common usage, an abuse, the one who accosts not only implies, literally, that the accosted should not affect him with his "bad" head (olori buruku, ma koo ti e ba mi), but also assumes, metaphysically, that his fate would protect him against the radiation of the "culprit" fate. In this sense, as Bascom rightly observes, to abuse someone thus can lead to a fight "because it is an insult to his ancestral guardian soul and thus almost a curse." [83]

The cursing instinct, however, is another dimension to the psychic recognition of fate, and one that concerns the main subject of this book. This shall be dealt with more fully in the next chapter. The instinct applies when an individual acknowledges his own fate, not only to protect but, primarily, to effect a retribution. Again there are various expressions of this mode, for instance, a warning thus expressed: "Majee k'ori mi mu e" (Don't let my head "get" at you), or, more directly, "Ori mi a mu e!" (My head will "get" at you)—the "get" in both suggests a retaliation for something done to the accuser. It also implies the efficacious power of Ori or fate as a thought-transmitting agent, and sometimes the suppliant has some knowledge as to what retribution he wishes: "Ori mi a je ko padanu" (My head will make you suffer total loss). The frequency of these and similar expressions among the Yoruba may lead one to believe that they are a tribe of cursers; but the instinct is in fact consistent with, one could expect, fatalistic societies, as we shall see. However, another way of looking at it is its association with the Yoruba belief in the power of the word Ase, therefore the power of Esu—since the fate god is its "divine enforcer." His devotees are very much aware of the fatality of his power, hence their instinct to wish to divert any oncoming evil vibrations of fate to someone else (Esu ma semi elomiran ni o se).

A more visual illustration and parallel of this psychic process and the individual's or "ori's" fatal power of efficacy is readily seen in a ritual that calls up and employs Esu's power for a catastrophic action. Here, Esu is approached as the keeper or authority of Ase, and the person seeking revenge or a retributive action on another goes to Esu's earth symbol (yangi) with palm kernel oil (adi). At the laterite mound, the person relates his grievances and what he wishes done, pouring the palm kernel oil on the mound with something like the following expression:

Esu "Laroye" . . . (recites Esu's praise-name). Here, I have brought you "adi" (palm kernel oil). You detest it, I know, and I personally would not have dared to give it to you. But somebody you know very well wants me to give it to you. He knows it is abominable to you, yet he swears it is your food. Here, Esu, I bathe you with it in his name.[84]

For Esu, as implied in the Ifa verse quoted earlier, is allergic to palm kernel oil, which supposedly touches his venomously angry spot.

There is no definite reason why the palm kernel oil should have such an effect on Esu, although for the purposes of the concept being developed, one could be suggested. The retributive oil is extracted from the nut inside the kernel which Ifa uses in his divination of fate. The oil, therefore, from another point of view may be seen as a fate agent, with retributive or malicious powers. It is an agent that induces the negative aspects of Esu, of fate, the evil aspect of the good and evil complementarity—that is, as opposed to palm oil, its good aspect and agent of the cool, which is produced by the fleshy outer covering of the same kernel. The efficacious power of "adi" is in fact a foundation of the vitriolic or satiric potency with which Esu is identified.

The ritual that acknowledges Esu's fateful, fatal powers is therefore both physical and psychical. Regarding the latter, the ritual does not necessarily limit itself to an Esu devotee but rather implies everybody as a potential devotee—even though the implication is seen from the Yoruba viewpoint. Furthermore, the ritual presupposes a need and anticipates a fulfillment of that need. It also involves the fate of an individual or individuals. The individual performs a ritual on account of another individual over whose fate the doer seeks to gain control. The ritual expression has a potential for a satiric action and gesture that will be discussed in the next chapter.

NOTES

1. David Worcester, *The Art of Satire* (Cambridge, Mass.: Harvard University Press, 1940), chap. 1.

2. M. Baudin, *Fetishism and Fetish Worshippers* (New York: Benzinger Brothers, 1885), 14; Verger, *Notes,* 110. Also see Bascom, *Sixteen Cowries,* verse A37.

3. A. B. Ellis, *The Yoruba-Speaking Peoples of the Slave Coast of West Africa* (London: Chapman and Hall, 1894), 66.

4. See Ogundipe, *Esu Elegbara,* 1:114–115.

5. For various theories on myth, see "Myth and Symbol," in *International Encyclopedia of the Social Sciences;* "Myth," in *The Encyclopedia of Philosophy;* Richard Chase, *Quest for Myth* (Baton Rouge: Louisiana State University Press, 1949).

6. Dos Santos and dos Santos, *Esu Bara Laroye,* 135–137. See also the Ifa texts "Atorun Dorun Esu" and "Orisirisi Esu" in the same work; and Thompson, *Flash of the Spirit,* 21–22.

7. Insight from Chief "Esulani" Ojeyemi, interviewed at Ikirun, Oyo State, Nigeria, July 1981.

8. See Verger, *Notes,* 109; also Ogundipe, *Esu Elegbara,* vol. 2, praise-poems 7 and 9.

9. For versions of this theme of creation, see Bascom, *Sixteen Cowries,* 36–37; Idowu, *Olodumare,* 19–22; Robert Smith, *Kingdoms of the Yoruba* (London: Methuen, 1969), 12–13; Ojo, *Yoruba Culture,* 194–195; Ogundipe, *Esu Elegbara,* vol. 2, tale 16.

10. See Idowu, *Olodumare,* 85–89. For an aesthetic explanation of this version, see Soyinka, *Myth, Literature,* 140–160.

11. Both gods are interchangeable in Yoruba creation myths. For versions that identify Oduduwa specifically as the "Creator of Earth" and Obatala as "Creator of Mankind," see Bascom, *Sixteen Cowries,* 36–37; Idowu, *Olodumare,* 19–29. For historical origin of Obatala and Oduduwa, see S. Johnson, *History of the Yorubas,* chap. 1; Benjamin C. Ray, *African Religions* (Englewood Cliffs, N.J.: Prentice-Hall, 1976), 42–45; Idowu, *Olodumare,* chap. 3.

12. Babalola Fatoogun, interviewed in January 1986 at the University of Ife, Oyo State, Nigeria. For an odu that explains this, see dos Santos and dos Santos, "The Orisa and the Odu Which Accompanied Them with Their Esu," in *Esu Bara Laroye.*

13. Babalola Fatoogun; see also dos Santos and dos Santos, "The Orisa and the Odu."

14. See Bascom, *Sixteen Cowries,* 36–37; Idowu, *Olodumare,* 19–22; Ojo, *Yoruba*

Culture, 194–195; Ogundipe, *Esu Elegbara,* vol. 2, tale 16. Also Ray, *African Religions,* 42–45; S. O. Biobaku, "Myths and Oral History," *Odu* 1 (1955): 14–15; H. U. Beier, "The Historical and Psychological Significance of Yoruba Myths," *Odu* 1 (1955): 18.

15. See Idowu, *Olodumare;* 19–22; Bascom, *Sixteen Cowries;* 36–37; Ojo, *Yoruba Culture;* 194–195; Ogundipe, *Esu Elegbara.* vol. 2, table 16.

16. Compare with Chase's view: "gods are made out of human passions in operation upon the event of human life"; *Quest for Myth,* 17.

17. Ojo, *Yoruba Culture,* 194–195.

18. Bascom, *Sixteen Cowries,* 36–37.

19. Ogundipe, *Esu Elegbara,* vol. 2, tale 16.

20. Idowu, *Olodumare,* 19–20.

21. Ibid.

22. Ibid., 20, n. 1.

23. Part of a praise-poem of Esu chanted to me by Chief Ojeyemi at Ikirun. For a longer text of this poem, see H. U. Beier and B. Gbadamosi, trans., *Yoruba Poetry* (Ibadan, Nigeria: Ministry of Education, 1959), 15.

24. See Oyin Ogunba, "The Agemo Cult in Ijebuland," *Nigeria Magazine* 86 (1965): 184.

25. Ojo, *Yoruba Culture,* 222.

26. Idowu, *Olodumare,* 20, n. 1.

27. Ogunba, "Agemo Cult."

28. Ibid., 184.

29. Ibid., 172.

30. Ojo, *Yoruba Culture,* 222.

31. See Ogunba, "Agemo Cult," 179.

32. My translation. For a poem that contains this, see Ogundipe, *Esu Elegbara,* vol. 2, praise-poem 14. See O. Ijimere, *The Imprisonment of Obatala,* in *The Imprisonment and Other Plays,* ed. Ulli Beier (London: Heinemann Educational Books, 1966), 19, 24. For various interpretations of this, see Beier and Gbadamosi, *Yoruba Poetry,* 15; Pemberton, "Eshu-Elegba," 25; Pelton, *Trickster in West Africa,* 163. For an essay based on this, see Judith Hoch-Smith and Ernesto Pichardo, "Having Thrown a Stone Today Eshu Kills a Bird of Yesterday," *Caribbean Review* 7, no. 4 (1978): 17–20.

33. For comparisons of Esu and Hermes, see Pemberton, "Eshu-Elegba," 6–7; Wescott, "Sculpture and Myths," 351–352.

34. Chief Ojeyemi, 1981 interview.

35. Bascom, *Sixteen Cowries,* 40; dos Santos and dos Santos, *Esu Bara Laroye,* 28.

36. Ogunba, "Agemo Cult," 184.

37. Idowu, *Olodumare,* 85.

38. Ogundipe, *Esu Elegbara,* 2:42.

39. Ogunba, "Agemo Cult," 179.

40. See Verger, *Notes,* 117–118; also Pemberton, "Eshu-Elegba," 22–23.

41. See Idowu, *Olodumare,* 154–156.

42. A Yoruba traditional song; see ibid., 155. English translation by the author.

43. Part of "Ose Otura," in *Iyere Ifa: The Deep Chants of Ifa,* ed. R. Armstrong et al. (Ibadan, Nigeria: University of Ibadan, Institute of African Studies, 1978), 120.

44. See Ogundipe, *Esu Elegbara,* vol. 2, praise-poem 7.

45. On this topic, see O. Lucas, *The Religion of the Yorubas* (Lagos: C.M.S. Book-

shop, 1948), 243–257; Bascom, *Ifa Divination*, 102–119; Bascom, *Sixteen Cowries*, 32–52; Idowu, *Olodumare*, 169–185; Abimbola, *Ifa*, 113–149.

46. See Bascom, *Sixteen Cowries*, 38–39, and verses K2 and A18.

47. See Abimbola, *Ifa*, 113–114; also Idowu, *Olodumare*, 75–80. For the story of Esu's rebellion against Ela (Orunmila), on account of responsibilities to human destiny, see Ogundipe, *Esu Elegbara*, vol. 2, tale 41.

48. Idowu, *Olodumare*, 174.

49. Bascom, *Ifa Divination*, 103. See also Idowu, *Olodumare*, chap. 6, particularly p. 53.

50. Idowu, *Olodumare*, 140–141. On this subject as regards various parts of Africa, see Geoffrey Parrinder, *Religion in Africa* (London: Penguin, 1969), 39–46.

51. Bascom, *Ifa Divination*, verse 111–1, p. 355.

52. See Bascom, *Sixteen Cowries*, 33; Idowu, *Olodumare*, 171.

53. Abimbola, *Ifa*, 116–132.

54. Idowu, *Olodumare*, 171.

55. See Ogundipe, *Esu Elegbara*, vol. 2, tale 18.

56. Bascom, *Ifa Divination*, 118.

57. Ibid., 106. See also Robert F. Thompson, *Black Gods and Kings* (Los Angeles: University of California Press, 1971), chap. 4, p. 3; Ogundipe, *Esu Elegbara*, vol. 2, tale 7.

58. Ogundipe, *Esu Elegbara*, vol. 2, tale 23.

59. See Bascom, *Ifa Divination*, 107; also Ogundipe, *Esu Elegbara*, vol. 2, tale 9; Abimbola, *Ifa*, 9.

60. See Bascom, *Ifa Divination*, 117; Ogundipe, *Olodumare*, 77; Abimbola, *Ifa*, 115.

61. See Pelton, *Trickster in West Africa*, 144–145.

62. See a version of this in an Ifa text that includes it; Bascom, *Ifa Divination*, iv.

63. Idowu, *Olodumare*, 171.

64. Abimbola, *Ifa*, 114; The foolishness of a piece of yam is perhaps suggested by the unprotesting way it submits to being eaten or pounded for eating.

65. See ibid., 134–146; also Bascom, *Sixteen Cowries*, 34–35 and verse A34.

66. Bascom, *Ifa Divination*, 114. But see contradiction of functions between Esu and Ifa in Abimbola, *Ifa*, 115, 116.

67. Bascom, *Sixteen Cowries*, verse A34.

68. Ibid., verse A18. On Esu assuming power over all the other gods, see J. E. dos Santos, *Os Nago E A Morte* (Petropolis: Editora Vozes, 1976), 171–175.

69. See Bascom, *Ifa Divination*, 34; Abimbola, *Ifa*, "Notes on Plates," plate 4.

70. See also Abimbola, *Ifa*, plates 10, 11; and Thompson, *Flash of the Spirit*, plate 15, p. 29.

71. Ogundipe, *Esu Elegbara*, vol. 2, praise-poem 7.

72. See Abimbola, *Ifa*, 145.

73. See ibid., 116–118.

74. For a constructed dialogue between "Onibode" and "Person," see Idowu, *Olodumare*, 174; see also Bascom, *Sixteen Cowries*, verse A35.

75. See Bascom, *Ifa Divination*, 116–118; Bascom, *Sixteen Cowries*, 33–35; Abimbola, *Ifa*, chap. 5; Idowu, *Olodumare*, 169–174.

76. Dos Santos and dos Santos, *Esu Bara Laroye*, 50–65 (Yoruba original); 66–82 (English translation). See also Pemberton, "Eshu-Elegba," 68.

77. On Esu's capacities to propagate himself, see "Atorun Dorun Esu" and "Orisir-isi Esu" in dos Santos and dos Santos, *Esu Bara Laroye*.

78. See "The Orisa and Odu Which Accompanied Them with Their Esu," verse 36, in dos Santos and dos Santos, *Esu Bara Laroye*, 147.

79. Pelton, *Trickster in West Africa*, 147.

80. Ogundipe, *Esu Elegbara*, vol. 2, praise-poem 7. Translation is slightly revised. See also 1:146–148.

81. Thompson, *Flash of the Spirit*, 22.

82. Ogundipe, *Esu Elegbara*, vol. 2, praise-poem 2. Vol. 2.

83. Bascom, *Ifa Divination*, 103.

84. See Idowu's version in *Olodumare*, 84.

2

Archetypes: Satire and Satirist

The implication that was made at the beginning of the last chapter, that fate has to do with satire, now demands some attention. With Esu established as a fate god and essence, this implication should become clearer and more obvious as we resolve the relationship between the god and satire. To do this effectively, we shall have to establish a definition of satire, especially one that will eventually apply to Esu and that emphasizes his satiric power—his appellation, Elegba (short form of Elegbara, which means "the tough or problematic encounter").

The trouble with the term "satire," as many scholars on the subject have explained in the attempt to define it, is its protean image, since the word has acquired so many meanings and forms in its development through the ages.[1] Unlike tragedy, comedy, and so on, the term, as G. L. Hendrickson points out, is "an indispensable label not only for scenes and situations of private and public life, but especially for the characterizations of almost every form of literary expression."[2] Edward and Lilian Bloom, taking a similar point of view, evoke an image of Mercury for satire's chameleon nature:

Like the god Mercury, satire is elusive and variable, wearing many disguises and satisfying many explanations. Even as the deity adroitly roamed from high to low—as orator and trickster, as fleet messenger and patron of the marketplace—so satire has always demonstrated its adaptability to circumstance and intention.[3]

This latter observation is in fact very useful, from our knowledge of Esu so far, and it obviously anticipates, in part, our conclusion about Esu as satire and satirist.

A general definition describes satire as an attack on vices, follies, and so on, "raised to the level of art and employing weapons of wit and humor."[4] While this definition is basic to the many forms of satire and highlights its two essential qualities, attack and humor, it nevertheless seems limited in scope with regard to satire's literary development. Indeed, satire, long before the word entered the English language in 1509, has been in existence not only as a literary form in classical Greek and Roman literature, as in the works of Aristophanes, Lucilius, Horace, Juvenal, and others, but also has been part of the cultural and ritual activities of the so-called primitive or traditional cultures, as many scholars have observed.[5] For instance, the invectives, verbal personal assaults, or lampoons found in Old Comedy and in the drama of Aristophanes have descended from the phallic invocations and raucous banter of Saturnalia and fertility rituals.[6]

It could therefore be said that the development of satire as literary art had its origins in the less formal, although more serious, invectives of the Greek tradition as well as in the more formal "satura" of the Roman tradition; this development should be seen more in terms of tone and spirit than of form.[7] In this sense, we can deliberately extend this origin, as the English Renaissance scholars erroneously conceived it, to the Greek "satyr."[8] And, as indicated in the introduction, R. C. Elliott has brilliantly traced satire back to the magical power of curses and rituals, citing adequate examples from the ancient literature of three cultures—the Greeks, the Irish and the Arabs.

With Esu-Elegba as a potential "satyr" or a satiric figure and power in the African or black tradition, these "primitive" origins obviously should interest us. Matthew Hodgart, in fact, in his book on satire, mentions the god as a figure in the line of traditional trickster representations among which we can locate the origins of satire.[9] While his observation takes the right direction, being derived from one of the earlier studies of Esu, it is nevertheless incidental. Our task, therefore, is to explore reasons why and how the god happens to be thus associated, and, more than this, whether we could classify him as a satirist of all times.

I shall go directly to what I think is a common factor, and therefore the most important element, in all satire, whether traditional or modern in concept, drawing support from what, for me, is by far the most influential study on the subject, R. C. Elliott's *The Power of Satire*. This common factor is the power of the word, for it is a factor on which all satire depends for its efficacy, whether in poetry, prose, drama or any other form. Elliott cites copious examples of this "magic" of satire from his three cultural sources: the Irish poets, whose verses could rhyme rats to death or deal injury to stingy patrons; the Arabs, who could, with their cutting and witty verses, weaken their war opponents to the point of surrender; and the death-dealing iambics of Ancient Greece. It is the last source that is of particular interest in many ways to my concept. At the forefront is Archilochus, the earliest recorded poet after Homer, whose legend about his efficacious verses or his satiric powers is well known to scholars of satire. Although Homer's *Margites* is usually considered the first poem to use the iambic meter, Archilochus was the first to use it in a particular way as a satirist.[10]

According to the story, Archilochus, whose marriage vows were flouted by Lycambes, his fiancée's father, wrote a scathing verse in iambics to curse Lycambes and his household. This verse, recited in public at the festival of Demeter, caused Lycambes and his daughter (or daughters) to hang themselves for shame.[11] Unfortunately, the bulk of the cutting power can be found only in fragments.[12] But from reconstructions and interpretations of scholars and by collecting views from classical authors, an image of a powerful satirist emerges.[13] Archilochus is thus usually considered the archetype of the satirist. I must, however, clarify immediately the likely confusion between Archilochus and Thersites, another archetypal figure. While Thersites predates Archilochus, he is a fictional character in *The Iliad* and not an actual person like Archilochus.[14]

Archilochus, after his death, was apparently honored as a god; he "became the center of a heroic cult on his island of Paros."[15] At any rate, according to some classical authors, for example Dio Chrysostom, Apollo had predicted that Archilochus would be immortal.[16] Also, epigrammatic epitaphs were written in his honor; a famous one by Julianus reads:

Cerberus, whose bark strikes terror into the dead, there comes a terrible shade before whom even thou must tremble. Archilochus is dead. Beware the acrid iambic wrath engendered by his bitter mouth. Thou knowest the might of his words ever since one boat brought thee the two daughters of Lycambes.[17]

This power associated with Archilochus has vibrated for centuries after, felt by later satirists who use the archetype as a warning to offending, vice-ridden men. Ben Jonson, for instance, a powerful satirist in his own right in the seventeenth century, at the end of his play *Poetaster* raises a justification for his satire:

> I could do worse,
> Arm'd with ARCHILOCHUS fury, write Iambics,
> Should make the desperate lashers hang themselves.
> Rime 'hem to death, as they doe Irish rats
> In drumming tunes.[18]

Satire, if no less venomous in tone and spirit, has since Archilochus been less personal and less efficacious. At any rate, that power has since been transformed into, or watered down by, art in its more aesthetic forms. But the power or the essence of it strikes a chord at which point we could begin to assess Esu as a satirist with similar and perhaps greater power of the word.

Elliott's thesis, backed by adequate history and theory, is that satire developed out of ritual,[19] and that in its earlier, more serious form, that is, when its efficacy was more seriously desired or realized, or when it was less an art form and more a personal invective or curse, its emphasis, which condemned vice and sought to punish it, was "bitterness, hatred and abuse."[20] The ritual, carrying with it "a sense of outraged justice," involved the transmission of a charge in the form of a ridicule, an abuse or a curse, from a subject to a recipient so accused. The charge is launched, so to speak, through a medium implicit in the power of the word, hence the magical quality it assumes. Since Archilochus did sometimes actually call on the gods to effect his desire (for instance, his invective on Lycambes and his daughters was recited at the festival of Demeter, his patron goddess),[21] we can assume, at least temporarily, that the agent in whose charge he placed the efficacy of his verse was Demeter, or any other god so invoked. For Archilochus, it seems, also often called on Apollo.[22]

In a fragment that gives us some sense of the power of his satires, Archilochus leaves the fate of the accused, a former friend going on a journey, to the elements and to the ferocious, warlike barbarians:

[May he be] driven out of his course by the waves; and at Salmysessus may the top-knotted Thracians seize him bare of friendly [kinsfolk], there to eat the bread of servitude and fill the measure of many ills, seize him frozen with the cold; and may he have upon him much tangle of the surges, and his teeth be chattering, as he lies on his belly like a dog, helpless on the edge of surf, spewing out the wave. This I fain would behold, because he wronged me and trod a covenant underfoot, he that once was my friend.[23]

This indictment, imbued with the preternatural power of Archilochus, in fact recalls the Esu-centered directive quoted at the end of the last chapter. I have reconstructed this a little to emphasize its tone and attack:

Esu "Laroye"! . . . (recites Esu's praise-name) On my right hand is palm oil. I know you like it because it soothes you. Consequently I, Ishola Lawal, give it to you. Grant me your favor and protection. . . . But here, on my left, is your detestable palm kernel oil. I personally would not have brought this to you, but Rafiu Salako, who has done me great injustice, wants me to bathe you with it. He knows this is an abomination, yet he swears it is your favorite food. Here, I give it to you in his name, go and avenge yourself. He has cast dirt on my honor, avenge me. Let him suffer dearth. Strike him down with an incurable disease . . . etc.

Both passages are vehement imprecations demanding justice for the guilty person, although, noticeably, the former is more direct than the latter. Nevertheless, Esu obviously serves as the agent of the imprecator—Esu provoked with palm kernel oil. The anger-provoking oil, "adi," to which Esu is allergic, may be seen as a symbolic gesture for Salako's offense and as the medium of expression used to coerce Esu into action. Esu nevertheless is the agent of the imprecator in whose charge is placed the efficacious power. And based on the remarks so far made about Archilochus, Demeter's votary, the devotee of Esu is the satirist. But here we must take caution, for our background of Esu, so far, will not allow us simply to designate the satirist status to his devotee and assume Esu only as agent. We will have to reconsider the situation.

In the Esu passage, the god is called upon to act by provoking him. The provocation assumes Esu's capacities, the retributive power that punishes and the satiric power which is effected on the person named as the offender. Actually, this makes Esu an agent of the imprecator as well as the power itself, the medium of satire (Table 1). But then we may remember that the imprecator's desire is conditioned by his will, his Ori or Esu (fate), and that the efficacy of the desire may be considered a result of an interaction of two fates. It is in this light that we can see Esu as both the satirist and satire, and the devotee becomes the satirist, indirectly, by virtue of his fate, or as a devotee of Esu. I shall come back to this.

With Archilochus the situation is slightly different. Demeter and the other gods are not provoked; rather, they seem to be merely called upon, or are assumed, as witnesses to the action or to assist in implementing the fatal indictment, the efficacy of the satire. Also, none of the gods was especially known to have destructive powers, like Esu, or like the gods of the underworld that were usually invoked in the Roman cursing tablets.[24] In fact, Demeter was basically regarded as a kind and gentle goddess who "takes no part in war and strife and seldom is aroused to wrath."[25] As for Apollo, the Delphian oracle, he should be regarded in this case as just that, an oracle whose pronouncements are to be feared in matters affecting law and order. It is in this capacity that Archilochus implored him for help. He is called upon to sanction Archilochus' pronouncement as opposed to effecting an appropriate pronouncement.

This distinction makes neither Apollo nor Demeter a satirist; but Archilochus is, as the one who is provoked by the falsification of the oath of marriage. Against this falsification he launches his satire, the medium for which is the iambic verse potent with venomous, magically efficacious power (Table 2). Demeter, or any of the gods usually called upon, may be considered indirectly a satirist only in the sense that she is meant to support Archilochus' desire and the power he has as the "servitor of the Muses." For as Elliott points out, the power of the word resided in the poet himself, and Hendrickson, taking a psychological approach, argues that the gods were not necessary for the efficacy

Table 1
Agents of Satire

Imprecator	Agent/Medium/Power
Isola Lawal	Oil (for satire) . . . .
	SATIRE
	Esu (for imprecator) . . . .

Table 2
The Satirist

Imprecator/Satirist	Agent/Medium (Satire)	Efficacy
a. Lawal/Esu	Oil/Esu	Disaster on Salako
b. Archilochus	Iambus-invective (with power)	Suicide of Lycambes

of the power.[26] In fact, the gods called upon may be said to be built into the fabric of the iambic power of Archilochus. Leonidas seems to have implied this in the following inscription:

Stand and look at Archilochus, the old maker of iambic verse, whose infinite renown hath spread both to utmost East and furthest West. Sure the Muses and Delian Apollo liked him well, such taste and skill had he to bring both to the framing of the words and the singing of them to the lyre.[27]

He is also said to have been one "who first dipt a bitter Muse in snake-venom and stained gentle Helicon with blood."[28]

Archilochus indeed admits that the power he has is god-given: "Wretched I lie, dead with desire, pierced through my bones with the bitter pains the Gods have given me." Although possibly a "censure of Aphrodite,"[29] the fragment nevertheless seems to reflect the power of Archilochus, since its venom could be said to derive from the "pains" of "desire" when oaths taken on account of such a desire were flouted. With this interpretation, the fragment reinforces the notion that the gods' sanction and support are built into the fabric of the iambic power. Therefore the satiric indictments of Archilochus, it must be emphasized, are not preceded by, or said simultaneously with, an act similar to that which provokes Esu into satiric action. Consequently, without doubt Archilochus, as the one provoked, is the satirist, and the gods, if we must have it so, are surrogate satirists insofar as they complied with or sanctioned his proposal—strictly speaking, they are part of Archilochus' or the satirist's medium.

In this regard, perhaps the Esu passage has more in common with private curses or the Roman curse tablets, "defixiones," which called upon the gods, usually of the underworld, to effect disaster on a victim. For this directive makes the gods directly, and the writers of the tablets indirectly, satirists. This distinction may be further emphasized by the clandestine nature of the procedure, especially if we consider the fact that satire usually is a public indictment. The invoker of Esu and the writers of the defixiones make their curses in secret, whereas the gods that are provoked or coerced by them could be said to effect the curse publicly, since the disaster wrought on their victims inevitably comes to public notice.[30] It is, of course, arguable that this "public" disaster is only a result of the "secret" imprecation or curse. But it can also be argued, as will be done later, that this result is a visual expression of the satiric power. In the defixiones and the invoking of Esu, this power appears to belong to, or is demanded from, the gods as opposed to being a direct power of Archilochus' imprecation.

These distinctions are necessary in order to have a clearer perspective of Archilochus and Esu-Elegba as satirists and, for the purposes of this book, in order to be able to place Esu in an archetypal role of satire and satirist. However, we may quite rightly be halted for a moment by the fact that one personage is historically real and human, while the other is a mythological figure or concept—although myth could be as real as history to its particular society, not only by way of euhemerism but also by the belief of the particular society from which the myth originates. It may be that Esu, in reality, should be classified with mythological figures like Thersites of *The Iliad* and his descendants, like Loki of the Norse legend;[31] or figures like Cerberus, the three-headed dog guarding the gates of Hades, whose monstrous bark has been compared with the slanderous, satiric tongue of Archilochus;[32] or at best he should be classified with the Greek and Roman gods of the underworld. We may remember, nevertheless, that Archilochus, after his shocking death in battle (his killer was later expelled from the temple of Apollo), became mythicized and was worshipped as a god.[33] Conversely, Esu's personality, perhaps like any other god's through the confusion of historical and mythical identities, could assume or characterize the personality of the votary. In other words, it is possible for the god to have become anthropomorphized through the processes of oral tradition, as suggested in the last chapter. Hence, the point of reference that distinguishes between myth and reality, between the mythic Esu and the human Archilochus, should not be a deterrent. In fact it should help to determine the question of archetypes, as we shall see.

Both Archilochus and Esu, we can therefore agree, have some common satiric characteristics. Both have, as established, the magical or satiric power, a command of the word, with the efficacy to punish vice. This power, to agree with Elliott, "could kill and in popular belief it did kill." But by such belief, what, in effect, one may ask, is the satirist doing to the life of the person thus accosted by his power? Is it not a fact that he has control over the life of the person—that the satirist holds the life of his victim, as it were, in the palm of his hand or, more precisely, in the center of his thought? Of course, this is assuming the fact that the assaulted truly offended the satirist—and there are traditional beliefs that hold that an unjustly levied satire, like an unjust curse, will not only fail but also boomerang back efficaciously on the utterer.[34] Breaking the oath of marriage, Lycambes placed his life in the hands of Archilochus, who had the power to punish offenders who accosted his personal dignity. A reconstruction of the extant fragment of Archilochus' satire in fact reflects this.[35] Whether Lycambes or his daughters' death were psychological (and this is one way of looking at it) would seem to be immaterial to the efficacy of the power.

At any rate, in fatalist or, as Elliott calls them, "shame" societies, the belief is real and holds true—although this belief may also be looked at in terms of psychological cause and effect.[36]

The same thing goes for the person who is a victim of Esu's provoked wrath, if we assume that the provoker has an axe to grind with the offender. In a society that believes in retribution, this offender as well as Archilochus' are victims of fate. As architects of their own demise, they flouted the traditional codes of conduct, for which they cannot escape the retributive power of fate.

Consequently, satire—at least personal satire—we can establish more firmly, has to do with fate, as described by Esu and Archilochus. The fate of the individual, because he has wronged the satirist, is at stake. Its natural course or process, whatever that may be, as endowed in the sky-world (going by the Yoruba world view) has been arrested, as it were, and is therefore subject to a change or a redirection (fatal or otherwise) by the satiric power. However, it is possible to argue the obverse and say that whatever happens to the offender is his fate as chosen in the sky-world, that it is his fate to be so arrested and punished. It all depends on the way we conceive fate, whether as something preordained and immutable or as something changeable. It also depends on whether we view a natural process of fate as implying life from childhood through adulthood to old age, which includes marriage, having children, a job, and so on, or whether the process ends anywhere the life of the subject ends. In view of its complexities and what has been expressed already on the matter, we need not concern ourselves with it further at this stage.

However, we may observe that Archilochus, presumed as the archetype of satirists, is only an agent of that fatal or fateful change, whereas Esu, the Yoruba fate god, is not only an agent but also a medium. In other words, if Archilochus is a satirist, Esu as fate is both the satirist and the satire. We shall have to explain later why the latter is actually so and how this relates to the individual in terms of "ori" (head) as established earlier. What should be obvious so far in the argument being proposed is that with Esu we are looking at something or somebody (that is, its human manifestation) beyond Archilochus—at least for the purposes of our concept. We are looking at something, going by the Yoruba creation stories, that preceded man or came down with man when he was created. This is so even by what Archilochus acknowledged—that his power was a gift from the gods.[37] For satire presupposes a power without which there can be no satire. In fact, satire is a fusion of both medium and power. With Archilochus, it is the fusion of power and the iambus which produces his efficacious imprecation; but it should be noted that the power comes from outside of himself, through him and out again, metamorphosed in iambics. Perhaps Callimachus' characterization of Archilochus will serve as a good illustration of this: "he drank the bitter wrath of a dog and the sharp sting of the wasp; from both of these comes the poison of his mouth."[38] With Esu, on the other hand, he himself is that fusion of medium and power which is invoked to act in favor of an individual, or which, as fate, satirizes

Table 3
Satirist and Satire

Satirist/Agent	Satire (Medium/Power)	Efficacy
a. Esu	Esu	Disaster (Ogun's massacre; Obatala's deformities)
b. Archilochus	Iambus-invective, with gift-power from the gods	Lycambes' suicide

an individual (Table 3). The proposition, therefore, is that Esu is an archetype of satire and the satirist, and we can begin to appreciate him fully as such in the light of Archilochus and the early seriously intended satire.

First, we should note that early satire is not only ritual-based, whether it derives from fertility rites or war chants or a curse, but also compounds the ideas of efficacy and ridicule. As regards the satirist, he launches his attack, filled with a sense of outraged justice, and seeks punishment as a moral example for his society.[39] Archilochus' satire of Lycambes, whether it was actually effective or not, was seriously directed and desired to take effect. But a ridicule was also implied. The attack was publicly directed during the festival in honor of Demeter. Thus exposed, Lycambes became an object of ridicule to the public, who would have been sympathetic to the satirist's indictment, since its aim was to expose a violation of the traditional code. It was the shame of this exposure that may have killed Lycambes and his daughters.[40] Viewed this way, satire, even at its early stage, is both conservative and instructive. For as Elliott observes, a satirist "is the preserver of tradition, the true tradition from which there has been grievous falling away."[41] Lycambes falsified an oath of marriage, a principle of custom and culture. As we shall see, Esu not only levies this conservative moral action, but he is also the moral action that is levied. There are basic facts about him that should support this conclusion.

As pointed out earlier, Esu-Elegba is more than just a trickster. Yet it is from this view of him that we can begin to perceive something of ridicule in his satiric qualities. Esu, as a trickster, is supposed to be responsible for all the tricks, serious or comic, that life (fate really) plays on us. In this regard, we may go so far as to agree with the appellations with which he is commonly labelled: "mischief maker"; "agent provocateur"; "confuser of men" who "so confuses the head of the queen / That she strips and goes naked";[42] "a past master in the trickery of deception";[43] or even as "the instigator who tricks men into offending the gods, thereby providing them sacrifices," as Joan Wescott would, rather erroneously, have it.[44] In sum, and metaphorically, we could say he is one that puts sand in the soup, salt in tea, or blows pepper into people's eyes. But for what, we may well ask in curiosity? Why would he do all this? Is it for the fun of it, as some interpretations tend to imply? Or is there something significant other than pure deceit that these tricks signify? Locating trickster qualities in schizophrenia and in the treatment of it, John Layard identifies two types of tricksters, with opposite characteristics: "The one tricks in order to deceive," the other, which is the positive aspect and "a function of the autonomous psyche," has a dual teleological aim by first bringing the "opposite complexes [of the first type] into consciousness and then uniting their opposite contents in a creative and one pointed union."[45] In other words, the trickster has both destructive and creative qualities. These are also qualities which identify Esu as an embodiment of good and evil.

In any of the stories about Esu, it will be obvious that his "trickery" actions are moral-based and that the seeming deceit is for a particular effect. Also, the stories almost always contain both the serious or cautionary and the shaming element of ridicule, all of which he not only brings to bear but also physically manifests. For instance, there is a story of two friends who vowed that nothing could tarnish their unique friendship, which Esu, however, put to the test.[46] As the two farmers were working on their respective farms one afternoon, Esu, wearing a black and white hat, walked along the path separating the farms. The farmers, each seeing a different side of the hat, began to argue about its color. When the argument seemed to subside, Esu passed by the second time with the colors now turned in reverse to each farmer. The argument picked up again and turned into a brawl that would have destroyed both farmers. It was at that point that Esu revealed himself and showed them the ridiculousness of their quarrel and, of course, of their vow. Esu himself supplied the satiric moral that jolted the two friends back to a traditional awareness: "When you vowed to be friends always to be faithful and true to each other, did you reckon with Esu? Do you know that he who does not put Esu first in all things has himself to blame if things misfire?"[47] In one version he symbolically drove the point home by showing the red inside of his hat[48]—the danger and the destruction that await such lack of awareness, the third significant color that completes the symbolic and satiric presence of Esu.

Perhaps a more visual satire is the story of the discontented favorite queen and her "inattentive" or negligent husband, the king. I have combined two versions of the story, Ogundipe's and Verger's.[49] Esu went to the queen and promised that her husband's waning love would be revitalized if she could cut, with a razor, a tuft of hair from his head with which to make a love charm. But Esu also went to the king to say that his wife was planning to kill him with a razor. That night, the queen took a razor and walked stealthily to the king's bedroom. The king, pretending to sleep, was on guard and watched all her movements. As she was about to go into action he caught hold of her hand and disarmed her. He was about to kill her when the queen's ambitious son, having been previously alerted, no doubt by Esu, entered the bedroom with warriors and attacked the king for wanting to kill his mother. The king screamed for police guards, and a bloody massacre ensued.

Taken at face value, it is difficult not to see Esu, especially in the latter story, as a confusionist and bloodthirsty sadist, as some scholars imply. For instance, Joan Wescott's Hermes-conditioned interpretation simply makes Esu an irresponsible, impulsive confusionist and a totally destructive sadist.[50] But a highlighting of each personage's character (a discontented wife, a negligent husband and an ambitious son) should make the horror more visually satiric as it points the moral to the traditional code of conduct. For it is none other than each person's fate (each person's Esu or Ori), conditioned by his or her character, that has directed each respective action. It is the lack of control of their character's obsession, which presumes a lack of awareness of that obsession and a flouting of the traditional code of conduct, that has provoked and fated the end-product—the satiric grotesquery.

This grotesquery, whether mildly effected as in the farmers' case, or brutally demonstrated as in the royal household, is supposed to bring the personages or the public, or both, to an awareness of the obsessional drive in man's nature and a reaffirmation of the traditional codes of conduct. The grotesquery is the product of the satirist, the satire, in this case, of Esu—a product of each individual's Esu or fate. The satiric exteriorization of self will be discussed more fully in the following chapter, which explores satire and its victims.

Most of Esu's stories, as the above tales show, have this satiric double edge in which a personage or personages are thrown, or find themselves thrown, into a shameful, ridiculous situation by their actions, and then are horribly jolted into awareness, which also informs the moral integrity of the public. This is obvious in the royal tale. In the story of the two farmers, we shall have to consider my informant's version for its full emphasis, in which the visual of horror is literally and metaphorically demonstrated by revealing the red inside the cap to the friends. This signification emphasizes the multicolored practicality of the cap, but no doubt also the awareness of the dangerous trait in man's character that could destroy friendship.

It is also clear from these stories that nobody, man or god, is immune to Esu's satiric exposure, and quite naturally so, since everybody, man or god, has his or her own fate. For instance, in the stories referred to earlier, we find that gods have been satirized with impunity for their lack of control. Obatala, the creative molder of the human form, unable to control his palm wine drinking habit, was ridiculed by Esu into such a drunken stupor that his fingers went awry and molded deformities—the grotesque manifestations of satire. The same is true of Ogun, the metallurgical deity, creative essence and warlord. In a drunken fit, having lost control of his superhuman power, he massacred both enemy and ally on the battleground, at which satiric horror he (and no doubt the public as well), when the fog of drunkenness cleared from his eyes, was jolted into an awareness of his error.

A point I would like to clinch immediately, for subsequent reference, is the visual grotesquery of the satiric image. For it clearly explains the more realistic, modern (as opposed to traditional or mythical) manifestations of Esu, which will be discussed in the next chapter. The final image we get from Archilochus' satire, that is, its efficacy, is the dramatic suicide by hanging of Lycambes and his daughters. This compares with the final images of Esu's satire, described above: king, queen and prince in the web of a triangle murder; Obatala's stark deformities; Ogun's outrageous massacre. Here, in fact, we see the physical nature of satire's magical power shot and frozen right at our faces, which action in turn freezes the expression of ridicule-turned-horror on our faces. Here, the power that has satirized its victim or victims is not only satirizing us, the public, but also making us perform another function of satire—its thought-provoking, mind-searching, resolution-compelling function. In this sense, the double-edged power is seen in a frozen movement which is instructive, castigating and therapeutic in its sobering effect. I shall come back to this.

What has been evident from the stories and my interpretation of them is that Esu is definitely more than just a trickster or "a past master in the trickery of deception." Indeed, there seems to be a technical difference between Esu's trickster qualities and those of, say, Hermes, often erroneously cited as the Greek counterpart of Esu.[51] It seems to mark a subtle distinction between irony and satire. While irony can be a component of satire, the same can hardly be said the other way round. This is precisely the point Norman O. Brown raises when he says, "A review of the mythology of Hermes the trickster shows that his trickery is never represented as a rational device, but as a manifestation of magical power."[52] In other words, Hermes' trickster power, like a theatrical device, effects a breathtaking (magical) theatricality, but for its own sake. For instance, we will never know exactly why Hermes stole his brother Apollo's cattle and persisted in his denials other than to show himself as an infant wonder. Although there is an indication that he was hungry, he ate none of what he stole.[53] At their best irrationality, his magical skills effect a comic action or comedy for the activist and an irony on the recipient. For instance, in stealing Apollo's cattle, he effects an irony on him—the all-powerful Apollo, tricked by his mere baby brother.[54] At their worst rationality, the ironies they produce often do not go beyond being bathetic contrivances for the artful satisfaction of a latent misogynist, as in the story of Pandora, who was used as a tool to inflict punishment on Prometheus. For the story reflects a psychological motivation which goes back to Zeus. Zeus wanted attributes for Pandora which could best inflict punishment on Prometheus, who stole fire from heaven to give mankind. Hermes therefore equipped her with "lies and deceitful words and a stealthy disposition." Brown parallels the misogynist attitude with the various interpreters of the evolution of the female figure—Hesiod and "the authors of Genesis 3 and Paradise Lost."[55]

Although the surface reading of the story would seem to exonerate Hermes as a mere tool of Zeus, in reality we cannot let him off completely from his father's despotic attitude. For he sees Zeus' request as an opportunity to show off his magical art. In equipping Pandora with questionable qualities, he betrays his own sadistic whims (since the choice is left entirely to him) rather than following Zeus' directive on the matter. In fact, the magical product casts an ironic stroke on Zeus, the powerless despot.

In comparable stories of Esu, about the confused queen who strips and goes naked or the royal triangle murder, we will not find a baseless, opportunistic theatricality such as that which describes Hermes' actions and effects. Although both stories, especially that of the naked queen, appear to derive from a misogynistic conception of the mythmaker, nevertheless, in terms of content, Esu's motivations are purposeful and moral, therefore his effects are dramatic and satirical. As a satirist, Esu is the artist of the dramatic denouement—which brings us back to the grotesque product of the satiric action.

As stated, the difference between Esu and Archilochus may be considered in terms of the relationship between satire and the satirist. This difference is even more explicit in the consideration of the grotesque end-product. With Archilochus, the power and the medium which constitute his satire originate from outside of himself, the person endowed with the gift. Through words, Archilochus levies his satire, and the physical product, Lycambes' suicide, describes the equally physical (verbal) grotesquery. With Esu, he himself is the power and the medium, and the grotesque product—the naked madness of the queen or the royal blood bath—is a propagation of himself, the satirist. This idea will become clearer when the satire is later related more specifically to fate, which is Esu and which also propagates itself. Here we can begin to see it from the point of view of his victims. On the surface, the manipulation by Esu of the three personages (the king, queen and prince) is nothing more than the common tricks of a sadist. That they all fell susceptible to the "trick" without questioning it is, itself, ridiculous, although a drug power is implicit. More realistically, though, each personage's character would tend to account for much of the susceptibility. And that is precisely the point. They all suffer from two common faults—a mistrust of one another and a lack of knowledge of, or lack of confidence in, their own nature and capabilities. The end-product, the grotesque image, is a visual and physical representation of satire which, itself, is psychical and radiates through the image as a certain power, a certain art, a certain poetry. Comparatively, therefore, we may note that Archilochus' satire is from the physical (verbal) to the physical (the final image of suicide); whereas that of Esu is from the psychical (Esu as power and medium) to the physical (the nakedness and murder). Both powers, however, whether from an outside physical source or from the psychical, are a propagation of themselves.

To be able to grasp fully the physical reproduction, or the verbalization, of Esu's "psychic" satire, we will have to consider some of his praise-poems. Perhaps the most visually direct image of it is the one that describes Esu's rather fatal action: "Having thrown a stone today / He kills a bird yesterday," or its variation: "Having thrown a stone yesterday / He kills a bird today" (previously cited).

The thrown "stone," whether delayed for the past or the future, as suggested by the variations, implies an artful calculation of the thrower, but also comments on his ironic character—one that seemingly but never really forgets and one that is unpredictable. Furthermore, it comments on the victim to whom the "stone" is directed, the satirized who is being punished for an act of which he

may not really have been conscious, or which he has waved off or forgotten as
an offense. Striking its victim, the "stone" stamps on him an unmistakable
mark of the thrower, which the satirized then recognizes if he but reflects on
his offense. This satiric stone with its verbalized expression (the throw) is, like
Archilochus' iambic verse, morally charged, and it magically assaults its victims with poetic justice.

The following excerpts from praise-poems will serve as examples of the poetic expressions of Esu's "psychic" satire:

> Eeeee, t'Esu Odara
> (It is the matter of Esu Odara)
> Lo soro o
> (That is difficult)
> T'Esu Odara lo soro
> (It is the matter of Esu Odara that is difficult)
> Bakere o j'adi o
> (A Councillor—that he is—does not eat "adi")
>
> . . . .
>
> T'Esu Odara lo soro
> (It is the matter of Esu Odara that is difficult).[56]

> Esu Odara, confuser of men!
> The owner of twenty bondsmen sacrifices
> So that Esu may not confuse him.
>
> . . . .
>
> Esu so confuses the head of the queen
> That she strips and goes naked;
> Esu cudgels her to make her cry.[57]

> Ooosa ti o lolua laiye
> (A god without a master in the living-world)
> Beeni o ni lorun
> (Without a master in the sky-world)
> Akorii-gbaje tii so laaarin apata
> (Special calabash fruiting in the heart of a rock)
> Owara ojo tii ba onle ogba leru
> (Torrential rainfall that terrorizes the owner of a bamboo-fenced house)
> Okuuse o baraiye nu
> (An indigent person does not bother anyone)
> Alagbalugbu obe tii yopin lenu
> (Overabundance of stew frothing forth—like an infection)
> Alagbalugbu obe tii ro komukomu
> (Overabundance of stew with awesome bubbling)
> Yeepe o ni bi taaa gbaa mu;
> (A burning nettle has no hold)
> Gbogbo ara nii fii joni.
> (The burn irritates the entire body)

Otakiti ponwo la
(An acrobat who somersaults and licks his hand)
O bomi enu fena jo
(One that blows up the fire with a mouthful of water)[58]

Firi o, oju alaa o
(Swift as a dream)
Olowo aiye l'emi o momo sin
(Lord of world-wealth, he will I forever worship)
Alaketu ere ja ju'wo lo
(King of Ketu whose curse hits harder than poison)
Epe a ja j'oogun
(Curses are more effective than medicine)
Esu l'omo ereele
(Esu is the ''child'' of the household curse)
Omo ere ode
(Offspring of the curse that derives from without)
Omo okunle-l'ogungun
(''Child'' who kneels on medicine)
Ere mo kunle l'ogunbere
(''Curse,'' I kneel on medicinal leaves)
Ere mo kunle ngo r'elejo
(''Curse,'' I am on my knees with no knowledge of my accuser)
Elejo ti gb'ebi, o ba tire lo
(The accuser has accepted the terms of justice and has gone his way)[59]

The first two verse passages have been referenced earlier. The difficult ''matter'' which the first verse acknowledges, as applied previously, is the difficulty of maintaining an equilibrium between the good and evil complementary forces embodied in one's Esu or one's fate. ''Odara'' must be seen in relation to Esu's ironic function—the one who ''throws'' (tricks, confuses, deceives) his victim for attempting to ''throw'' him—in other words, for attempting to cheat fate. This difficulty can either be manipulated by perpetual sacrifices, or provoked by an agent, palm kernel oil (adi), which manifests Esu's satiric power.

The second verse explains the ''matter'' further, describing its implications. Sacrifices are made so that we escape the confusion of Esu, the disorientation of the good and evil equilibrium, a disruption that causes the queen to go naked and masochistically to inflict punishment on herself—a satiric gesture. If we ask what actually laid her open to such an assault, we may recall the story of the king, queen and prince and the character traits that evoke the grotesque image of the triangle murder—suspicion through guilt (king), jealousy (queen) and ambition (prince). The queen of this passage therefore may be given to any obsession, like these, which results in certain madness—the mark of Esu's satiric ''stone'' on her. Therefore, what on the surface looks like a sadomasochistic act—the beating administered by Esu's cudgel (kumo), which makes her cry—is a satiric chastisement or punishment. Of course, by chastising her,

Esu has also chastised the public, since it is a warning against such an obsession frowned upon by tradition.

Because Esu is a "confuser of men," he has to be reckoned with either by heeding such warnings or by acknowledging his attributes. Such attributes, as expressed in his praise-poems, often give full value to his ironic as well as his satiric capacities through implied and suggestive images. In the third and fourth texts above are examples of such images. For instance, an image of Esu's indomitable strength and indestructibility is a "special calabash fruiting in the middle of a rock." Apart from the fact that it is an unusual calabash in the middle of a rock, one wonders whether there is any connection with or implied reference to "Igba Odu" or "Igba Iwa, the calabash of existence." In this special ritual container, Bascom observes, "wonder-working charms are stored by a great babalawo who gives directions as to how it should be worshipped, with the strict warning . . . that it should never be opened except [unless] the devotee is exceedingly grieved and therefore anxious to leave this world."[60] Interestingly, Bascom goes on to explain that, according to diviners at Meko, the type of calabash used contains a crude figure, "like those which represent Eshu."

With these fateful yet fatal consequences in mind, we will find Esu's satiric power more revealing and compelling in the images drawn of him. For instance, he is the "torrential downpour that terrorizes." He is the overabundant stew that is bubbling over, that probably attracts one and makes one salivate; but the "ipin" (an infection of the eye) that comes with the line is particularly arresting and somewhat ironic. It makes one cautious of the likely fatality of the "frothing" and awesomely bubbling stew. We all have to be cautious of the dangers of life, of the satiric potential of our different fates. For the power of Esu is as touchy as the nerve-racking, body-convulsing irritant "yeepe" (werepe), whose "burning" is hard to control or soothe. Esu is also, above all, the efficacious "curse" that humiliates and vindicates. This satiric power is often implied even in single praise-appellations like "Oteekoyade," literally, "conspiracy brings suffering"; but it suggests one who turns the malice of conspiracy into war, which brings unnecessary suffering to all, innocent and guilty alike. Or "Asorebiengo," the one who is kind to a fault, like an idiot; by implication, the one whose kindness is often misunderstood because of its deceptive nature, and therefore can be dangerous. Or, quite appropriately, his most common appellation, "Elegba" (Elegbara)—one whose power-encounter is problematic.

Venturing further into the real character, or the magic, of this power, we can even make parallels with what Elliott calls the psychological factor in ridicule and shame, which is capable of driving an individual to violent acts like suicide—and we can go by the example of Archilochus' iambics on Lycambes and his family. In the two stories already cited concerning the consequences of the palm wine habit of Ogun and Obatala, we get a clue to the "psychological" character and potential of this power. In versions of both stories, Esu is rarely mentioned but is assumed as the one that intoxicates with the traditional drink—the power in the palm wine that has provoked the devastating consequences. A draught of the drink is not, itself, necessarily intoxicating. But the inability of the gods to control their consumption, because of the drink's "tricky" mellow sweetness, results in the ridicule-tempered intoxication. The intoxication, as a power of Esu, confuses to such an extent that it turns their heads and drives them to madness, thereby producing images of mad ecstasy—Ogun's massacre and Obatala's deformities. We would recall that both gods realized the shame of their intoxication and reacted accordingly. But regarding the grotesque images of satire, we are again confronted with the characteristic nature of the power that reproduces images of itself, recalling the Osun-Esu story, cited in chapter 1, which describes Esu as a self-propagator. What this implies, in essence, is the notion that an individual is satirized by his own Esu, that is, his own fate, which, as has been established, has to do with his character. In this regard Ogun and Obatala were each satirized by their individual fate. This idea may also be applied to Archilochus' story by shifting emphasis from the satirist to the satirized—Lycambes is satirized by his own fate.

If we follow this psychological consideration of fate, we may note a technical difference between the satire of Esu and that of Archilochus in terms of emphasis—although this difference, in reality, simply presents alternative ways of looking at the same satiric action. With Archilochus as the imprecator, the satire is seen primarily from the point of view of the satirist. With Esu as fate, however, we perceive the satire from the viewpoint of the victim, the satirized, in whose eyes, or rather in whose satiric condition, we see the satirist, the fatal self-propagator. For since fate is not palpable, Esu as satirist is not immediately obvious; his image, however, becomes visible and palpable through the curser or the devotee, the surrogate satirist. This perspective also enables us to see Lycambes, ultimately, as a victim of his own fate—which is consistent with the psychological view of Lycambes' death through the guilt-ridden, suicide-compelling imprecations of Archilochus. This view, in fact, poses Archilochus' god-given power itself as a generative satirist through Archilochus, the surrogate satirist. However, surrogate satirists may become satirists by looking at satire precisely from the point of view of their own fate, which satirizes their victim. Furthermore, it is possible, by a boomerang effect, as with a curse, that the satirist whose fate satirizes becomes satirized by the same fate.[61] This reversal will be considered more fully in the next chapter.

These perspectives of satire, it should be noted, are made obvious through the consideration of Esu-Elegbara as fate god and fate-essence. Esu, we can conclude, embodies the two possibilities—for he is a regenerative satiric power as well as a satirist. As both, he has archetypal claims and status beyond Archilochus.

But if Esu indeed is fate itself, is it justified to assume that fate therefore is satire? Somehow, this sounds a bit odd and needs some qualification. We are considering a potential and tendency of Esu, which also happens to be a potential and tendency of fate. For Esu, a god attributed to fate, is capable of satire, and at such moments he, by derivation, is the power of satire. Similarly, fate in general is potentially satiric and can satirize. While we may not say, strictly speaking, that fate is satire, because then we shall have committed our whole existence and state of being as an expression of satire, we may, however, propose the fact that we often get satirized by our own fate or, through interaction, by someone else's fate. We can examine this possibility, first in general, and then relate it more specifically with the individual and Esu.

For instance, it is possible, as stated before, to see, free of any associations, how fate can seem to play us many tricks, especially when these actions seem to be rather unnecessary and undeserved. The expression "life is a joke" comes up as appropriate here, a "joke" that is often assumed to have gotten out of hand. A random survey of the misfortunes and accidents in life will inevitably reveal that compulsive power that seems to render individuals powerless in embarrassing or disastrous situations—the loss of property by fire; loss of wealth through gambling, litigation, burglary, and so on; minor or fatal motor accidents from sudden mechanical failure or carelessness. These situations, aside from scientific explanations, or in the absence of any known causes, would appear to be mysteriously directed by some unknown force. Or how does one comprehend the case of an individual who sits at home, at peace with himself, but suddenly (to take an extreme possibility) meets his death when a motor car goes out of control and crashes into his house? The victim, if he survives, must wonder what he has done to deserve such a catastrophe, although he thanks his stars for having escaped death. Against such misfortune or accident, sacrifices or prayers are made, but even supplication sometimes appears to be futile, and disaster happens in spite of it—which makes the situation all the more bewildering and mysterious.

To begin to see the satiric content in misfortunes and accidents such as those just mentioned, we will have to note a belief common to fatalistic, or what Elliott refers to as mythically bound, societies. This is the fact that nothing happens for nothing, that, although reasons can be somewhat elusive, everything can be explained as a phenomenon of the gods. Incidentally, this conviction is, to a certain extent, also a scientific theory. But while science seeks and waits for proof in the cause and effect of physical interactions, a fatalist mythologizes and taps his or her cultural resources for ready answers. In this way, illuminations of difficult answers often involve consultations with special people who are gifted in the cosmic processes or in the art of determining fate. With this in mind, we can begin to probe the satiric power in terms of fate-power.

For instance, it is easy to see Archilochus' episode from a fatalistic point of view. Lycambes' death is caused by his violation of a sacred oath of marriage "made by salt and table."[62] He was caught up, as it were, in the satiric meshes of his own fate, which, of course, through interaction, was retributively conditioned by Archilochus' fatal (satiric) power. However, not so easy are the reasons for the death of Lycambes' daughters, whose fates were also caught in the same mesh, rather undeservedly, as we are made to understand by an epigram by Dioscorides in which the daughters complain about their deaths.[63] A random fatalistic justification might be that they were accomplices to the breaking of the vow. This process will be explained more clearly in the following chapter, but as far as our limited source can probe the situation, we may note that Neobule and her sister(s) did not resist their father's decision to falsify the vow. And if such resistance by women is questioned as rare or frowned at in classical Greece, we can suggest, be it inconclusively, the examples of strong-willed figures like Antigone, Hecuba and Medea.

Esu-Elegba, however, presents a better and more direct example of a fatalistic conception. In the example of the motor accident given above, a fatalist who identifies Esu as fate will say that the god is responsible for the accident, for a reason that is accountable. It is with such a reason that we can relate to the satiric power of fate. It is obvious that this reason, whatever it is, must be sought in the man himself, who is being retributively punished.

Even where it is a case that is attributed to the witches, as is often affirmed in the Yoruba locality, it is still possible to say that the victim is so assaulted because of a previous disruption in the fate process for which he is responsible. And, at any rate, a Yoruba rationale would seem to support this notion: "A man's surest protection against the Witches is his Ori," that is, his fate.[64] The punishment thus inflicted on the victim of accident is effected, by a fatalistic reasoning, to jolt him, or any others around him, into awareness of a past offense for which he must make amends. In other words, the satiric levy, as it were, is a moral corrective. In this regard, survivors of such measures often make sacrifices (saraa) to purge themselves of their offenses as well as to celebrate their good luck in surviving.

Hence, without even looking for specific reasons—and we can suggest some by seeking parallels from the palm wine indulgences of Ogun and Obatala—the Yoruba fatalistic world view seems to have assumed a reason, with the implication that the satiric action of fate is brought on the individual by himself. This, on the surface, sounds like an argument that contradicts the concept of fate, an argument that presupposes the individual's free will and the responsibility of the individual for the consequences of his free-willed actions. But the Yoruba concept of fate, to my mind, has resolved that contradiction. As stated before, an individual, god or human, is endowed with his own Esu, his own Ori or fate. This fate is associated with the person's character in the sense that it is conditioned by the person's will, which in turn is conditioned by character. This idea is further made explicit by the concept of Ori in which the metaphysical Ori is represented by the physical head, the seat of will and character. It is in the light of this that we can conceive more clearly the fact that, even to a fatalist, the individual is responsible for the action brought upon him—in this case, the satire with which he is afflicted. Therefore, taking up the case of the accident once again, we can say that the satiric power of fate, activated by the individual's character and will, on account of some known or unknown action, has brought the disaster on the individual. And, as a probing thought to the action, we may ask the puzzling, fatalistic questions: Why is the individual at the place he was at that particular time of accident? What *will* brought him there? What was his character? What deed, for which he has been censured, brought him to this end? These I call fatalistic questions since they seek moral and cultural (social) answers. But then, are they really different from a scientific probing that seeks the psychological explanation of things? Are they really different from, for instance, the analytic probing in schizophrenic cases by Philip Metman, or John Layard, whose case studies and suggested treatment are, interestingly, based on the trickster concept?[65] To these probing questions we can only go so far for answers without consultation with a fate quester like an Ifa priest, or with the person himself—that is, if he acknowledges Esu and probes his own mind, or regularly consults a priest for knowledge.

But mythology has constantly given us examples, which Ifa priests also consult for answers. Some of these examples have already been cited. For instance, in Ogun's military massacre, that action was brought on him by his stubborn character and combative will. He challenged his Esu, his fate, into a drinking feat, which roused his riotous temper to such awesome proportions that he massacred friend and foe alike on the battleground. He had gone too far, unguardedly, with drinking the potent palm wine. When he became sober, he stared with horror at the grotesque manifestations of his satiric power of fate. He immediately became aware of this characteristic potential.[66] It is this potential that also supposedly describes the character and will of his devotees. Obatala, in a similar vein, although with a different character and will, also drank to much palm wine. The satiric result was the deformities that his creative fingers molded. The realization of this potential describes the characteristic nature of his will—the quintessential calm and endurance that is required to forestall any temptation to acts of violence. Significantly, he forbade palm wine to his devotees. We shall return to these myths, but here they clearly show not only the questioning mind of a fatalist but also the satiric power of fate, which every individual possesses by way of the fact of fate, and for which he is responsible. Making a psychological justification for the death of Archilochus' victim, Hendrickson states that Lycambes had resorted to suicide through a feeling of guilt and shame.[67] But more than this is the fatalistic view—it is his head (ori), his stubborn and irresponsible character, that brought him to the halter through the falsification of an oath. In relation to this view is Archilochus, the provoking agent of that power through the interaction of characters, of wills, of fates.

With regard to satire as a manifestation of the interaction of fates, or a conflict of the wills, it should be noted that its power, whether with Archilochus or with Esu, is not necessarily effective. It can simply be rendered abortive or, as previously observed with curses, it can boomerang back on the person that launches it. Again, the Yoruba proverb that represents Ori as the best defender against witches applies. A person who is innocent (and innocence can be relative, like truth) or whose Ori is stronger than that of the person satirizing, can resist, and therefore may not be touched by the satire launched at him. In fact, a fatalist would insist that one's Ori or Esu or fate cannot satirize one for what one has not done. On the contrary, the satirist can be satirized by his own Ori or Esu because of his satiric action on an innocent person. At any rate, human beings being far from perfect, are continually getting satirized for one thing or another by their fate-power. This conception can be understood in terms of the good and evil complementarity in human nature which constantly seeks balance, constantly seeks a therapy. Satire, a result of its imbalance, also seeks therapy, an "epidemic" therapy. As stated in the introduction, "epidemic" implies both the contagion of delirium and the attendant cathartic cure. This therapy is also consistent with the psychological treatment of a schizophrenia, described by Layard, in which the "autonomous psyche" seeks to counteract and unite the opposite elements of "autonomous complexes."[68]

Satiric power, therefore, we can conclude, has to do with fate. It is, in fact, the power of fate, and in Esu-Elegba as fate-essence, more than in Archilochus, we see its fullest expression. In the light of what we have been considering, it is possible to see Archilochus' satiric power as a manifestation of Esu (fate). To express this power, Archilochus utters iambics which, indirectly, condition the expression. Esu, on the other hand, directly launches his psychical action, which reproduces itself physically on his victims, who in fact are victims of their own fate. Archilochus, or any other satirist, is in relation to fate as are Esu's devotees to Esu. But then, as already implied, we are all potential devotees of Esu, at least in the black tradition.

The next chapter deals more formally with the victims of satire, that is, Esu's victims, specifically in the Yoruba culture and, more generally, in the black tradition. These victims are satiric characters or subjects of the Drama of Epidemic.

NOTES

1. See Worcester, *Art of Satire;* Ronald Paulson, *The Fictions of Satire* (Baltimore: Johns Hopkins University Press, 1967); Michael Seidel, *Satiric Inheritance: Rabelais to Sterne* (Princeton, N.J.: Princeton University Press, 1979); Northrop Frye, "The Nature of Satire," *University of Toronto Quarterly* 14 (1944–45): 75–89.

2. G. L. Hendrickson, "Satura Tota Nostra Est," in *Satire: Modern Essays in Criticism,* ed. R. Paulson (Englewood Cliffs, N.J.: Prentice-Hall, 1971), 37; see also Worcester, *Art of Satire,* chap. 1.

3. Edward Bloom and Lilian Bloom, *Satire's Persuasive Voice* (Ithaca, N.Y.: Cornell University Press, 1979), 15.

4. John Gassner and Edward Quinn, eds., *The Reader's Encyclopedia of World Drama* (New York: Thomas Y. Crowell, 1969), 741.

5. See *Oxford English Dictionary* (Oxford: Clarendon Press, 1933), 9: 119–120. For historical and theoretical origins, see Elliott, *Power of Satire,* chaps. 1, 2. Also Matthew Hodgart, *Satire* (New York: McGraw-Hill, 1969). For the origins of Greek invectives, see F. M. Cornford, *The Origin of Attic Comedy* (Garden City, N.Y.: Doubleday, 1961).

6. Cornford, *Origin of Attic Comedy,* 35–52; Elliott, *Power of Satire,* 5–6.

7. For various arguments with regard to origin and development of "satura" as a literary genre, see Elliott, *Power of Satire,* chap. 3. For a technical distinction between "satura" and "satire," see Hendrickson, "Satura Tota Nostra Est"; also B. L. Ullman, "Satura and Satire," *Classical Philology* 8 (1913): 172–194.

8. See Elliott, *Power of Satire,* 102–104. On the etymological error of the Renaissance, see O. J. Campbell, *Comicall Satyre and Shakespeare's Troilus and Cressida* (San Marino, Calif.: Huntington Library Publications, 1965), 24–34. But see argument for the false etymology as favorable: Seidel, *Satiric Inheritance,* 4–6.

9. Hodgart, *Satire,* 21–22.

10. See Elliott, *Power of Satire,* 4; J. M. Edmonds, ed. and trans., *Lyra Graeca,* 3 vols. (London: Heinemann, 1926–1928), 3: 603–605.

11. For a discussion of Archilochus and his efficacious power, see Elliott, *Power of Satire,* 3–15. For fragments and comments on Archilochus, see J. M. Edmonds, ed. and trans., *Elegy and Iambus,* 2 vols. (London: Heinemann; New York: G. P. Putnam's Sons, 1931), vol. 2.

12. See Edmonds, *Elegy and Iambus,* vol. 2, fragments 94–96.

13. See Elliott, *Power of Satire,* 14. For original reconstruction of Archilochus' satire on Lycambes, see G. L. Hendrickson, "Archilochus and Catullus," *Classical Philology* 20 (1925): 155–157.

14. For a discussion of Thersites and other figures in literature, see Elliott, *Power of Satire,* 130–140.

15. Ibid., 7.

16. See Edmonds, vol. 2 *Elegy and Iambus,* 93.

17. W. R. Paton, trans., *The Greek Anthology,* 5 vols. (London: Heinemann, 1915–1919), 2: 43. Quoted in Elliott, *Power of Satire,* 9.

18. C. H. Hereford and Percy Simpson, eds., *Ben Jonson,* 11 vols. (Oxford: Clarendon Press, 1932), 4: 322.

19. Elliott, *Power of Satire,* chaps. 1, 2. See also chap. 7, esp. pp. 282–283.

20. See ibid., 11–15. For a full analysis of satire and ritual, see ibid., 49–87.

21. Ibid., 7. See also Edmonds, *Lyra Graeca,* vol. 3: 605.

22. See Edmonds, *Elegy and Iambus,* vol. 2: 113; also vol. 2: 91–93, 97, 99.

23. Fragment 97A in Edmonds, *Elegy and Iambus,* vol. 2: 151; see also translation by Hendrickson in "Archilochus and the Victims of His Iambics" *American Journal of Philology* 56 (1925): 101–127.

24. See W. Sherwood Fox, "Cursing as a Fine Art," *Sewanee Review Quarterly* 27 (1919): 460–477, esp. 466–469.

25. Catherine B. Avery, ed., *The New Century Classical Handbook* (New York: Appleton-Century-Crofts, 1962), 383; see the myth of Demeter in ibid., 300–384, and in *Oxford Classical Dictionary* (Oxford: Clarendon Press, 1970), 324.

26. Elliott, *Power of Satire,* 14–15; Hendrickson, "Archilochus and Victims," 116.

27. Recorded in Edmonds, *Elegy and Iambus,* vol. 2: 97.

28. Gaetulicus, recorded in ibid., vol 2: 97.

29. See fragment 84 and comment in ibid., vol. 2: 141. See also Edmonds, *Lyra Graeca*, vol. 3: 606.

30. For an example of "defixiones" and the procedures taken, see W. S. Fox, "Cursing as a Fine Art," 446–449.

31. For the satiric characteristics of such figures, see Elliott, *Power of Satire*, 130–140.

32. See epigrams 69 and 70 in Paton, *Greek Anthology*, vol. 2: 43.

33. See Elliott, *Power of Satire*, 130–140.

34. Ibid., 288–289, 291.

35. Ibid., 14; Hendrickson, "Archilochus and Catullus," 155–157.

36. Elliott, *Power of Satire*, 20, 76–78.

37. See Edmonds, *Lyra Graeca*, vol. 3: 606; compare with fragment 84 in Edmonds, *Elegy and Iambus*, vol. 2.

38. *Callimachus and Lycophron*, trans. A. W. Mair (London: Heinemann, 1921), 239; also quoted in Elliott, *Power of Satire*, 11.

39. See Elliott, *Power of Satire*, 11; also Frye, "Nature of Satire," 78–79. But see Wyndham Lewis' argument against this moral mission: "The Greatest Satire Is Nonmoral," in *Satire: Modern Essays in Criticism*, ed. R. Paulson (Englewood Cliffs, N.J.: Prentice-Hall, 1971), 66–79.

40. See Elliott, *Power of Satire*, 77.

41. Ibid., 266. On this conservative tendency of a satirist, see R. W. Corrigan, "The Aristophanic Comedy: The Conscience of a Conservative," in *The Theatre in Search of a Fix* (New York: Dell, 1973), 53–62.

42. Part of a Yoruba traditional chant for Esu; see translation in Beier and Gbadamosi, *Yoruba Poetry*, 15.

43. Pemberton, "Eshu-Elegba."

44. Wescott, "Sculpture and Myths," 337.

45. John Layard, "Note on the Autonomous Psyche and the Ambivalence of the Trickster Concept," *Journal of Analytical Psychology* 3, no. 1 (1958): 21–28.

46. For various versions of the story, see Ogundipe, *Esu Elegbara*, vol. 2, tales 24, 25; Pemberton, "Eshu-Elegba," 25–26; Verger, *Notes*, Hoch-Smith and Pichardo, "Having Thrown a Stone," 17–20.

47. Ogundipe, *Esu Elegbara*, vol. 2, tale 24.

48. Supplied by Chief Ojeyemi, the head of the Egungun cult in Ikirun.

49. Ogundipe, *Esu Elegbara*, vol. 2, tale 20; Verger, *Notes*, 113.

50. Wescott, "Sculpture and Myths," 341.

51. See Pemberton, "Eshu-Elegba," 26; Wescott, "Sculpture and Myths," 370–371.

52. Norman O. Brown, *Hermes the Thief* (Wisconsin: University of Wisconsin Press, 1947), 11.

53. See "Hermes," in Avery, *New Century Classical Handbook*, 553.

54. For a different perspective of Hermes and his action, see Karl Kerenyi, "The Trickster in Relation to Greek Mythology," in Paul Radin, *The Trickster: A Study in American Indian Mythology* (London: Routledge and Kegan Paul, 1956), 173–191.

55. See N. O. Brown, *Hermes the Thief*, 9.

56. Previously cited in chapter 1; part of Armstrong, *Iyere Ifa*.

57. Part of a Yoruba traditional chant for Esu; see translation in Beier and Gbadamosi, *Yoruba Poetry*, 15.

58. Ogundipe, *Esu Elegbara*, 2: 20; praise-poem 6, lines 5–15. My translation.

59. Ibid., 2: 24–25; praise-poem 7, lines 17–26. My translation.

60. Bascom, *Ifa Divination*, (quoting D. O. Epega, *The Mystery of the Yoruba Gods*), 83.

61. On the satirist satirized, see Elliott, *Power of Satire*, chap. 4.

62. See fragment 96 in Edmonds, *Elegy and Iambus*, vol. 2.

63. See Hendrickson, "Archilochus and the Victims," 120–121.

64. See Abimbola, *Ifa*, 152. On Ori's potential in general, see ibid., chap. 5.

65. See Philip Metman, "The Trickster Figure in Schizophrenia," *Journal of Analytical Psychology* 3, no. 1 (1958): 5–20; Layard, "Note on the Autonomous Psyche."

66. For a conceptual recreation of Ogun's myth, see "The Fourth Stage," in Soyinka, *Myth, Literature*. For a dramatic exploration of the myth in relation to Esu, see Femi Euba, *The Gulf* (Lagos: Longman), forthcoming.

67. See Hendrickson, "Archilochus and the Victims," 119.

68. See Layard, "Note on the Autonomous Psyche."

II

DEVELOPMENTS

3

Victims of Satire

In terms of Esu-Elegbara, then, the most important factor of satire is hardly the satirist but the satirized—the victim of satire. This seems to be consistent with an observation made in the introduction—that it is not so much the "problematic" of Esu that is significant as that of his devotees. And since these devotees are after all Esu's people (specifically, every black person in Esu's black tradition, although in general mankind as a whole), his victims, that is, victims of satire, must necessarily be located first and foremost in the black tradition. As has been noted, these victims will constitute the potential characters of the satirist-dramatist, whose theme and action will express the concept of what I have called the Drama of Epidemic. I hope to emphasize, in the light of Esu as the archetype of satire and satirist, that these characters are bound up with the ritual and archetypal role, and in the disposition of the satirist. Also, by relating to the fateful and fatal manifestations of satire, the victim may be seen as an agent of his or her own satiric action or destruction. The implication here is related to what Peter Morton-Williams observes as a traditional fact, that Esu cannot lead an individual into misfortune unless the individual provokes the event.[1] With Esu, as Hendrickson argues in the case of Archilochus, the victims are agents of their own satiric destruction.[2]

Because it deals with two general localities, this chapter falls into two sections. The first considers the victims in the Yoruba (Nigerian) locality from where Esu originates. The second section extends the black milieu to the Americas, mainly by virtue of the presence of Yoruba descendants in the locality and, more important, by the obvious influences of the Yoruba religion.[3] But the assertion that the victims in these localities are representatives of the black tradition must be taken in broad terms, since little or no attempt is made to identify specific characteristics of Esu in each of the black cultures. As we shall see, the situations considered readily lend themselves to such generalizations since they are concerns not only of the Yorubas or their descendants, but also of the interacting cultures in those localities. In fact, in the case of the Americas, these generalizations inevitably involve the white cultures as well.

The preceding chapter examined certain features of satire in relation to the satirist. One obvious feature, and one we now return to, is the grotesquery that satire assumes. In the examples already given, it is obvious that a satiric attack involves and stamps on its victims a grotesque image visible in one form or another.[4] For instance, the attack on Lycambes results in his suicide and that of his family. The grotesquery therefore is visible in the image of suicide. Or, relating to Esu, we have seen the grotesque product of satire visible in Ogun's massacre, Obatala's deformities, and the nakedness of the queen. Furthermore, perhaps more conceivable to us in the modern world, in motor accidents may be seen grotesque satiric images. Precisely because of the concern for the rate of accidents in our technological age, this aspect is discussed in greater detail here.

It has also been noted that this grotesque image of the attack is, as regards Esu, not only an expression of the poetic power of satire but also in fact an extension of the satirist himself, so that the real link between the satirist, satire and the object of satire is the grotesque image. Esu himself serves as a model in his stories, as in the Osetua tale in chapter 1, in which we see him as capable of propagating himself. And in terms of grotesquery, we not only identify him with the grotesque expression of his victims or in his praise-poems, but in certain physical images of him as well, such as the image inside the divination bowl of the Meko diviners,[5] or images of him in localities like Dahomey or in the transatlantic world in Cuba and Haiti.[6] At any rate, the symbol of Esu, found at the threshold of houses, is a crude mound of red laterite. And, incidentally, an attempt to evoke visible or concrete images of fate will almost certainly yield some form of grotesquery, what with its tricks, unpredictability, ironies and fatality.

But taking a survey of satirists as a whole, we find that the conceptual image of satire as well as that of satirists is generally grotesque. Satire is the "bitter venom" of the snake, the bitter wrath of a dog, the sting of wasps,[7] the curse, the "acrid wrath,"[8] "the viper's gall [that stains] mild Helicon with blood,"[9] the "reductio ad absurdum."[10] Or, more to the dramatic concept of this book, its nature and objective can be construed, metaphorically, in terms of an epidemic process. But then satirists, true to the weapon they employ, are also characterized as grotesque. Archilochus, for instance, is often implied as a wasp; significantly, the passerby at his tomb is warned to tread softly lest he "rouse the wasps that settle" on the gravestone.[11] Hipponax, another Greek iambic satirist who lived about a century after Archilochus, is described as a "small, misshapen man, sensitive about his appearance" or as a "lame deformed beggar"; a sculpted exaggeration of this grotesque figure by the brothers Bupalus and Athenis apparently resulted in their suicide through the caustic imprecation of the satirist.[12] Classical Roman satirists were even more open-minded and uninhibited about their image, which they self-satirized. Quintus Ennius (239–169 B.C.), usually considered the originator of the Roman verse satire, satura, addresses himself thus: "Hail, poet Ennius, you who hand on to men the flaming verses from your very marrow"; but then he also recognizes the grotesque state in which he writes satire: "I never poetize unless I am laid up with gout."[13] In like manner Horace, who always sees himself as a bull, "admits to being short in stature and prematurely gray."[14] Making an analogy between himself and Archilochus and Hipponax, he says, "Beware, beware! I'm a tough fellow with horns, ready for the wicked, like him to whom the false Lycambes would not give his daughter, or him that was so fierce a foe to Bupalus."[15]

In the Renaissance, an age littered and inflamed with medical imagery, an age when satire was a contagious disease and the satirist a "barber surgeon," an executioner, or "a doctor physik," images of satirists were often projected as "Saturnian men," descendants of the planet Saturn, "of all planets the most malignant and most baleful with the greatest power for evil and the spread of incurable disease."[16] The saturnine disposition, it was believed, inevitably manifested itself in their physical appearance, for, as with the Celtic satirists, these men were afflicted by some "bodily ailment and deformity."[17] Examples of this grotesquery abound through the ages, even in the criticism of modern satirists. For instance, Roy Campbell was known to have boasted that "just as a lion breaks the spine of a giraffe, so his verse will drive hated rival poets to their doom."[18] And when Northrop Frye sees the satirist's victim in all institutions as a "gigantic monster," we may imagine the monstrosity or the ironic contrasting dwarfness of the satirist, who must match, as it were, grotesquery with grotesquery in order to effect a satiric attack on his victim.[19]

Indeed, reasons for the monster image of the satirist are not far to seek. Perhaps the most obvious, and one that has been dealt with here at length, derives from antiquity—that is, the archetypal idea that the satirist has the power to kill. But even where this is debatable or is regarded as a superstition, there still remains the threat which the satirist poses with his "blighting," "stinging," "barbed," "vitriolic" indictment. Such words describing his attack not only reflect the personality of the satirist, but also, whether conceived or factual, point to a sort of psychosomatic deformity of the satirist. It is this deformity, in all its monstrosity, that is in turn projected on the victim. In this regard we see Frye's "gigantic monster" from the satirist's point of view, and this process relates with what has been established before, that is, the idea of satire propagating itself. Michael Seidel makes a valid point when he says of Thersites, the first satirist represented in literature, "Perhaps Thersites has become a satirist because he is ugly, or, in a more intriguing variant, perhaps being a satirist has made him ugly."[20] For since the attack, when directed, makes its impact on the victim, the grotesque image inherent in the attack also makes its impression and propagates itself one way or another, depending on the constitution of the satirist. The impression could range from expressions of fear or nervous tension, through states of misfortune, to images of death. Thomas Randolph's *The Muses' Looking Glass,* in a scene where the characters, Comedy, Tragedy, Mime and Satire, are talking about their individual attributes, perhaps clearly establishes the link of grotesquery among satire, the satirist and the victim. Distinguishing himself from the others as the one most fit to prepare the masque about to be enacted, Satire describes himself

> As one whose whip of steel can with a lash
> Imprint the characters of shame so deep,
> Even in the brazen forehead of proud sin,
> That no eternity shall wear it out.
> When I but frown'd in my Lucilius' brow,
> Each conscious cheek grew red, and a cold trembling
> Freez'd the chill soul; while every guilty breast
> Stood fearful of dissection, as afraid
> To be anatomis'd by that skilful hand,
> And have each artery, nerve, and vein of sin,
> By it laid open to the public scorn.
> I have untruss'd the proudest: greatest tyrants
> Have quak'd below my powerful whip, half-dead
> With expectation of the smarting jerk,
> Whose wound no salve can cure. Each blow doth leave
> A lasting scar, that with a poison eats
> Into the marrow of their fames and lives;
> Th'eternal ulcer to their memories![21]

It is with this view of grotesquery as regards the satirist, satire and the victim that this chapter approaches the victims of the satirist Esu. As noted, since Esu has already been established as fate, this view also implies that fate with its satiric power is grotesque. As a sort of parallel, the Moirai, the Greek metaphor for fate, suggest such an image. Although usually depicted more as a fact of nature than as an actual power that dispenses, that is, as the "Doom" of the destruction that the gods dispense, they are sometimes personified as the off-spring of Night.[22] Esu, however, whose symbolic color is black, or part black, has been noted as a confuser whose contorted actions on victims not only mirror his satiric power but also his image. It is on this end-product of victims that I dwell here.

To be able to see clearly the nature of the grotesquery of the end-product, it is perhaps inevitable to have a sense of the magnitude or the prevalence of the "evil," "folly" or "crime" which satire attacks. Logically, this evil should be proportionate to the satiric impact producing the grotesquery. For satire, it can be assumed, exists only when it has a cause to denounce, ridicule or indict, something that unconditionally releases its calamitous venom. And while we may agree with Juvenal that whatever men do is the subject of satire,[23] we cannot but note, using Archilochus as a case in point, that there has to be some sort of corruption or injustice in people's action which is offensive to the satirist or to his sense of propriety, on account of which he seeks a moral judgment or punishment. Juvenal, writing at a time when evil and corruption were rife, demonstrated this reaction by his overwhelming satiric rage.[24] The greater the violation of an attitude, code of conduct or accepted standard, the more prevalent its corrupting influence, the more contagious the epidemic, so to speak, the greater the satiric urge or the counteracting "epidemic" impulse to sanative prospects. This would seem to support Juvenal's apocalyptic level of satiric impulse against the "existence of numinous evil . . . [for] Rome has lost contact with her own sacred tradition, and this loss of the old virtues and customs has led to degeneracy and perversion."[25]

Furthermore, one may not overlook the rather counterproductive effect that prohibitive laws seem to impose on the satirist's impulse.[26] As Lord Shaftesbury noted in eighteenth-century England, one of the high periods of satire, "The greater the weight (or constraint) is, the bitterer will be the satire. The higher the slavery, the more exquisite the buffoonery."[27] And although direct attack may not be possible under stringent, prohibitive laws, satire will find its expression through camouflage or in other ways, in a climate in which it cannot be avoided. For, as Elliott puts it, the general protective image of the satirist is that of "a public servant fighting the good fight against vice and folly wherever it meets it."[28] Thus, at the risk of legal consequences, there seems an inevitable compulsion of the conscience greater than the penalty against satirizing or the punishing of vice and folly. Horace, although writing in the first century B.C., a rather liberal age, says, "Whether rich or poor in Rome, if chance so bid, in exile, whatever the color of my life, write I must."[29] Juvenal, however, writing the first century A.D., a less liberal, more violent age, made a similar but more legitimate claim. He explains, with his customary caustic rhetoric and mocking ridicule, how it is difficult not to write satire.[30] In the case of Archilochus, we find that his society even permitted personal abuse that killed with impunity, as is proven by the death of Lycambes and his daughters.

It is, of course, difficult to measure the intensity of Esu's satiric impulse in terms of historical developments of satire and prohibitive laws. In this regard, it is pertinent to consider Frye's argument that, in order to attack anything effectively, satirist and audience (that is, the satirist and his particular society) must agree on its undesirability—which "commits the attacker, if only by implication, to a moral standard."[31] With regard to the frame of reference which we have so far considered, that is, satire in its primitive, more personal origins, we may see Frye's "agreement" in terms of traditional codes of conduct or societal norms. And against the background of these codes of tradition we may perceive the victims of satire. Lycambes and his daughters died because the family flouted the traditional codes of marriage. As will be seen, Esu's victims are struck by similar fates, for similar reasons. But the intensity and the efficacy (or the hope of it) of both expressions may be considered not only as a reflection of existing traditional beliefs, but also as a reflection of the nature of the societies from which such beliefs emerge.

For instance, regarding Archilochus, Hendrickson observes:

[A]part from his artistic endowment, which was far in advance of his time, he has not yet emerged from the crude passions of social and political middle age, an age of cruelty, hatred and self-help in lieu of law . . . [for] that which survived pre-eminently in the judgement of posterity was the unparalleled intensity of his hatred and its expression.[32]

The superstition and cruelty of this middle age, says Hendrickson, "contrasts unfavorably with the humanity and rationalism of the earlier Homeric society."[33] In a way, the contrast perhaps made up the conservative moral outlook and sense of justice of the satirist, the background of which inevitably reinforced his satiric thrust.

Since satire in general indicts vice and folly, it is possible to relate the cruelty and hatred of Archilochus' age, and its attendant satiric intensity, with any age or society in which curses or vehement satire also thrived, such as the Roman and Elizabethan ages, the eighteenth century, and certainly the modern age, which has produced two world wars. It is with the possibility of such contrasts in mind that I wish to look at the society that potentially postulates Esu as a satirist and therefore identifies its people as victims of his satire. Indeed, as should now be obvious, Nigerian society contrasts favorably with the age and society of Archilochus in many ways.

In a modern society whose tradition is, to a large extent, still mythically bound and whose historical construct therefore developed from oral as opposed to written records, it is impossible to assert facts of history regarding the nature of that society and its development through the ages—that is, facts similar to Hendrickson's observation regarding Archilochus. Beliefs, of course, may be strong enough to make a sort of euhemeristic assertion, and archaeological finds may do much, as they have for scholars of classical Greece. But on the whole, without written records there is no way we can follow, or effectively speculate upon, the satiric trends of such a society, let alone attempt to isolate periods of intensity. Neither can we trace legal strictures applied to satirists and their effects on the satiric mode, as we could in the European tradition.

However, it is possible to determine the quality of life in a contemporary society, with all the influences from other cultures imposed by modern civilizations, if this life is set against a background of traditional life as reflected in, or established by, oral history. And since the satirist is by nature conservative, it is possible to describe the intensity of satire by the extent to which the contemporary society has wandered away from the traditional. James Ngugi, writing about features of satire in Nigerian literature, implies this much when he says: "Satire takes, for its province, a whole society and for its purpose, criticism. The satirist sets himself certain standards and criticizes society when and where it departs from these norms.''[34]

THE AFRICAN MODEL

The model I have been using—the Yoruba society from which Esu-Elegbara derives—still stands. But using this model implicates Nigerian society as a whole because the present realities to be discussed embrace the whole of it. In other words, the whole society, as represented at any rate in the big cities, participates in these realities. But the satiric implication may also extend to other societies in Africa which share such realities. Ngugi, for instance, has similarly used Nigeria to locate some of these realities as common trends in Africa.[35] The second section of the chapter extends the Yoruba society to include the diaspora, and, using Esu as a common factor, discusses other realities that embrace the black communities as a whole in the Americas. In consideration of the obvious influence of the Yoruba tradition on the other black cultures that intermingled through the Atlantic slave trade, especially as regards Esu-Elegba, probably the most influential of the transported gods, I will assert that it is possible to relate to the satirist and satiric developments in the black tradition. My analysis of Nigerian society is based primarily on firsthand experiences and reports in local newspapers (the most critical years for this survey were 1976–1984).[36]

A random survey of the present society in Nigeria, as constituted in the big cities, especially within the Yoruba States, should reveal at least two prevailing factors which seem to express, at once, the traditional love of life and the reckless flouting of the traditional codes of conduct regarding that love of life. As will be examined, these factors in fact raise a justification for the satiric impulse and intensity of the present day.[37] One factor is the materialistic tendency to accumulate wealth and property; the other is a certain optimistic confidence that all is well, or, if not, that it can be made so through the right procedure, enabling one to acquire the ''essential commodities''[38] for well-being. As such, nothing is impossible to achieve. Both factors, as we shall see, are related.

These two factors are not in themselves despicable tendencies, for tradition supports them. The latter, when one reflects on it, is rooted in the strong belief in the cleansing and therapeutic power of rituals. The constant need to probe the unknown, the need to return to seek knowledge on the oracle board, the need to avert dangers and fatality, for a successful passage or transition from one moment and state of existence to the next, are all traditional expectations and requirements to promote a well-ordered and natural process of fate. They all therefore acknowledge some sort of support for Esu.

While the constant need to perform these rituals and rites of passage does imply, I will argue, the desire and will to live and avert death, it does not imply the fear of death, as some have interpreted.[39] To suggest the fear of death is to overlook precisely the confidence and the sort of regenerating impulse that the communicants receive after each ritual, which appears to have fulfilled their needs. At any rate, there is the belief in life's continuity linking the world of the living with the worlds of the dead and the unborn. The continuity assures the cycle of birth, death and rebirth.[40] But the renewed confidence appears to function as a therapy for taking risks and daring death itself. I shall come back to illustrate this fact.

Similarly, acquisition of wealth and property is not necessarily frowned upon by tradition, especially if it commands and supports followers. Rather, it is when the accumulation is done in a spirit of individualism and personal gain that it seems to disturb the social and communal balance. Making a proverbial link between the Yoruba traditional concept of destiny and the economic or market enterprise (aiye l'oja, oja l'aiye: the world is market, the market is world), Bernard Belasco rightly identifies personal fortune in Yoruba belief, as a corporately determined process of fate between Ifa, Esu and the ancestral pedigree.[41] Once the individual's "market of destiny" is determined, and the idea suggests that one's destiny is marketable, a fortune or an accumulation of wealth thus fated assumes a communal sharing. One may go along with this idea of marketable destiny in terms of the conflicting notions of the Yoruba concept of fate: on the one hand, fate is fixed; on the other, it can be altered by adequate bargaining with sacrifices. However, as Belasco suggests, any tendency to exploit such a fate by individual hoarding is blocked or countered by the existing forces of "existential reversals" such as the witches, the Ogboni, and so on.[42] He argues that the emergence of new cults to maintain the social equilibrium, that is, "the new imperial dimension imposed on translocal ritual," came with new trade opportunities and new resources of accumulation.[43]

Furthermore, it could be assumed that a society that had gradually developed a well-established system of exchange through barter, market dues and trade route taxes—even before direct contact with Europe—one in which trade became a major element in the growth of towns and cities, and one that was receptive to new trade resources surely must acknowledge the delights and advantages that accompany possession of wealth.[44] Wealthy traders were recognized by the king and the community. Status and power were usually determined in terms of wealth and property, which included a number of wives and slaves, or servants.[45] Thus, administrators of a community within the society could be presumed to be men of wealth and property. But, as explained, what tradition seems to frown upon is the selfish, individualistic or despotic attitude that an accumulation of wealth and power may foster, especially if acquired by dishonest means, or if followers are ignored. Peter Lloyd records the unpopularity of a Chief Agbaje in Ibadan, who was accused of exploitation, "insatiable ambition and soulless tyranny . . . [which] have never been the characteristics of the Ibadan nobility."[46] Similarly, misers are often strongly criticized.

Wealth—whether in terms of ready cash or property—being a symbol of social status, traditionally commands many privileges in Yoruba society. As is usually acknowledged, it is the fate of a man of wealth to be thus endowed.[47] Privileges accorded the wealthy man include acquisition of an important office in the community, support of followers around him, and a general respect by the community.[48] But these privileges have to be won by the person of wealth by proving himself through spending, sharing and general hospitality. For his wealth can only be seen or appreciated as well deserved by his generosity and his keeping a hospitable house. These are expectations that portray him as a man of good character, one capable of maintaining the well-being of the community; without these obligations, he is nothing.[49]

Without going into the ramifications of the Yoruba system of etiquette and the expectations and disapprovals of society regarding the wealthy man, we may just note that there are quite a few proverbs that draw parallels between character and wealth. For example, "Owolewa," literally, "Money is beauty"— "beauty," however, suggests both physical and inner character, as implied by a variant of the proverb, "Iwalewa," literally, "Character is beauty." Both assume an act of sharing. With this in mind, I would like to immediately implicate Esu with the traditional concept of wealth and the wealthy man and by so doing show wealth as a major target for satire in present-day Nigerian society in which the exploiters of wealth are potential victims.

According to the traditional concept of fate, acquisition of wealth, through luck or economic success, has to do with fate endowed in the sky-world or heaven before the individual is born. For he is an "olori rere" (a lucky person), with a head fated for good fortune, as opposed to an unlucky person with a "bad" head (olori buruku). As has been established, this state of existence or fortune assumes Esu the fate god as the giver whose essence is the given. Consistent with this idea is the sculpted image of Esu, which often prominently displays, among other things or fate implements, a vestment of cowries, a symbol of both wealth and the essence of fate.[50] Indeed, to be endowed with wealth is basically to be endowed with a good fate, which also implies a good head. However, tradition does not seem to distinguish between acquisition of wealth through using one's given head, that is, being industrious (and this is a traditional requirement), and through luck by effortless means.[51] Although one could argue that the latter means may require some sort of intelligence, a flair for business, or that the source of wealth may simply be an inheritance, such an acquisition would tend to materialize through sheer luck, since it is fated, than through personal effort. To this extent, the process of acquisition is often deliberately misconceived and therefore exploited. This throws another light entirely on the fate of the individual that engages himself thus. For in a way, it would seem that fate could be manipulated. This, in fact, is the metaphoric link between market and destiny which Belasco makes.[52] But such an attitude, which cannot be dissociated from character, an integral factor of fate, has its fatal or satiric consequences. An illustrative analogy of the manipulation (of fate) and its consequence was supplied by two informants.[53]

Both of them, natives of Iworo, an important Badagry village of Esu, which

Fate implements of Esu.

some claim as the god's village of origin,[54] describe what is obviously a satiric comment on foreign exploitation. As the story goes, the central market at Iworo, by the lagoon, was once the center of cowrie transactions for all its Yoruba neighbors, including the present-day Lagos. Once some strangers of an alien race and culture came to its shores in a dinghy. They saw at the approach of the market an enormous mound of cowries, the accumulation of years of wish and ritual tokens, for Esu-Elegbara. Knowing nothing of the indigenous culture, the aliens insisted on removing the cowries. On the first attempt to get away with the cargo of loot, the dinghy sank, and down with it went all the foreign capitalists. From that day on, my informants conclude, the incident, with its resounding "chinks of money," has continued to serve as a retributive warning to exploiters and all those who attempt to manipulate a "wealth pact" with Esu.

Actually, the story, however far-fetched it seems as a real occurrence, nevertheless has snatches of historical truth. Badagry was one of the chief slave markets along the West Coast of Africa in the nineteenth-century slave trade,[55] and presumably cowries would have been used for buying slaves to be transported across the Atlantic; the Yoruba were supposed to have pursued cowries as far as the Forcados River for ritual purposes.[56] There also could have been an incident of a sunken dinghy, although it would have carried slaves rather than cowries. At any rate, the carrying of cowries was plausible, and some sort of exploitation may have been involved—the Portuguese were said to have pursued both slaves and "coris" at Forcados as early as 1503.[57] But the conviction with which the story was told sprang from a belief in the retributive agency of a god whose emblem, going by the vestment on his statues, is the cowrie. As such the interpretative analogy of capitalist exploitation holds good.

Wealth pacts (that is, "seso owo") with Esu are a corruption, in the living-world, of the fate endowment of wealth as given in the sky-world. It is a traditional concept in which, interpretatively, Esu is coerced by an individual into a pact for an abundance of money. That Esu is coerced is a conclusion based on my analysis so far of Esu as the fate-power of each individual. In fact, when asked whether Esu is involved in the process, my informant Babalola Fatoogun claims an indirect involvement: "Esu will sanction whatever sacrifice the individual makes for a particular purpose."[58] I have taken this to be a naive answer which, however, supports my argument. The pact and its coercion assume an unendowed fate of wealth and the inability of the individual to make money by natural means. In other words, the individual does not have the patience and perseverance it takes to live at least bearably well, if not luxuriously. By derivation, it also assumes that the individual possesses a bad or unwanted fate originally endowed in the sky-world. He therefore wishes to improve his lot and alter, by coercion, the natural process of his fate. To be sure, tradition allows for improving one's lot and the offering of sacrifice for such an improvement, such as an acquisition of money. However, as my informant noted, the normal process favored by tradition is a long one, and because of this some people prefer the quick but hazardous route. For such a pact, like its much milder forms, exploitation and robbery, is not without its consequences—since it is not to be assumed that Esu can be coerced, or can allow himself to be coerced, without consequences. Tradition, indeed, relates fatal consequences at the end of the time span stated or assumed in the pact—the violent death of the individual or of his child or children, abject poverty worse than death, a long period of suffering through illness or another misfortune, and so on. My informant states that the pact itself assumes a shortened life span, since it shortens the amount of time in which the individual may have made the money in a normal process. He also states that death may affect his children since the wealth requested may be a sum total of that with which he and his child or children may have been endowed. Lloyd records that a ''man is believed to be able to use medicines which ensure his success yet at great personal cost—his wives are barren, his children die.''[59]

Actually, however absurd it may sound, such a pact is hardly far-fetched, for there are parallels in Western literature. For instance, there is the pact of Faustus with Mephistopheles, dramatized by Christopher Marlowe in the Renaissance and by Johann Wolfgang von Goethe in the Romantic period.[60] Both versions derived from the medieval concept of a pact with the devil, which also derived from the Judeo-Christian concept of a pact with Beelzebub. The difference between the Western and the Yoruba concept is that in the Western concept Mephistopheles, the devil, or Beelzebub is a totally negative force, whereas Esu is an embodiment of both good and evil.

The traditional Yoruba concept perhaps more vividly illustrates the ironic and satiric repercussions of such a pact, although it must be stressed here again that it is not so much the fact of the stories that matters as the fact of the belief. In coercing Esu—the ritual usually involves a human sacrifice and the fate of the victim of sacrifice—the individual is in effect coercing his own fate (Esu) into altering its natural process for a given period of time, at the end of which is a fatal consequence.[61] Hence he becomes his own victim. But we will have to see this in the light of what has already been established as the concept of satire in terms of Esu. In fact, since the individual is directly involved with Esu, the satirist and satiric power, it is possible to see the whole situation as a satiric process with the individual as the victim of satire.

As implied, the individual, by making a pact with Esu, is not only denouncing his own fate but also forcing a reordering of the same fate. This would seem to be consistent with a belief, even among the Yoruba, that fate can be altered. But then, like all pacts, the reordering process, if it is to be effective, demands an oath of contract which involves some sort of violent repercussive action on the individual, that is, after a period of happiness and abundant wealth. The pledge therefore may be seen as a curse, an indictment on self, the efficacy of which is the satiric grotesquery, the propagated image of the grotesque pledge. Ronald Paulson comes to a similar conclusion about a pox-efficacy of ''the primitive satirist's curse'':

The curse itself derives from the idea that external appearance should correspond to inner reality, a diseased body to a diseased soul. . . . A pox is both a painful punishment for transgression and an externalization of an internal corruption. . . . It fastens on the delicate spot, exaggerating it, inventing it, or in some way distorting it.[62]

An analogy can now be made between this pact and the more realistic tendencies of exploitation. The contact with European culture and trade had gradually accelerated the concern for and importance of money in Nigeria. William Bascom, from field work done in 1937–1938, observed that although tradition acknowledged social status over wealth, two high-ranking officials of the king whom he interviewed would prefer wealth to their traditional status.[63] The availability of new resources has gradually brought about increased consciousness of money as an essential commodity, which in turn has encouraged the exploitation of traditional concepts and promoted new devices for making money fast, such as bribery, money doubling, robbery, and so on. This consciousness received its fullest expression with the belief that emerged with the abundant flow of crude oil—that money is inexhaustible and is free and accessible for any individual to spend. The only problem, if ever there was one, according to the belief, was devising a way of getting it. This idea, in fact, is ironically consistent with another idea apparently inspired by a former military head of state: that the problem was not money but rather how to spend it. A solution to this "problem of spending" was therefore as easy as physically confronting the mountain of "gold cowries" and lifting huge amounts of it with impunity. There were many newspaper reports of such exploits and mind-numbing deliberate depletion of the Nigerian economy, especially between 1979 and 1983. Furthermore, the abundant, easily accumulated wealth resulting from the exploitation of the oil resources encouraged a social pastime called "spraying." This term, with its visual association with the spraying bullets of the machine gun, describes the preoccupation, on social occasions, with flaunting and dealing out large amounts of cash to musicians, celebrants and sycophants.

Spraying, an appropriate symbol of wastage and its many forms, is a result of the accumulation of easy, as opposed to hard-earned, money through bribery, corruption and open robbery. It is a social disease that has infected and corrupted the traditional concept of sharing and has gradually grown to epidemic proportions in recent years. More important, the dishonest methods of accumulation can be seen as modern capitalistic forms of wealth pacts, since they involve a forced reordering of fates, therefore an encounter with Esu. Although there is no conscious pledge made, it is logical to assume that such wastage cannot continue indefinitely without disastrous consequences; hence the country's present bankruptcy and stagnant growth. Putting this malaise in satiric perspective, we cannot but momentarily consider the ironic versatility of spraying. A pleasurable term at social ceremonies, it nevertheless describes forms of economic wastage; consistent with its military derivation, it has effected a satiric coup d'etat in terms of economic bankruptcy. It is the fatality

Money spraying. (This cartoon, by Josy Ajiboye, appeared with the article, "The New Millionaires," *Sunday Times* (Nigeria), August 6, 1972, p. 6. Reproduced by permission of *The Daily Times* of Nigeria.)

of the pledge of contract in wealth pacts, the grotesque externalization of satiric power.

However much the onslaught was brought about by a series of individual pacts, a wastage which reflects a national attitude and which also affects a whole nation cannot be talked about in terms of the individual. Rather, we are dealing here with a communal fate, the fate of a society, in which and against which individual fates are set as interrelating, conflicting forces. Segun Osoba talks about the scramble to get rich quickly in all walks of life, before and after independence, so that there was "no room for creative intellectualism or idealism in Nigerian politics."[64] In other words, there was no primary effort to assess the fate and plan the future of the country properly. Capitalism, in any of its many senses, involves one or more individuals exploiting other individuals or a group of individuals.[65] This exists in any society. But the kind of capitalism that has been brought about gradually in Nigeria through economic contact with the Western world, one that encourages individualistic "private or corporate ownership of capital goods," is somewhat foreign to Nigerian society. For, as explained, the tradition of the society thrives on a system of sharing whereby a man of wealth draws around him wives, slaves and followers with whom he shares his money in order to prove his worth. In the modern political situation, it would seem that the converse is operative—the individual uses followers from his ethnic group to enrich and empower himself while pretending to help his community.[66]

This is not to say that misers and capitalistic tendencies did not exist in the tradition. As one of my informants explains, nothing is happening now that has not happened before, the difference in the modern world being its magnitude. In terms of such antisocial behaviors, tradition in fact makes disapproving, proverbial comments, for instance, "Akii l'ahun, ka niyi," which means, "We cannot be miserly and still command respect" or "If you're miserly, you cannot be respected." For to be tight-fisted is to be socially poor because one lacks a following; like a poor man, one will be treated with contempt—traditionally a miser is apparently considered worse than a poor man.[67] For miserliness can be taken metaphorically to embrace all forms of corruption through exploitation or questionable means of accumulation. Poverty, however, is often associated with laziness: "The god that favors a lazy man does exist; it is one's hands that bring prosperity" (Oosa ti gb'ole ko si . . .).[68] Although the latter proverb may be interpreted to favor capitalistic tendencies, capitalism, in which one individual or a group selfishly hoards many business concerns, is frowned upon,[69] as is suggested by the following proverb: "Okanjuwa ati ole, deede ni wonje." Literally translated "a hoarder and a thief are the same," it implies that the two individuals have similar tendencies and should be similarly treated, as malfeasors or criminals.

Encouraged by capitalism, hoarding in Nigerian society has escalated into modern trends in the wealth pact—the hoarding of goods bought cheaply but sold at exorbitant prices in the endeavor to get rich quickly. The more direct and daring trend, consistent with the last proverb quoted, is of course barefaced robbery—the lifting of huge sums of communal or national funds or, as what Osoba calls straightforward looting of the public treasury. An irony to the proverb, however, is the fact that neither the hoarder nor the robber in modern society seems to have received the merited criminal and individual punishment. It is as if the whole society, who for the most part have remained silent or were powerless to do anything, have condoned the act. Indeed, the general feeling one gathers is that the situation would be no different if the opportunity to hoard or steal presented itself to other hands. This can be supported by such frequently heard comments as "This is Nigeria," "If you can't beat them, join them," and so on. Talking about earlier tendencies immediately after independence in 1960, Osoba quotes remarks made by some of the leaders of the nation who justified their "looting."[70] The psychology of such effrontery is that of a person who assumes that people are stupid and will therefore accept any explanation or say nothing. Hence it is possible to relate to a kind of reordering of communal or societal fate.

Similarly, the wastage that this accumulation encourages, that is, spraying, seems to have been condoned. In a way, it is a kind of sharing, and the sprayer probably has made a case for himself that tradition supports his action. But spraying is a warped kind of sharing in terms of accountability (the easy acquisition of the wealth) and wastage. For tradition also recognizes that a rich man who has no control over his money will foolishly lose all to those who are ready sycophants to his money.[71] At the same time, the sycophants and all those who enjoy being sprayed are condoners of wastage. Hence again, with this argument, we can consider the reordering of fate and its consequences as a communal endeavor.

Therefore, with regard to the satiric perspective already established, what is increasingly clear in these developments can be stated in general as a conflict between tradition and contemporary society, a conflict that is raised through tendencies to subvert, change or exploit traditional values. Paralleled with the traditional ritual of wealth pacts, these tendencies are seen as a collective attempt to reorder the communal or societal fate, which, however, involves fatal consequences. Communal fate constitutes and involves the various interacting fates that describe tradition. Gradually influenced by contemporary values, there is a general reordering of societal fate through a reordering of the individual. The process is, in fact, a disruption of the traditional character and social equilibrium. The product of this disruption is economic bankruptcy and a total collapse of power. In satiric contrasts, wealth, which in tradition commands a following and keeps power in control, may be seen as an equilibrator. Against this balance we see malfeasors such as Chief Agbaje exploiting wealth to gain power, for which he died (the consequential and satiric death) before he could attain his objective.[72] This capitalistic singlemindedness has gradually taken over and become powerful in modern exploitation; thus power as a disequilibrator now controls wealth; hence national bankruptcy follows. Pursuing my informant's insight a little further, we can assert that there is nothing happening today that has not happened before, that it is only a question of magnitude and, therefore, the intensity of satiric assault. Perhaps then we can consider Belasco's idea in this light when he says, "Esu himself became more and more 'angry,' rather than capricious, until he ultimately emerged as a personification of evil, an abstract essence responsible for the disruption of the state."[73] The evil intent can only make sense in terms of the satiric intensity of Esu, the archetypal leveller.

The state of collapse in the Nigerian economy therefore can be seen as a satiric assault of the fatal powers of tradition on modern society. But then, since society describes tradition, and tradition constitutes society, we may say, in retrospect, that it is an assault of society on itself, just as the fate of an individual assaults or satirizes that individual, as previously established. Like that of the individual, the assault is supposed to create an awareness that should force society back within the limits of tradition, thereby maintaining an equilibrium. Of course, the equilibrium that needs to be maintained is that between the components of good and evil embodied by Esu, which is difficult to maintain.

However, it is not easy to explain the process of fate, its satiric assault and efficacy, in collective terms, for one is immediately confronted with a number of questions. For instance, can one really speak of the fate of a society at the expense of individual freedom of thought and action, or the individual effort to effect purposeful change? If a handful of individuals, severally or in groups, violates traditional norms or moral codes of conduct, why should the whole society suffer for it? To say that the Yorubas, not to mention the Nigerians as a whole, are a communally integrated society is an overstatement that must produce a cautionary clearing of the throat, and therefore demands some qualification. For the Yorubas are far from being united as a group, and individualistic tendencies among the subgroups were a cause for concern not only in the political breakups and disunity after independence in the attempts at democracy, but earlier resulted in the bitter internecine wars of the nineteenth century.[74] Even within the subtribes may be found communities that show subtle, if not marked, individual differences in their way of thinking. For instance, Ogunba talks about the power struggle in Ijebuland with the Agemo cult.[75]

However, the degree of communalism may not be measured by political disunity in the power struggle to gain economic control. While these differences are recognized as hindrances to communal effort, it is possible to talk in terms of, for instance, similarities in religious and social beliefs from one community or subgroup to another. If anything, it is a ritual relationship that binds all—the belief in the power of divinity, the belief in Esu or fate, even though in such a belief may be found shades of difference in worship and concept within and among the various communities. Although it is difficult to extend this consistency beyond the Yoruba communities without conducting some sort of survey, one may assume that there are likely parallels in belief among the different ethnic groups, especially those held together, however insecurely, by common frontiers or a central government. To be sure, the catastrophic collapse of power and the economy may be partly caused by precisely the differences existent in the tribal or ethnic groups lumped together by the imperial administration. Nevertheless, it is possible to see this demise not only as a tragedy of the inability to unite, but also, through its common belief in the fate process, as a satiric attack of fate on the society—although this idea may not clearly explain why the society is, collectively, a victim of the satiric assault.

Looking at the overall picture of corruption and licentiousness in the second civilian regime in Nigeria (from 1979 to 1983), one sees not only a depletion of the economy on a large scale by a few, but also a general tendency in all walks of life to emulate, in varying degrees, the corrupt leaders of the society. Everybody, it seems, wanted to have a slice of the huge whale of booty that on the one hand appeared inexhaustible, but that on the other posed a fear that the best part of it might soon disappear. The whale image is deliberate. The myth of inexhaustibility, as exemplified by the wasting of money in spraying sessions, seems a characteristic feature of belief. It recalls the story of the dead body of a "monster"—perhaps a whale or a shark—seen washed up on the Atlantic beach in Lagos, the present Victoria Island, around 1952. People who went to see it and to cut a piece of meat from the creature told of its foreboding presence and the inexhaustibility of its flesh.

Admittedly, a remarkably large number of people probably did not participate in the looting, but then neither did they try to prevent it, or if they did, the attempt probably had a wrong or indirect emphasis and therefore was not effective. There was nothing in the nature of, for instance, the people's (farmers') movement of the Agbekoya uprising (1968) during the previous military regime—a protest against high taxes and new modes of taxation.[76] The inability to prevent corruption can perhaps be explained as a tragic powerlessness on the part of the few who may have tried and failed—and to try was to face consequences such as prison detention. But such powerless attempts were certainly overshadowed by the general outlook of collective complicity. At any rate, a disruption in the economic flow, whether by an individual or by a few, is a disruption of the complementary forces of good and evil which, if not checked or controlled, would only lead to chaos. It is in this regard that one can justify the catastrophic demise as a satire on the collective consciousness of the society.

To illustrate this satire more concretely, a microcosmic case in point may be made from an insight by one of my informants about one of Esu's favorite rendezvous—the marketplace. Here, a representation of the macrocosmic society, a cross section of the community may be found—rich and poor, old and young, from various occupations and, more important, representatives of the various ethnic groups. Here everybody, exploiters and plain dealers alike, converges to be exploited by the market price inflaters, who have taken their cue, and are taking their toll, from the resounding chinks of "gold" waste being sprayed by the powers that be. In terms of my concept, this inflation may be regarded as a satire that Esu (fate) has exerted on his victims through the agency of the market sellers. Or perhaps, on another level of thinking, each individual's (seller's) fate in the marketplace may be seen to be provoked by the economic pressures of society that collectively levy a satiric attack, in terms of inflated prices, on the consumer. However, since the satire affects the whole community or the fate of the society (and the attack is brought about by the conditions within the society), a collective way to describe the situation is simply that the society is a satiric victim of its own fate, that is, the fatal power generated by its own fate or Esu. This may be illustrated by what has been established in the last chapter, the capacity of Esu, as the archetypal satiric power and satirist, to reproduce himself. In this regard, the grotesque inflation can be seen as the image of satire reproduced by the satirist, the fatal power, through the agency of the market, a locality for fatal possibilities. It is on this account that Esu's "problematic coolness" is sought through libations of palm oil, as Thompson observes. But, as explained in the introduction, surely no "coolness" can be maintained unless a balance is maintained in the society itself, a balance that marks the devotee's (individual's, community's, society's) own "problematic coolness."

For the stagnant economy, inflation, armed robbery are all manifestations of the fatal power of Esu generated to strike awareness of that imbalance and the necessity to maintain a balance. They are the grotesque images of the moral indictment levied to chastise the social contagion or epidemic of waste. To be sure, the wastage and the consequential bankruptcy describe a logical process that requires no analysis or special investigation; but the consideration here is a fatalistic view, based on the ritual concept of Esu-Elegba.

Perhaps a more expressive manifestation, in terms of the visual image of fatality, is the automobile accident as a claimant of lives in Nigeria. Statistics drawn over an eight-year period (1967–1974) show that Nigeria, compared with other developing African countries and leading industrialized countries, has the highest number of accidents per capita per year as well as the highest yearly rate of increase. Deaths from automobile accidents in Nigeria, recorded by RTA (Road Traffic Accidents), were greater in number annually than those from the prevalent communicable diseases, for instance, the cholera epidemic of 1971.[77] But in order to be able to put this epidemic in satiric perspective, we must examine some of the conditions on the Nigerian highway, the attitude of its users and the implications of this attitude in terms of the general recognition of Esu as a god of fate.

Indeed, the road, like the marketplace, is a world that attracts people from all walks of life, and where accident is no respecter of wealth or status. And since Esu is generally attributed as the cause of these unforeseen mishaps, it will be understood that whatever happens has to do with the fate of the victim. Because accidents happen so frequently there is a tendency to regard them as an inevitable fact of life. It is possible to conceive the network of interaction on the roads of modern Nigeria as a macrocosmic world of fatality in which a human being (driver, passenger, passerby), as a microcosmic individual, is inescapably exposed and constantly trapped by the unfathomable guiles of chance, the risks and challenges of life. Such a perspective assumes a world of strife in which anything can happen to anybody at any time, be it the most careful and excellent driver, the seemingly innocent passenger or passerby, or even the stay-at-home, as is sometimes the case.

But the implications go further. For the logical supposition that the number of accidents can be reduced by conscious effort is not reflected by the general attitude toward life on the Nigerian roads. In fact, that attitude poses an ironic statement on any attempt at such an effort. (The Road Safety Corps was such an attempt; it was established in 1977 to deal with lawless, reckless drivers on the highway.) Nevertheless, it does not mean that road users are not aware of the dangers on the road. But drivers have a sort of carefree attitude that seems to give them the conviction that nothing can happen to them on the road. This conviction, which seems to throw an ironic questioning on the fatalistic view, comes from what I have come to see as a certain mental or physical acknowledgment of Esu.

The expectation of drivers or passengers going from point A to B that they will reach their destination safely is itself a recognition of the god of fate. It is an indirect prayer to the god for guidance, or a pact between them and the god that there should be nothing to obstruct the natural process of fate. For death by accident is not natural. As stated previously, a natural process of fate implies a life span from youth to old age in which one has a spouse, children, a good education, etc.[78] But there are also physical identifications of this indirect invocation.

The vehicles that use Nigerian roads most frequently are those carrying passengers and goods—buses, taxis, vans and trucks of various forms and makes. They ply the cities, towns, villages and almost any road, tarred or graveled, smooth or crooked, narrow or tortuous, corner or hill. No condition of the road seems to present any problem to the economic prospects of the driver and vehicle, nor to the value-for-money demands of the passenger—although this is often at the expense of the physical and mental state of all. For the rough and tumble of this economic venture not only results in wear and tear on the vehicle's body and engine, but also can give the passenger mental and physical strain. This compulsive dependence on the Nigerian road is partly concerned with the problem of communication; the inefficient postal and telephone systems make road transport the most effective means of communication. However, the complexities of the equally wasteful procedures that have caused such deficiencies will not be dealt with here. Newspaper reports of abandoned or unfinished projects often imply that some sort of embezzlement of funds is involved.

Regarding the recognition of Esu, an interesting feature common to these vehicles may be focused on: the various captions usually inscribed on the front, back or side panels, or sometimes on all. To understand the often metaphoric meaning of these inscriptions is to have an idea of some of the concerns, apprehensions and preoccupations which condition the Yoruba, and in fact the Nigerian, mind. The captions are usually in the form of an assertion, a warning, a question or an abuse, or any combination of these. For the purposes of this study, I have collected the ones whose meanings and implications reflect a consciousness of fate and its possibilities on the highway. They were gathered randomly on Ife-Ibadan and Lagos-Ibadan highways and represent a cross section of the passenger vehicles found in the southwest region of Nigeria.

It should be pointed out, however, that these captions are not necessarily a conscious thought or signification of the inscriber or the driver, that is, within the frame of this interpretation. It is possible that most of them were written with no serious intention or primary objective other than to decorate the vehicles with catchy phrases or humorous expressions, like the naive art sometimes seen on some of them. Indeed, some may not be explained further than this—for example, "Uncle Omoge," which is just a humorous comment on a man that likes young, beautiful women. Regarding the dangers of interpretation, there is, nowadays, mass production of these captions on stickers, which makes any attempt at useful interpretation difficult. As such, the illustrations used here are somewhat selective in terms of what will more easily explain my frame of reference.

Furthermore, many of the traditional themes have been corrupted in recent times by a lot of foreign influences, like English, American, or Christian and Islamic concepts. Although some of these influences have not actually destroyed the basic meaning or interpretation, and some betray the fertile imagination of the writer, they have on the whole limited the range of choices because of the degree of ambiguity generated by these corruptions. For example, one panel of a vehicle reads: "Jesu O Seun. E ye binu Ori. Jesus saves." Here, a traditional thought (Don't be envious of Ori—that is, another person's good "ori") is flanked, almost nonsensically, by Christian-based thoughts, "Thank you Jesus" and "Jesus saves." Although the traditional thought could stand on its own, the juxtaposing is uncomfortable by the evangelical implication of the Christian thought. Nevertheless, a lot of the captions are common sayings revealing Yoruba traditional thought, ideal or moral, commenting on life. The selections have therefore been made with the view of showing their particular relevance to life on the highway in relation to the fate of its users. A few examples should illustrate this.

One reads: "The Young Shall Grow; Igbehin a dun." The first part, an affirmation of the natural biological process, is self-explanatory in its English form. Its verbal reminder is almost redundant, but it is hardly an overstatement in an environment where the process can suddenly be halted, or where the desirable natural process of fate is thought to be interfered with. The second part of the caption in Yoruba reinforces the desire by confirming the joy of it: literally, "The end shall be sweet" (pleasurable). For the implied desire, taking both expressions together, is a realization of a full life, consisting of at least a spouse, some children, an economically satisfying job, and the benefits and respect of old age. In other words, it hopes for a full span of fate in which the young shall grow to old age, a fate unhandicapped or unfoiled by unnatural forms of death like motor accidents. Hence it is a short prayer to the fate god, who is capable of materializing or averting such events.

A common caption, and one that is fraught with traditional concepts, is "Iwa," which ordinarily means "character." But as stated before, character has to do with one's personality, which traditionally is a condition of the physical and metaphysical Ori and therefore a condition of fate. Indeed, as Bascom translates, "iwa" is "destiny."[79] In this regard, the caption is a reminder of the Yoruba's most important moral value, "Iwapele"—good character, by extension, a good fate.[80] It is also a warning to those who may not possess one, the "olori buruku." A good character assumes a good "ori" (head) and fate, one which should bring good luck on the road. In other words, it is one which expects Esu, the fate-essence, to open up accident-free conditions on the road and a safe accomplishment of the journey. The caption therefore indirectly and mentally ritualizes the efficacy of an accident-free journey, a hope that, in the inevitable interaction of fates on the highway, one may not encounter personalities with bad ori whose bad luck or fate may infect a good one. There is an unusual but ironic combination of the good and the bad in the caption, "Iwa—Chop Life." "Chop Life" implies undesirable, high and carefree living which involves some sort of wealth pact and money wastage, the end of which is catastrophic.

But another condition the "Iwa" caption expresses as a prerequisite or quality of good character is the fact of patience,[81] since it is through patience that the journey on the road may be accomplished. Abimbola records a story from the Ifa corpus in which patience (suuru) is described as a quality of good character. This quality is implicit in another caption that is often seen, "Suuru Ni Baba Iwa" (Patience is the father of character). As we shall see, it is a quality that is often flouted on Nigerian roads, sometimes, ironically, by the driver of the truck or bus bearing the inscription.

Some captions appearing on the same or different vehicles easily lend themselves to various combinations that express in full the implications of the necessary awareness in life, especially life on the roads. For example, "Igba Laiye; Feso Jaiye; Ma Seka Ore Mi" (Life is a question of time span; Use cautionary discretion in living; Friend, do not indulge in evil). Surveying the process of fate in a life span, the captions warn that no condition is permanent, and that to misuse life is undesirable and against traditional precepts since it is fraught with consequences that shorten the natural process of fate. Again, as these expressions are written on a vehicle, one cannot but relate them to life on the road. In fact, nowhere else does one find the consequences of this lack of caution as vividly and demonstrably as on the highway.

Personalities that persist in disregarding such cautions, or in such an untraditional way of manipulating life, meet with direct but humorous abuse in some captions, for example: "Go on with Your Rocca (head?)—Sir Seleke"; "Esinmi Pomposity" (Stop being pompous); there are variations of this: "Esinmi Rascality"; Esinmi Ibaje"; "Onikoyi, Se Pele" (Onikoyi, exercise patience). The first seems to imply a person with a bad ori, suggesting that it should keep away so as not to infect a potentially good ori. "Sir Seleke," an example of ambiguity of language and thought from foreign influences, probably refers to a specific person, a sort of headstrong or no good character found on the motorways. It is a kind of shameless overbearing which the second caption also derides, perhaps relating to the selfish attitudes of some drivers, like holding up the flow of traffic (for instance, trucks that take up the road at a slow speed), or not giving proper signals, or passing illegally. A more common variation of this caption drives home the point: "Esinmi Ibaje" (Stop indiscipline). This has since received a stronger emphasis with the introduction of the WAI (War Against Indiscipline) crusade. The final captions may pass unnoticed or be waved off as just a warning. But if one considers the historical relevance of Onikoyi, the megalomaniacal, bloodhound-like warrior who, according to legend, was finally eaten alive by birds of prey,[82] then its ironic meaning becomes clear as regards reckless and selfish road users.

These captions, although only a small number appear here, cover a cross section of vehicles by the thought and consciousness expressed. As representations of Yoruba traditional thought on life, in this case life on the roads, they justify my contention that Esu, as fate god or fate-essence, commands a conscious acknowledgment of road users, even without an apparent or direct sacrifice offered to prove it. The acknowledgment is more psychic than physical, and the users in this world of roads include all whose daily transactions depend directly or indirectly on use of the road, whether on foot or by vehicle. The transactions include friendly visits from one house to another and business journeys to the market, office, school or farm. For these transactions inevitably bring the users of the roads in contact with the captions, which readily reveal their own inner feelings and apprehensions as they ply the roads. In other words, the captions parallel the travellers' own thoughts, their hopes and prayers, more so when a link is made between the captions and the many horrid accidents often encountered along the roads. For instance, an ironic caption on an accident vehicle will not fail to arrest the attention of passengers or passersby, who sometimes point up the irony further, with their verbal gift for punning, by directing a humorous or abusive remark at the vehicle or at the "olori buruku" that has effected the accident.

Such tongue-in-cheek use of words has fashioned some of the appellations given to the various types of passenger vehicles that travel the city and interstate roads. For instance, there is the "Bolekaja" (Alight and let's fight), implying the ramshackle character of the old "mammy-wagon" buses and the rough, tough breed that drives them. There is the "Oluwole" (God has entered), relating to the disastrous accident that occurred when one of the so-called buses crashed into the walls of a house. The appellation thus establishes the vehicle as an irony of fate which God, for reasons best known to Him, may again deflect from the road into another house. It also says something about the "olori buruku" whose fate it is to drive such buses.

The "Oku-Eko" (the dead-dilapidated of Lagos) refers to the type of municipal buses in Lagos that constantly break down anywhere and at any time. Both the name and the inaction, however, indict the government officials who engaged in buying these secondhand buses from Europe at supposedly firsthand prices. Then there is the "Danfo," which suggests uprightness, but ironically this type of vehicle, because of its high clearance and lightness, and also because of the way it is recklessly driven, is accident-prone.

Again, these appellations, like the captions, one way or another comment on and acknowledge the ironic function of Esu, that is, his peripetic ability to cause road accidents. Because the appellations are household words in Nigeria, we can also assume that the whole society, consciously or otherwise, acknowledges this ironic function. The awareness further suggests, by extension, that the people comprising the society are potential devotees of Esu. However, if this recognition is clear and conceivable, the fact that they are potential victims is less so. This needs a little clarification.

One way of looking at the reckless driver and the accident into which he or she is thrown is to see the accident as a just consequence of the driver's action. But this is too simplistic and does not take in all the complexities involved in the satiric process. Indeed, in vain we shall seek to find any logic or meaning in the action of a driver who is aware of the daily occurrence of motor accidents on the highway, and whose vehicle is the bearer of a caption or captions which recognize the possibilities of fatal consequences, and yet who drives recklessly, as if begging for death. This action, however, has a rational basis which gives us a new dimension of Esu's ironic function. For to relate reckless driving to the ritual concept of Esu is to understand how the driver is inseparably bound up with the drama of life to which fate commits him or her, and by which the driver becomes a victim of satire.

To be aware of consequences and yet plunge heedlessly into the abyss of fatality presumes a challenge, a dire will in the face of death. It is a challenge that recalls Ogun's combative will, discussed in the introduction. And since every motorist is technically a devotee of Ogun, by virtue of manipulating Ogun's metallic device, one could say that the challenge is a heroic act to be desired. In reality, therefore, the irony of the consequence seems to lie not so much with the awareness of Esu (at least not directly) as with that of Ogun, the god of iron. It lies between the level of awareness and what this awareness means to the driver, in other words, his commitment to what is actually thought to be desirable. The captions on the vehicles are more or less the anticipated hope, prayer or psychical sacrifice which the devotee-driver directs to the god and ancestral patron, Ogun. Thus directed (and traditionally the prayer or sacrifice is supposed to be conveyed by Esu as messenger), the devotee ritually absolves himself of all the human weaknesses and misdemeanors that caused the fatal ruptures of the past, and which are likely to fashion those of the immediate future. With a renewed sense of freedom like that which develops after an actual offering of sacrifice, he plunges recklessly into the unknown future. He confidently anticipates, on account of his ritual absolution, not fatality, but survival, through the magical power (Ase) of his god. With this conviction, he often gets carried away so that, intoxicated or possessed by the will of his patron god, he is invariably exposed to the same retributive punishment of his god's error of judgment, that is, the lack of awareness or recognition of Esu. Lost in the intoxication of the act of driving and the vision of accomplishment (reaching the destination), the driver is unwittingly blind to the fatal possibilities of that very act. In fact, this act—the speed, the recklessness, the intoxication—is a sort of pact with fate or Esu which, however, is fraught with consequences. Reiterating the story of Ogun's diabolical act, we will find a similar pact with fate and a similar fatal consequence. Intoxicated with his wilful prowess and his vision of conquest, Ogun massacred both friend and foe, a satiric action caused by his lack of awareness and self-control. Similarly, the motorist in his or her pact with fate loses self-control, a traditional imperative of Esu, a failing which may result in the satiric fatality of an accident. The fatality therefore may be construed in terms of the limitation of the driver's awareness—a confusion between what is desirable as regards one's patron god, and the desirable recognition of the fatal consequences of one's diabolic action, of the satiric action of one's Esu.

For to take cognizance of the director of fate is to recognize the limits of man's intoxication or possession, the limits of his will. It is also an attempt to maintain a balance, or a mediation, between the complementary forces of good and evil embodied by his fate, which is difficult but nevertheless necessary for the fullness of his life.[83] The difficulty of maintaining his balance is the irony of human action, which is tragic. In this respect, with regard to Esu, satire seems to bear affinities with tragedy. Relating to the boundaries, Frye states, "Satire at its most concentrated . . . is tragedy robbed of all its dignity and nobility, a universal negation that cheapens and belittles everything."[84] Seidel, however, observing Wyndham Lewis' "nonmoral" attitude to satire, says that for the poet-satirist "satire is a grinning tragedy."[85] In the macrocosmic world of the motorways, a manifestation of this irony is the grotesque satiric expressions of Esu in terms of motor accidents. It is a world in which man as the microcosmic entity is constantly satirized by his own fate.

However, this conclusion obviously raises some questions about the persons other than the driver who may be part of an accident. While the accident may be justified because of the reckless driving of the motorist, it does not account for the lives of the passengers in the accident vehicle—those the driver has infected, as it were, with his or her "bad head." But it is possible to explore the same theory established for the mass contagion of economic bankruptcy.

The act of setting out on a journey with an awareness of the dangers of the road is itself a commitment of one's fate to those risks, or to the daring of death. In another perspective, it is a risk that one takes with whatever pact one makes with Esu—a pact of business, trade, pleasure, and so on. For the driver as well as for the passenger there is a common and basic objective of the pact, a desired objective of the will, which is in conflict with the risks of the pact. It is the desire to reach their destination, to transact or accomplish their pact. It is a hope for the rewards of their pact. Toward attaining his desire, the passenger also projects a symbolic gesture of sacrifice, verbally or mentally by way of a prayer, a traditional thought like that implied in the captions; or the gesture could even be a more formal acknowledgment, a call for protection and guidance. But in fact, in the process, the passenger also often gets carried away by this gesture and betrays a characteristic impatience to reach the destination. It is possible, of course, that part of this impatience is due to the fact that this most effective means of communication can often be time-wasting and tedious as opposed to other means, like the telephone. For instance, making business deals on a first come, first served basis will naturally provoke such impatience. Nevertheless, experience shows that, being anxious to arrive quickly at the destination (sometimes a matter of life and death), the passenger very rarely challenges the recklessness of the driver. As such, his anxious silence may be tantamount to compliance. Consequently, because of the risks involved, his desire is in ironic conflict with his awareness of fatal consequences, for which limitation he may be brought into a satiric judgment through circumstances beyond his control. It is in this light that one can make sense of the carnage effected by the careless, reckless and inept drivers on Nigerian roads. These, along with the victims of other accidents of life, are manifestations of Esu's satire, or fate's power of satire. The grotesque forms and shapes of the accident vehicles that litter the roads are the physical exteriorization or expression of this power, the self-propagating image of Esu, the satire and master satirist, whose weapon is double-edged irony. (In recent times, fewer wrecks are seen, although it is doubtful whether the rate of accidents has been reduced considerably. The reason may be that the wreckage is now cleared from the roads almost immediately after accidents.)

Not only is the morbid art consistent with satire, which is equally morbidly grotesque, but so also is the morbid moralization that it seems to project. Confronted by the grotesquery, the initial reaction of the onlooker is probably a spontaneous laugh, because of the sheer ridiculousness of the mangled shapes. And wit or humor is one of the essentials of satire.[86] But the tragic implication of the impact soon takes over, jolting and halting the senses. In that moment of time, all ironies with which satire has been effected cease to be funny. The facial creases of the initial laughter immediately freeze into horrid grimaces, a mirror image of the satiric grotesquery of the accident. This is the moral impact of the satire, the double-edged irony that, as Alexander Pope may have implied, "heals with morals what it hurts with wit."[87] It recalls the impact on Ogun, when he was sober, of the stark, horrid reality of his involuntary, senseless massacre. Like that butchery, the carnage on Nigerian roads is that of the double-edged satiric power of Esu, the trickster-satirist whose "matter" (that is, the problematic condition in man) is the difficult ritual affirmation of keeping in balance the good and evil essence in man.

And if the impact of the grotesquery has not effected a radical change in the actions of humans (the recklessness of drivers, or the views of travellers), it is because satire in general, in spite of its objectives and castigating devices, has not effected much change in its public, society or audience outside its context.

Speaking about Aristophanes on the idea, R. W. Corrigan says: "For better or worse, Aristophanes failed in his attempts to change the patterns of Greek history. Quite predictably, the Greeks did not follow his advice and go back to the good old days."[88] One reason for this may be what Elliott sees as the relationship between society and the satirist: "Society, quite naturally, is dubious . . . it points to the inevitable discrepancy between the ideal image, projected by rhetorical convention, and what it takes to be the actual fact."[89] And F. E. Lumley, reviewing the question on all sides, concludes, "The proposition that satire is an effective instrument of control must be left in the air."[90] Lycambes and his daughters' deaths had not prevented the possibility of other indictments from similar actions of men. There is no evidence that Archilochus stopped satirizing individuals that violated oaths—what seemed to have touched his anger to the quick. Neither had Roman satirists, especially the biting anger of Juvenal, prevented the fall of Rome. Similarly, modern satirists have not succeeded much, if at all, in their objectives, although their venom seems to have been tempered over the years by the aesthetic function of art. Furthermore, people seem not to have learnt from the catastrophic product of wealth pacts. For as long as people interact with others, who have their own fates, they will continue to be satiric victims, as it were, of that fate, of Esu the archetypal satirist in humans.

THE NEW WORLD MODEL

The second part of this chapter deals with victims of a different kind, the main difference being one of environment. For I shall now focus on the Yoruba diaspora in the Americas, including those countries that have Yoruba descendants as a result of the transatlantic slave trade, countries like Brazil, Cuba, Haiti, the Caribbean nations, and the United States.[91] No attempt is made to consider the character of particular countries in relation to their actual assimilation of Yoruba culture conception of Esu. It is sufficient for the purposes of my concept to recognize that Esu is an important figure or force of worship in the orisa cults, that is, the Candomble in Brazil, Santeria or Lucumi in Cuba, Voodoo in Haiti, New Orleans and New York. At any rate, even though some of the countries are well grounded in Yoruba religion, or in the worship of the orisa, it is a fruitless effort to try to isolate Yoruba descendants, what with the inevitable mixture of African tribes that occurred during the slave trade.[92] Furthermore, the cults have attracted not only other black groups but also whites and various other ethnic groups. As already explained, the Yoruba religion, judging by the survival of its gods, and due to some historical considerations as well as the policies of slaveholders, seems to have taken a dominant hold on the black over other African religions.[93] And Esu, known by various names, including Papa Legba (Haiti), Exu Siu Legba (Brazil), Elegua (Cuba) and Pomba Gira (Brazil), is probably the most influential of all the African gods. It is these kinds of beliefs that have made generalizations valid and my concept of satire

a conceivable pursuit, and consequently one may, in a way that was not possible in the case of Nigeria, talk in terms of a black or an African consciousness
as opposed to a specific Yoruba reality.

But in the consideration of Esu as a fate god and satirist in the New World,
the theory hitherto proposed of Esu as a single satiric force of fate in his society
would seem to break down, for the simple reason that we are regarding him
within an alien society and culture. This cannot be successfully discussed without examining the historical event that caused the development of the African
community in the alien culture and therefore brought the god there—that is,
the slave trade. And in doing this, the satiric focus becomes a bit distorted.
For instance, going by the concept we have been following, slave trading,
along with all its grotesque manifestations in Africa and in the New World,
would tend to be a satiric gesture or expression of the fatal god on his people.
But for what offense, one may ask? And why should this involve the European,
who appears to be the principal agent of the satire? The fact that the alien
culture poses as an instrument of the satirist, Esu, throws an ironic incongruity
on the issue—although this could be disputed. We could, for instance, argue
that slave trading was not seriously opposed in Africa, but rather presented
some (kings, chiefs, warriors) with new opportunities to amass wealth and power,
which resulted in the internecine wars (especially in the nineteenth century) to
open up new trade routes, secure slaves and acquire specialized weapons, like
guns and gunpowder.[94] Consequently, the African did not hesitate to sell his
own people, a fact which the European exploited and which led to the subsequent horrors of the slave trade. All this may be used to argue that, fatalisti-
cally, the atrocities of the slave trade were a justified satiric consequence.

However, I am interested here not so much in the complex causes and the
nature of the slave trade as in its effects on the African who, inevitably, developed the satiric sensibilities of his fate god as a compelling communal force
and a means of black survival. The issue is not so much why the blacks became
slaves of the white culture, as how they were able to survive their common
fate within and against the communal fate of a different culture. This process
of survival, without complicating it with slave trading itself, although this must
serve as a background, inevitably should yield sufficient insights with regard
to the subject of satire and its victims.

An Olori Elesu (head devotee of Esu) and Ifa priest at Ife, Faloba, made an
observation, with an introspective conviction, that at first sounded naive—that
lamentably, Christianity and Islam were responsible for splitting Esu in three
different directions.[95] Actually, there is some truth in this, since both religions
have in fact attracted Esu into their respective religion's mythical history, locating his origins in the Garden of Eden and Mecca.[96] For instance, some of
my informants began our meeting with a Christian- or Islam-based interpretation of Esu before I diverted them from that line of thought. The Elesu at Ife
went on to elaborate on his stance regarding Christianity by asserting that the
white man, when he came, took the god away to his land, where he made him
the devil, and brought him back to Africa in that image.

There is obviously a distortion of facts or lack of historical coherence in the observation, since evidence of Christian conversion in Nigeria or Africa does not support Faloba's notion. Christian missionaries came to convert, not to take away and then convert. But on second thought, his is not an unusual observation, at least not any worse in distortion than other speculative interpretations, given people's inclinations to fantasize. Esu apparently is blamed for the coming of the British.[97] Another interpretation makes a case for the slaves: that the "migration of the Yoruba people to the New World was ordained by spiritual forces in order to insure a widespread belief in the Orisha."[98] The latter would make sense of the notion that Esu was the "civilizer, the one who opens your eyes to the way things really are."[99] Indeed, the Elesu might not have been thinking of the missionary invasion of Africa per se, but rather the events that occurred prior to the Christian bombardment, and that influenced or first established the devil interpretation. For the major contact with whites, which had occurred before any significant missionary work began, was the Atlantic slave trade. Although there was European contact with Africans prior to the Atlantic slave trade, Albert Raboteau notes that early missionaries in fact had little success and that the real missionary work and Christian conversion did not begin until "Christianized slaves began to return from Europe and America to Africa in the late eighteenth century."[100] Therefore, what Faloba might have implied was the European plunder that took away Africans, and no doubt their gods, as slaves—an experience out of which Esu syncretically emerged as the devil. As such, the Esu votary to a certain extent is logically correct, and his observation, if one goes along with it, opens up a number of questions and deductions that need to be examined. At any rate, his observation gives us a certain idea of Esu's versatility, and of course that of his devotees.

I reemphasize that it is a pointless exercise on the whole to try to determine why Yoruba religion, let alone African religion, has survived, or why its gods in particular have emerged as the most influential in the Candomble, or the Candomble de caboclo, which embraces other forms of religious worship.[101] David V. Trotman, in fact, attempted an analytic study of such survival or nonsurvival with regard to Trinidad and British Guiana.[102] The fact is that African religion has survived in certain areas, and the survival is prominent enough to make it an important institution of black culture.[103] It is also true that its survival, as in the Yoruba locality of origin, identifies Esu as either the most feared god or as a god that may not be slighted.[104] Yet, in spite of this, it is technically overpresumptuous and inaccurate to make Esu speak for all the transatlanticized slaves in the Americas and their subsequent descendants, precisely because of partial survival or nonsurvival of African religion in certain areas like British Guiana. I do not believe in the nonsurvival perspective; more extensive research in the future will bring to light evidences of specific, as opposed to speculative, shades of African survivals where survival has been assumed as nonexistent—researches that will look more closely into the Black Church, black music, and even black personality and concepts. But even where survival was discouraged, hindered or effaced by a strong existing Creole culture or Christianity, it is possible to relate in general to what Mechal Sobel suggests as a development of a quasi-African world view. This development, he says, "coalesced" the different cultures, "the various Sacred Cosmos, . . . under the impact of enslavement," which eventually developed the new Afro-Christian world view.[105] And if one relates to Esu's transliterative, fate-controlling role as a binding force in this coalition, a sort of metaphoric or mythopoeic interpretation, further to Faloba's conviction, can be suggested. By this, one is able to relate to the god as an expressive essence of the black experience in the collective struggle to establish an identity in the New World. It is in this struggle for survival that we can locate the satiric dimensions of the expression. First, we shall consider some of the characteristics that may have made the coalition inevitable.

Evidences of the brutal treatment of the slaves, who were manacled, whipped, packed like sardines in boats, branded or slave-driven, all point to the European conception of Africans as savage, barbaric, cannibalistic and, in short, devil-conditioned.[106] This conception was founded on false notions of their strange customs and the demons they supposedly worshipped which, subsequently, the Christian missionaries to the plantations and to Africa sought to exorcise so that the Africans could see the light of civilization.[107] This attitude, for instance, is implied in Mary Slessor's epitaph in Calabar, Nigeria: " 'The people that walked in darkness have seen a great light.' They that turn many to righteousness shall shine as the stars for ever and ever."[108] Seeing the light, however, did not mean that blacks could claim equality as human beings with their white masters since they were considered basically inferior and therefore must remain slaves—as several proslavery arguments of the planters have vehemently stressed.[109] In this regard, the black African's color was no help, but rather confirmed this devil nature. This idea was not only supported with forced references from biblical stories, like the story of Ham,[110] but also was determined by Western classical authors' conception of primitive Africa.[111] With this obviously stereotyped image of the black, it should be possible to build a theory of Esu within the plantation community of the various African cultures which later evolved as the Afro-American cultures in the Americas, a theory which identifies the generality as devotees of Esu.

It is possible to hold that Esu's symbolic color is black, although not the Western concept of black. This color may sometimes range between shades of black and red, or may be balanced with red or white. Esu's wood figures or dance wands, for instance, are usually colored black and sometimes draped with white cowrie beads. In some of his stories, his symbolic colors are either black and white, or black and red, or even black, white and red, as in some versions of the story of the two farmers already mentioned. The combination of colors suggests ambiguity, ambivalence, irony or even the complementary forces of good and evil which he embodies. But the color black, associated with the devil, had haunted the Christian fathers' imagination, subsequently influencing early European traders and the missionaries to Africa and the plantations. This color, by its more exotic evocations, apparently was related to the magical kingdom of the legendary Christian Emperor of Ethiopia, Prester John, which had captured the imagination of Europe and subsequently brought Spanish, Portuguese and English explorers to Africa. Ironically, the futile attempts to locate the holy kingdom eventually gave way to the equally "vivid and fantastic descriptions of black monsters and cannibals, related much more closely in size and shape to the ape than to European human beings." Ironically also, it was these explorations of the mythical African kingdom that led to the enslavement of black Africans.[112] In the process, the color had also become more definitive and more sharply focused as technical black.

Therefore, to insist on the complementary embodiment of good and evil (creative and destructive, really) and to recognize Esu still as the god of fate in the new environment is contrary to the Christian and European cultural ideas of the slave masters. But to do this is certainly one way of reevaluating the stereotyped image of the black and of establishing an expression of a black identity. It also identifies and puts in perspective the collective will of the black reacting in various ways against the hostile "peculiar institution" that threatened his survival. The reaction, therefore, can be considered in its expression as a satiric indictment on the slave masters. For the overall treatment of the slaves flouted the traditional codes of conduct and ethics of the black identity.[113] In this regard, the effort to identify and the struggle to survive may be seen in terms of what have already been established as fatal conflicts. Here, consistent with the general overview, it is a case of the communal fate or character (of the black slaves) in conflict with another communal fate (of the white masters). Here, also, fate may be understood in relation to the role of the slave and that of the master. The role of the master, that is, the slave owner or shareholder, was to make certain that the slaves worked and produced agricultural goods for maximum profit. Since these products were exported from the South not only to the North but also to Europe, one could say that this role extended to maintaining a national economic (and social) stability for the whites. In order to be able to achieve this objective effectively, the master's role further extended to coercing the slave by several means as well as seeing to it that the slave was strong and healthy. To this end, the owner tried to maintain a paternalistic relationship with the slave, although this paternalism was fraught with hypocrisies and ambiguities which were generated by the white hegemony projected through racism and dominant power.[114] The role of the slave, on the other hand, was to serve and be subservient to the master, whose property and chattel he or she was. In this role the slave was often regarded as a "perpetual child" and "the very mudsill of society," whose prerequisites were "vigor, docility, fidelity" because he or she was black and of an inferior race.[115]

The two roles each defined the character and will of the master and the slave. Because of the paternalistic concerns (genuine or otherwise) of the master, he or she tended to treat the slave like a child to be coerced, threatened and punished into doing the master's will. Also, because the master regarded the slave

as a savage and an inferior, the coercion, threat or punishment was often proportionate to the master's view of savagery—as demonstrated by severe, ani-
malistic whipping and lynching on the one hand, and proselytizing fervor of
evangelism on the other.[116] The role of the slaves also defined their character
and will. In spite of the fact that their health and well-being were maintained
by the master, the force of labor to which they were subjected, the savage
treatment they often received, the evangelistic imposition of the whites' religion over their own cultural beliefs, all combined to show up the ambiguities
and hypocrisies of paternalism, against which the slave inevitably reacted or
rebelled.

If we hold the Yoruba view that fate is conditioned by character and will, it
is possible to see the relationship between the master and the slave as one of
interacting fates that generate fatal conflicts. However, since the concept derives from an African perspective, I shall approach the satiric overtones of the
conflict purely from the point of view of the slave. In this regard, one point
must be understood from the outset: the white's conception of the slave as a
savage, a devil and a perpetual child was a violation not only of the character
of the slave, but also of the cultural dynamic that characterized and directed
the slave's fate and existence. This dynamic, from the Yoruba concept, is Esu-
Elegbara.

The slaves, in fact, certainly understood this condition of their existence
even by their often seemingly naive but ironical remarks, really their subtle
indictment of the white master. Apparently asked by a bishop why African
slaves "persisted in worshipping the devil instead of God," the response of the
slave was: "God is good, God is love and don't hurt anybody—do as you
please, God don't hurt you: but do bad and the devil will get you for sure! We
need not bother about God, but we try to keep on the good side of the devil."[117]
The curious question one may ask, however, is why the God that whites worship allows such brutality or violence against the slave. For such "badness" is
punishable by the African "devil."

This recognition by the slave, as an affirmation of the fateful and fatal capacities of the dynamic, proposes a relationship that is of utmost importance to
his or her well-being, a relationship, as implied in the remark quoted above,
that transcends that with God. Significantly, it is that which identifies the slaves
as Esu's children. For instance, exasperated and frustrated by his master's persistent attempt to win his slaves as Christian converts, a slave asserts the controller of his existence:

Master: In whose image were you made?
Slave: In the image of the devil, master.[118]

Of course, it is possible that the slave was being ironic or sarcastic. But this is
precisely the point, for Esu is a master ironist. It is the irony that links the
slaves, as devotees, with their god of fate, an irony which becomes clearer in
contexts such as the following:

White folk go to chu'ch,
He nevuh crack a smile.
Nigguh go to chu'ch
You heah 'm laff a mile.[119]

Here the "laff" imposes a comic relief on the lyric, but then it is also a satiric laugh of the Esu-conditioned "nigguh" deflating, rather grotesquely, the hypocritical piety of the Christian "white folk." Or, to use a black idiom which has been explored as a semiotic device by a black literary critic, Henry Gates, Jr., the "black" laugh is signifying upon the signified—white Christian solemnity or piety.[120] Apparently we can trace black Christian adoption of Esu by a later development. For instance, George Rawick identifies Legba (Esu), through metaphysical parallels, with "The Little Man" in the southern black conversion stories he collected.[121]

It should be clear from the foregoing that Esu is an ever-present consciousness among the slaves in the New World; that he is the ultimate controller of their fate; and that he is the black dynamic that is violated and provoked by the white community of slaveholders, overseers, slavemasters, proslavery advocates, and so on. If we accept this view, then it is only logical to think that he, as satirist and the satiric power and by a fatalistic justification, must counter the falsification of the whites with an avenging satiric action. Slaveholding in this regard can be seen as a component of the Western capitalistic system, or as a symbol of the extremely corrupting influence of Western capitalism, which violates the African traditional system of sharing. In terms of Esu, it is a wealth pact that inevitably manifests satiric consequences. It is with this view that we can probe the characteristic features of rebel slaves and their satiric overtures. For rebellion was the only choice left for the slaves in their dilemma. Inflicted on them by slavery, the dilemma made them vacillate between the role expected of them by the white slaver's culture and society and that which defined their own cultural character. But the rebellion came in many forms, although these can be examined within two main categories—direct rebellion in physical action against the given role, and indirect rebellion through accommodation of the role. The adoption by the slave of either alternative, in any of its forms, has been the subject of various historical examinations, since both tendencies offer clues to the character of the slave on the plantations.[122]

At one extreme, we have the so-called rebel slave, as evidenced by slave insurrections such as the ones led to Toussaint L'Ouverture in Haiti (1791), Denmark Vesey in Charleston, South Carolina (1822), Nat Turner in Southampton County, Virginia (1831), and "Sarah," who was described as the "biggest devil that ever lived."[123] At the other extreme, we have the docile slave, as evidenced by slaves who seemed to have internalized their masters' expectations and therefore appeared loyal and content with their lot.[124] Both these tendencies are forms of rebellion, as I shall argue, and there were others that fit into these categories, for instance, running away, self-mutilation and suicide, all of which were attempts at resistance against the peculiar institution.[125] To be sure, most of the insurrections failed in their physical objectives to kill the whites and exterminate slavery, for the slaves were soon suppressed and their leaders killed. Nevertheless, the rebellions showed the capacities of the "Negroes" to summon up or invoke their "devil" power to strike the evil of slavery with "evil." It is their ability or potential to "indict" the slave master with catastrophic "imprecations." But then, we must not forget that these violent attempts at freedom eventually led to the Civil War by bringing an awareness of the inhumanity of the peculiar institution, which justifies Esu's role as "manumitter."[126]

In order to be able to reflect on the full implications of the satiric power of the slaves and, by extension, that of their descendants, we shall have to come to terms with the supposed submissiveness and loyalty of the "docile" slave. Ironically, various studies have shown him to be the more notorious of the categories, especially as conceived by white culture. His principal stereotyped image, much exploited in antebellum literature, entertainment and art by anti-slavery and proslavery advocates alike, is "Sambo."[127] Implicated as the image of the black, he has many contradictory characteristics. He is loyal, ignorant, docile, stupid, and yet irresponsible, outrageously hysterical, ridiculously given to wild and wide laughs. And he is also a runaway. Furthermore, his African features (eyes, teeth, lips, nose) have been exaggerated to suggest savagery, barbarism, cannibalism—in short, the incarnation of the devil.

Although these incongruous generalizations represent an obviously unacceptable legitimation of the image of the black, with which no black person would wish to be associated, this image has nevertheless provoked various inquiries. These include the psychological impact of slavery and plantation life;[128] the paternalistic relationship between master and slave;[129] slave personality types and the contradictions of Sambo characteristics;[130] Sambo characteristics as representative of many slave societies, etc.[131] Such studies have made generalizations about Sambo as an image of the black particularly limited and limiting.

Yet Sambo, apparently a West African name,[132] remained a real appellation of North American slavery. In fact, the image, by the various arguments it provoked, seems to have lived in the minds of Americans, white and black, well into modern times, in an effort to relate modern tendencies realistically with the past. As recently as 1972, a group of teachers reacted against the use of Sambo stories in the school system because of their racist implications.[133] Contrarily, there was, more recently, a bid to bring back the television series "Amos 'n' Andy," which depicted stereotypes of Sambo and had been taken off the air in 1966 at the height of the civil rights movement.[134] Also, a major new book exclusively on Sambo has not only placed him deservedly on a heroic pedestal among a long line of world fools, but has also recognized the American jester as the longest surviving in any popular culture.[135] In this respect, perhaps there is no need to justify or disclaim Sambo's stereotypic image; rather, it might be more profitable, at least for the purposes of this book, to consider the image in the light of the fatal conflicts of black survival in a new and alien culture.

Kenneth Stampp has an insight in this direction when he concludes that the art of Sambo is "the art of conscious accommodation along with all its psychic consequences [and] is one of the skills that Negroes carried with them from slavery to freedom."[136] The observation supports my contention that the seemingly derogatory stamp of the Sambo stereotype can, in fact, be turned to more productive use apropos black survival and the black communal fate in the New World. For rather than merely looking at the image of Sambo as an unwanted one, we can begin to perceive it as a product of two contradictory choices to which Africans were fated in the "forced" ordering of their existence—the choices of rebel and docile slave. The forced ordering of their fate as opposed to the traditional ordering in their African locality is, as has been noted, a violation of their cultural values and may be construed as a capitalist wealth pact from the point of view of Esu. This ordering, again as suggested, tended to commit Africans to a dual role playing as they vacillated between the role demanded of them by the white culture and that of their own cultural character. Hence the contradictory choices of which Sambo is a product can be considered, whether singly or as a fusion of both, as an ironic characteristic of survival. Since the survival clearly expresses the fate process of the African slaves and their descendants, it would seem appropriate to consider it in the light of what has so far been established of the fate god with whom, after all, they had weathered the Atlantic crossing. For the irony of their existence mirrors the god's, the archetypal satiric power and satirist. It is in this light that the rebellion of the slave (whether through docility, insurrection, or running away) can be seen as an emanation of the satiric power of Sambo, the satirist.

To start with, parallels can be made between some of the already established ironic attributes of Esu and the stereotyped evocations of the slave-Sambo to show up the latter as a manifestation of the former. For instance, regarded as a messenger (slave) of both gods and humans, Esu, far from being a common messenger or slave, is not only dependent on the propitiation of his seeming "masters" but—and this is more important—is also depended upon for his fateful services for their existence. This would seem to be consistent with stories of Esu which describe him as the master or the greatest of all the gods. In such stories, superiority is gained only by deception using calm wit and intelligence.[137] Because of the dependency, he is a god that may not be neglected. Standing at the "gate" or the threshold of experience in any event, celebration, preoccupation (social, religious, political, etc.) or activity known to man or god, he has to be regarded first or nothing can be guaranteed. But then, to propitiate does not necessarily spell success, what with the chains of complex, error-suffused relationships between humans and their gods, between their will and the laws of the cosmos. This fact establishes Esu's designation as god of fate and embraces all that is associated with fate—chance, fortune, misfortune, magic and the concept of good and evil—all of which Esu expresses one way or another. Hence his tricks, deception, shiftiness and unpredictability, manifest confusion, irony and satire among men—although he is only in effect projecting character tendencies in the conflicting interactions of men. However, as an enigma to the uninitiated, he is a much maligned god. His deceptive personality has suffered from anthropological and psychological interpretations which emphasize his rebellious, childlike and phallic tendencies. For instance, the figure of Esu with a finger between his lips evokes from some scholars an image of a suckling child.[138] But this interpretation probably is a misconception. One of my informants, more to my conception, interprets it as Esu's calculatingly thoughtful pose as he surveys his next fateful move or calling.[139] However, perhaps some of the anthropological or psychological interpretations are influenced by the Fon concept, in West Africa, which emphasizes attributes like sexual potency.[140] Also, cast in the role of the devil by proselytizing missionaries, he is thus implicated, by association, as one who has committed blacks to their barbaric, savage, indolent, immoral and polygamous nature.

Placed against this background of Esu, characteristics evoked by the image of Sambo are very revealing. As a slave on the plantation, he was formally made dependent on the master, who provided his food and clothing to sustain his health and general well-being. But consequently he was also indispensable since his existence provided the master's family with subsistence and perhaps wealth, and sustained the economic relationship between the plantation South and the outer world. Because African slaves were so indispensable, the master had to think of ways to get the maximum amount of work out of them, for instance, "by threats, by promises of rewards, by flattery and a dozen other devices he knew of."[141] John Blassingame speaks of the difficult task of the overseer, whose job could be jeopardized by exerting excessive coercion likely to be detrimental to the slave's potential.[142] Advertisements in newspapers for runaways also tell us a great deal about how anxious masters were to recover their slaves.[143] Yet, if we consider the fact that the slave was responsible for provoking the guilt feelings of the abolitionists and the confusion between the North and the South in antebellum America which led to the Civil War in 1860, and subsequently to slavery's downfall,[144] we may note in the slave something of Esu's satiric attack on his victims. Indeed, we see, through Sambo, Esu the satiric manumitter.

To recognize the irony underlying the slaves' compliance with the master's cajoling and subtle coercion, to acknowledge their rebellious reaction to these psychological traits of dependence, is to understand the superficial nature of the relationship between master and slave. It is also to begin to understand the dissembling ability which Sambo shares with his god, Esu, from whom he derives his satiric power. In order to put Sambo in the right perspective of his art, we can briefly consider what antebellum literature makes of him.[145]

Interpretations of him on the whole would appear to embrace the two broad types already established—the contented slave and the rebel slave—which constitute the conflicting character features of Sambo. The first, the faithful and long-suffering, is the "noble" black of Uncle Tom and Uncle Remus or Jim Crow calibre.[146] He falls within the conception of Stanley Elkins' infantilized stereotype.[147] The second type, which John Blassingame implies as the "fugitive" Sambo,[148] is the more complex and probably the more realistic as a human being. He is a cross between all the individual plantation stereotypes, such as Nat, Jack and Sambo himself. Therefore he is rebellious, happy-go-lucky, irresponsible, intelligent, stupid, lazy, dishonest and pretentious—although he does not assume all these characteristics at once. His rebelliousness, if explored at all, is often underplayed on the antebellum stage, for understandable reasons.[149] But it may sometimes be underscored, however unwittingly, by rumors or news of a rebellion that is taking place or has taken place, as in John Murdock's *Triumphs of Love; or, Happy Reconciliation.*[150] Here Sambo, used as an abolitionist device, eventually receives his freedom by the good turn he does his master in an act of disguise which he has stage-managed. But there is also news from Santo Domingo about the successful rebellion of Toussaint L'Ouverture.[151]

It is also possible to conceive the actual existence of the first type, the docile slave, since there were slaves who had internalized the plantation expectations and the subservient roles to which the master had committed them, to the point of becoming resigned to their lot. And since there also existed some exceptionally kind and sympathetic masters, as some of the slave accounts reflected,[152] it is conceivable that a slave might be honest, faithful and loyal to his master. Yet we cannot rule out the possibility that slaves were more likely to receive rewards by assuming a character that would delight the master than by being themselves. For instance, one may imagine that some of the house slaves who often received the castoffs of their masters probably developed the art of playing up to their masters in order to win such favors. But in terms of survival, what with the punishments, the work demands, the temptations to act or "sin" as a result of poverty, status imbalance, demographic conditions, etc., a character with the kind of sustained religious austerity of Uncle Tom is difficult to conceive. Such a conception is only possible through the deliberate evocations of a proslavery activist like James Henley Thornwell, who believed that slavery was a condition of such an experience.[153] However, the character, as exemplified by Uncle Tom, may also favor antislavery or abolitionist hyperbolic projections against the grotesque evils of plantation life.

It is through these mystifications that the character became a stereotype. Ironically, we owe the sharp perspective of Uncle Tom's image of Sambo not to the southern master or the proslavery advocate, but to an abolitionist, Mrs. Harriet Beecher Stowe, daughter of a New England minister, in her very popular novel, *Uncle Tom's Cabin.* But this only reflects how manipulable and versatile the image is as a means of serving different ends.[154]

The second Sambo, by embracing the qualities of various types of characters that may have existed on the plantations, is also by that fact a stereotype. But at least he has all the possibilities of a fuller, more human existence and the full-bodied complexity of a normal individual, even though his "bad" qualities were often emphasized. Precisely because of his stereotyped image, this second type is more interesting to probe, for at least two reasons: it pretends, more realistically than the first, to be a collective portrait of the black; and since his portraiture more often reveals him as a rebel, a happy-go-lucky, or an evil character, he seems to owe allegiance to nothing but his own individuality. He is free, in a way, to react (run away, resist correction, etc.) according to the dictates of his will. It is also through him that we are able to see the satiric power of the image.

Interestingly, again, we get a good idea of the "realism" of this type through Stowe in the same novel—in the recalcitrant, irresponsible character of Topsy. In a somewhat racist description, she introduces the complexity of the character:

She was the blackest of her race; and round shining eyes, glittering as glass beads, moved with quick and restless glances over everything in the room . . . the expression of her face was an odd mixture of shrewdness and cunning, over which was oddly drawn, like a kind of veil, an expression of the most doleful gravity and solemnity.[155]

The recalcitrant, wicked behavior presented is a subtle, grotesque image which is taken for granted by the other characters in the novel, including Topsy herself. However, without intending to, Stowe inflicts, with the character's wild laugh, satiric stabs on all who regard her as an unrepentant image of the black. This image and ridicule developed and received its highest expression in the blackface minstrelsy of the antebellum era. In these minstrel shows, white actors wore grotesquely exaggerated black paint masks, delineating what were supposedly authentic African characters and types found on the plantations.[156] It was a satiric, projected gesture that bounced back, unintended, on the white actors and audience, similar to a curse, described previously, which boomerangs back on the curser. I shall come back to this.

But apparently in real plantation life, an important characteristic of the second type of Sambo was that he could put on a "mask" when he wanted to. In fact, with this ability as a protective power over his master's power, he often became the first type, so that he appeared docile and loyal—for example, Topsy's "doleful gravity and solemnity." It is this art of dissembling that an Alabama planter suspected when he consequently warned other whites to beware of the fugitive slave who was a "smooth tongued fellow and when spoken to used the word 'master' very frequently, particularly when accused of any misdemeanor."[157] The question therefore arises, What was this African or black "makeup" (a grotesque distortion) which fired the imagination of the white actor, writer or artist, at the lucrative expense of stereotyping? And what may it mean in the reality of the plantation survival of the black in the New World?

Obviously, the shareholder or the planter who was often a victim of this art was not by any means ignorant of it. As one planter diagnosed it:

The most general *defect* in the character of the Negro, is *hypocrisy* [my emphasis]; and this hypocrisy frequently makes him pretend to more ignorance than he possesses; and if the master treats him as a fool, he will be sure to act the fool's part. This is a very convenient trait, as it frequently serves as an apology for awkwardness and neglect.[158]

We may ignore the glaring hypocrisy of the thought itself, which, however, justifies the slave's assumed "hypocrisy"—since we do not know exactly why the master should have treated him "as a fool" in the first place, although his conception of the slave is very easy to guess at. What seems to be more important is the fact that the master's awareness of the deception did not mean he knew how to deal with it, for no punishment seemed to have corrected it. Furthermore, it is quite possible to have knowledge of something and yet still be baffled by it each time it is encountered afresh. Thus the master could find himself constantly befuddled and frustrated by the wiles or the so-called hypocrisy of his slaves. And we may note that, for survival, the versatility of the slave's art increased with the master's attempt to grapple with that art. But let us take up the dilemma of the master from another point of view.

The act of running away by a slave, for instance, suggests some kind of resistance or rebellion against the plantation system. This is more apparent in cases where runaway slaves, when recovered by their masters, destroyed themselves.[159] This resistance did not augur well for the planter either, because it was an economic liability or because it justified the abolitionist propaganda on the inhumanity of slavery. The slave's action, or reaction, was one more example signalling his or her agitation for freedom. Therefore there was need to prevent such notions. The planter, with the help of proslavery activists and southern literary men, launched deliberate full-scale counter-propaganda in an effort to mask anything that might be detrimental to slavery and to securing the slave on the plantation.[160] It is this propaganda that may have evoked the ironic image of Sambo's dissembling—the docile, loyal and contented slave.

The artistic and symbolic delineation of this masking, which capitalized on the propaganda, was the projections of the black in antebellum American literature and, more significantly, in the entertainment world of blackface minstrelsy. We can consider the somewhat inverted satiric process at work in these grotesque images in the light of the planter's or proslaver's "realism" or belief in the image. This process may be illustrated by an advertisement in the *South Carolina Gazette* of May 1, 1786, by a South Carolina master who describes his runaway slave as "sensible and artful, speaks quick, and sometimes stutters a little." The advertisement then goes on to state the cause of running away:

He may possibly have a ticket that I gave him two days before he went away, dated the 6th of April, mentioning he was in quest of a runaway, as I did not mention when he was to return, he may endeavour to pass by that.[161]

There is no reason to doubt the accuracy of the planter's description—the more accurate the description, the more likely he was to find his slave. But one wonders with Blassingame whether the characteristic speech defect of the slave was part of his "artfulness" or bag of tricks. And it could be that the master was doubly fooled for failing to recognize the characteristic stutter as an art. The notice, in fact, betrays this ignorance, because the master took his slave for a fool by providing him with a ticket to search for a previous runaway. This gesture makes the master a bigger fool and a victim of satire.

We will never know the whole truth about the advertisement, but we can make a case for the satiric potential of Sambo's art through a historical analogy with the South Carolina master's experience. Nat Turner fooled his master and many whites with his excessive religiosity, making them unaware of his rebellious character and planning until he struck with his surprise insurrection, a satiric indictment and attack on the inhumanity of slavery.[162] The point is that the master could often be genuinely deceived and fooled by Sambo's art, which was a product of the image that the master himself had evoked. When thus deceived, the impact of the irony on him was satirically more lethal, just as it was on a Maryland slaveholder who lamented the loss of his slave:

That this Slave should run away and attempt getting liberty, is very alarming, as he has always been too kindly used, if any Thing, by his master, and one in whom his Master has put great Confidence, and depended on him to overlook the rest of the Slaves, and he had no Kind of provocation to go off.[163]

This is another case of a "Nat Turner" and the unsuspecting but fooled eyes of the slaveholder. The provocation that he or the proslavery writer failed to see, or found hard to accept, is, of course, the inhumanity of slavery itself.

It was this ironic impact and satiric process that was operative in blackface minstrelsy. Considering all the implications of the image of the black, the grotesque features of the mask cast a satiric brand on the faces that wore them and on the white audience that saw them. While the whites thought they were laughing at black foolishness, they, without knowing it, were satirizing themselves as the bigger fools.

In fact, we will find that this realism of throwing into satiric relief (on the white victim) a projected mask-image of the black is a familiar characteristic of black survival, one that has persisted among Africans in Africa and among their descendants in the New World. For instance, it was characteristic of the Christian conversion in Africa, which may have succeeded superficially in substituting the name Esu with the devil, but not in obliterating the essence of the god. Broadly speaking, it was a characteristic that fashioned the Africanization of the Christian mode in churches across Africa.[164] In the New World, the masking was characteristic of the slaves who tricked their masters into believing that they worshipped the Catholic saints by superimposing the physical features of the saints on the psychic images of their gods. The white masters encouraged the syncretism because they thought it kept the slaves out of mischief. At any rate, such a compromise was possible as long as the Christian saints were "visible" objects of worship and Christianity was uncompromised. Nevertheless, there were known objections to the syncretism.[165] However, in both cases what was compromised at best, as in the image of Sambo, were the syncretic adaptations, an "art" at which Africans are adept, as Albert Raboteau rightly points out.[166]

But Sambo's artful realism has also persisted into the present. It is what fashioned the two arms (peaceful and violent) of the black civil rights movement of the sixties in America. It has reacted against itself and sought blackness as beautiful, or Negritude as an art, indicting the aping victims of white culture. It is a realism that is constantly being explored by modern artists and writers, both in Africa and in the New World, which is the subject of the concept of the Drama of Epidemic, and which links these practitioners with the satiric archetype, Esu-Elegbara.

Regarding this satiric process, we can now take another look at Stampp's conclusion to the observation, quoted earlier, on Sambo's "art of conscious accommodation . . . with all its psychic consequences." He says:

To escape this problem seems to be one of the aims of the present black revolution, for the search for identity is in part a search for a role clarity. To end all dissembling, to be all of a piece, to force the white community to accept them as they really are, not as it so long wanted to see them is quite obviously one determined goal of the new generation of blacks.[167]

I will go along with the stated objective as insightful. In fact, the act of forcing the white community to a specific acceptance is consistent with the realism of the art of Sambo, and one that has satiric implications. But the "art," to my mind, like the Sambo stereotype itself, need not be looked at as an undesirable defect, but rather as a necessary consequence of fate. It is very much part and parcel of the search for and affirmation of the black identity, a search to find, acknowledge and assert the essence of being black in the face of seeming deprecation of itself through dissembling. For he is the ironic man of American cultural history, and his dissembling, an ironic expression in his power, is the satiric power of identity over anyone who resists or fails to acknowledge that identity. It is the propagating satiric power of his god.

The foregoing has tried to examine the satiric tendencies of the black and the victims of their attack. Highlighting the victims, two broad types have been examined, the black as the victim of his own satire in Africa, and the white as victim of black satire in the New World. But the former also embraces the capitalist white who may have ventured into Africa, and the latter embraces any black aping the white culture. The following chapter looks at the "epidemic" process of satire in relation to these victims and the various plays in which they have appeared as characters.

NOTES

1. See Morton-Williams, "Yoruba Ogboni Cult," 373.
2. Hendrickson, "Archilochus and the Victims," 118–119.
3. On influences of Yoruba religion in the Americas, see Bastide, *African Religions of Brazil;* Simpson, *Black Religions in the New World;* Tallant, *Voodoo in New Orleans;* Sheila S. Walker, "African Gods in the Americas: The Black Religious Continuum," *Black Scholar* 11, no. 8 (1980): 25–36; M. Gonzalez-Wippler, *Santeria* (New York: Julian Press, 1973); Haskins, *Witchcraft, Mysticism and Magic;* A. Adeyemi Smith, "African Religion in the Americas," *African Mirror* (June–July 1979): 33–40; Pierre Verger, "Yoruba Influences in Brazil," *Odu* 1 (1955): 3–11; Deren, *Divine Horsemen.*
4. On the grotesque images of satire, see Frye, "Nature of Satire," 80; Seidel, *Satiric Inheritance,* 4–6.
5. See Bascom, *Ifa Divination,* 83.
6. See Thompson, *Flash of the Spirit,* 23–24, 26, plates 11, 12, 13.
7. Elliott, *Power of Satire,* 11; Frederic Will, *Archilochus* (New York: Twayne, 1969), 70.
8. Paton, *Greek Anthology,* 2:43.
9. Ibid.; also Will, *Archilochus,* 71.
10. Frye, "Nature of Satire," 88.
11. Edmonds, *Elegy and Iambus,* 2:97; Will, *Archilochus,* 71.
12. Elliott, *Power of Satire,* 13; Avery, *New Century Classical Handbook,* 572. See also *Oxford Classical Dictionary,* 519–520.
13. See Edwin S. Ramage et al., *Roman Satirists and Their Satire* (Park Ridge, N.J.: Noyes Press, 1974), 16.
14. Ibid., 65.
15. Edmonds, *Elegy and Iambus,* 2:85.
16. See M. C. Randolph, "Medical Concept," esp. 125, 141–143, 151.
17. Ibid., 152.
18. Elliott, *Power of Satire,* 12.
19. Frye, "Nature of Satire," 79–80. See a similar conclusion in A. P. Kernan, "A Theory of Satire," in Paulson, *Satire: Modern Essays in Criticism,* 265–267. For false etymology for satire, see Seidel, *Satiric Inheritance,* 5.
20. Seidel, *Satiric Inheritance,* 4.
21. Thomas Randolph, *Poetical and Dramatic Works* (London: Reeves and Turner, 1875), 176–266. Quotation from pp. 189–190.
22. *Oxford Classical Dictionary,* 430.
23. See Frye, "Nature of Satire," 79.
24. Juvenal's conception of evil and corruption is very pertinent to the modern world; see section on him in Ramage et al., *Roman Satirists,* 136–169.
25. Ibid., 143.
26. On the laws and pressure limiting satirists' freedom, see Elliott, *Power of Satire,* 261–265.
27. Anthony, Earl of Shaftesbury, *Characteristics,* 2 vols., ed. J. M. Robertson (Indianapolis: Bobbs-Merrill, 1964), Vol. 1:51; also quoted in Elliott, *Power of Satire,* 264.
28. Elliott, *Power of Satire,* 264–265.
29. Satires 2, i, in *Horace: Satires, Epistles and Ars Poetica,* trans. H. Rushton

Fairclough (Cambridge, Mass.: Harvard University Press, 1932), 131; quoted in Elliott, *Power of Satire*, 262.

30. Satire 1, *Juvenal and Persius*, trans. G. G. Ramsay (London: Heinemann, 1918), 3–15; see also Frye, "Nature of Satire," 79. For a comparison between the satiric styles of Horace and Juvenal, see John Dennis, "To Matthew Pryor, Esq.; Upon the Roman Satirists," in *The Critical Works of John Dennis*, 2 vols., ed. Edward N. Hooker (Baltimore: Johns Hopkins University Press, 1943), 2:218–220. For the social functions of satirists, see Elliott, *Power of Satire*, 112–125, 266. On Roman satirists and their works, see Ramage et al., *Roman Satirists*.

31. Frye, "Nature of Satire," 77–78.

32. Hendrickson, "Archilochus and the Victims," 114.

33. Ibid., 124. For a comparison between Archilochus' world and the periods preceding it, see Will, *Archilochus*, chap. 1.

34. James Ngugi, "Satire in Nigeria," in *Protest and Conflict in African Literature*, ed. Cosmo Pieterse (London: Heinemann, 1969).

35. Ibid.

36. On the various causes of the Nigerian economic crisis, see Yusufu Bala Usman et al., "Debate on the Nigerian Economic Crisis," *Studies in Politics and Society 2 (1984)*. For a cultural analysis of economic and political development in Nigeria, see Bernard Belasco, *The Entrepreneur as Culture Hero* (New York: J. F. Bergin, 1980); Segun Osoba, "The Nigerian Power Elite, 1952–65," in *African Social Studies*, ed. P. Gutkind and P. Waterman (New York: Monthly Review Press, 1977), 368–382.

37. For justification as based on Yoruba traditional characteristics, see observations in S. Johnson, *History of the Yorubas*, esp. xxi–xxii, 101–102; John Ferguson, ed., *The Yorubas of Nigeria* (Buckinghamshire, England: Open University Press, 1970); Ojo, *Yoruba Culture;* R. Olaniyan, "Element of Yoruba Diplomacy in Oral Tradition," in *Yoruba Oral Tradition*, ed. Wande Abimbola Ile-Ife, Nigeria: University of Ife, 1975), 293–332; William Bascom, *The Yoruba of Southwestern Nigeria* (Prospect Heights, Ill.: Waveland Press, 1984).

38. The term "essential commodities," commonly used for food products intermittently distributed and rationed by the government, seems appropriate here.

39. For such interpretations, see Pemberton, "Eshu-Elegba," 68. Cf. Pelton, *Trickster in West Africa*, 145–147.

40. See Belasco, Entrepreneur, 32. For a ritual explanation of the concept, see Soyinka, *Myth, Literature*, 10–11. Soyinka also develops this concept with his tragic idea in *Death and the King's Horseman;* see "Author's Note" in the play.

41. See Belasco, *Entrepreneur*, chap. 2, esp. pp. 31–34.

42. Ibid., esp. 32.

43. Ibid., 29, 33–34.

44. For the effects of the new resources on the development of Yoruba centralized kingdoms in the eighteenth and nineteenth centuries, see Peter C. Lloyd, *The Political Development of Yoruba Kingdoms in the Eighteenth and Nineteenth Centuries* (London: Royal Anthropological Institute, 1971).

45. For a concise description of this and its implications, see W. R. Bascom, "Social Status, Wealth and Individual Differences Among the Yoruba," *American Anthropologist* 53 (1951): 490–505; Peter C. Lloyd, *Power and Independence: Urban Africans' Perception of Social Inequality* (London: Routledge and Kegan Paul, 1974), chap. 2.

46. Lloyd, *Power and Independence*, 52–53.

47. See Bascom, "Social Status," 496–497; see also Belasco, *Entrepreneur*, 40–49.

48. See Bascom, "Social Status," 492.

49. Ibid.

50. For the ritual and monetary implications of the symbolic and versatile cowrie, see Belasco, *Entrepreneur*, 49–58.

51. See Bascom, "Social Status," 492, 502–503.

52. Belasco, *Entrepreneur*, 31–34.

53. Joseph Oyediran, Oba Arojomo, the Oniworo of Iworo, Badagry; Chief Ojomo Josiah Apata. Both were interviewed in Iworo at the Oba's palace, August 1981.

54. See Verger, "Notes."

55. Badagry, as well as the neighboring Lagos, had grown as a center late in the slave trading, in the nineteenth century. See J. H. Kopytoff, *A Preface to Modern Nigeria* (Madison: University of Wisconsin Press, 1965), 11–14.

56. See Belasco, *Entrepreneur*, 52–53.

57. Cited in Belasco, *Entrepreneur*, 52, from Duarte Pachecho Pereira, *Esmeraldo de Situs Orbis*, ed. R. Mauny (Bissau: Centro de Estudos da Guine Portuguessa, 1956), 125.

58. Interviewed at the University of Ife, January 1986.

59. Lloyd, *Power and Independence*, 52.

60. Christopher Marlowe, *The Tragical History of Doctor Faustus* (1588?); Wolfgang Goethe, *Faust* (begun mid-1770; completed 1831).

61. My informant, Fatoogun, gives an idea of some of the ways the pact is made, all of which involve the fate of the individual.

62. Paulson, *Fictions of Satire*, 12.

63. Bascom, "Social Status," 505.

64. Osoba, "Nigerian Power Elite," 376–378.

65. For the etymology of the term and development in usage, see Raymond Williams, *Keywords: A Vocabulary of Culture and Society* (New York: Oxford University Press, 1976), 42–44.

66. See Osoba, "Nigerian Power Elite," 378–379. For a comparison between the dominant ideology of liberal capitalism, the "selfish pursuit of economic gain," and the traditional Yoruba concept of shared economy, see Belasco, *Entrepreneur*, 23–34, esp. 31–34.

67. Bascom, "Social Status," 496.

68. Quoted in Beier and Gbadamosi, *Yoruba Poetry*, 62.

69. See the case of Chief Agbaje in Lloyd, *Power and Independence*, 52–53.

70. Osoba, "Nigerian Power Elite," 370–373.

71. See Bascom, "Social Status," 496.

72. See Lloyd, *Power and Independence*, 53.

73. Belasco, *Entrepreneur*, 33.

74. For a comprehensive account of the breakdown in Nigerian politics in the 1960s, see A.H.M. Kirk-Green, *Crisis and Conflict in Nigeria: A Documentary Sourcebook, 1966–1969*, 2 vols. (London: Oxford University Press, 1971), vol. 2. On the internecine wars of the nineteenth century, see R. Smith, *Kingdoms of the Yoruba;* Lloyd, *Political Development of Yoruba Kingdoms*.

75. Ogunba, "Agemo Cult."

76. See *Ayoola Report*, Report of a Commission of Enquiry into the Civil Distur-

bances which Occurred in Certain Parts of the Western State of Nigeria in the Month of December 1968 (Ibadan, Nigeria: Government Printer, 1969).

77. For figures and tables, see *Proceedings of American Association for Automotive Medicine, 22nd Conference,* Ann Arbor, Mich., 1978, 37–53.

78. On the powers that prevent achievement of fate, see Abimbola, *Ifa,* 152.

79. Bascom, *Ifa Divination,* 117.

80. See Abimbola, "Iwapele: The Concept of Good Character in Ifa Literary Corpus," in Abimbola, ed., *Yoruba Oral Tradition,* 387–417. On Iwa as an aesthetic force, see Rowland Abiodun, "Identity and the Artistic Process in Yoruba Aesthetic Concept of Iwa," *Journal of Culture and Ideas* 1, no. 1 (December, 1983): 13–27.

81. Abimbola, "Iwapele," 402–414. As a quality of all types of art and craft, see Abiodun, "Identity and Artistic Process."

82. See the poem "Onikoyi" in Beier and Gbadamosi, *Yoruba Poetry,* 46.

83. Compare Horton's idea of this using the Freudian concept of the conscious and the unconscious in the individual: Robin Horton, "Destiny and the Unconscious in West Africa," *Africa* 31, no. 2 (1961): 110–116.

84. Frye, "Nature of Satire," 86–87.

85. Seidel, *Satiric Inheritance,* 3–4. With regard to the cathartic affinities of tragedy and satire, see Alice L. Birney, "Introduction," in *Satiric Catharsis in Shakespeare* (Los Angeles: University of California Press, 1973), esp. 6–12.

86. See Frye, "Nature of Satire," 70; and Northrop Frye, *Anatomy of Criticism: Four Essays* (Princeton, N.J.: Princeton University Press, 1957), 224.

87. Quoted in Elliott, *Power of Satire,* 111.

88. Corrigan, *Theatre in Search of a Fix,* 58.

89. Elliott, *Power of Satire,* 266, 270–271.

90. Frederick E. Lumley, *Means of Social Control* (New York: Century, 1925); 237–259, esp. 251–255.

91. Evidences are based on the worship of the Yoruba gods (orisa) in these countries; see Sheila S. Walker, "African Gods in the Americas"; A. Adeyemi Smith, "African Religion in the Americas"; Albert Raboteau, *Slave Religion* (New York: Oxford University Press, 1978); Bastide, *African Religions of Brazil;* Serge Bramly, *Macumba,* trans. Meg Bogin (New York: St. Martin's Press, 1977); Haskins, *Witchcraft, Mysticism and Magic;* Tallant, *Voodoo in New Orleans;* Simpson, *Black Religions in the New World.*

92. See Philip D. Curtin, *The Atlantic Slave Trade: A Census* (Madison: University of Wisconsin Press, 1969).

93. For possible reasons for this influence, see Raboteau, *Slave Religion;* Simpson, *Black Religions in the New World.*

94. For some of the historical details that suggest this, see John H. Franklin, *From Slavery to Freedom: A History of Negro Americans,* 3rd ed. (New York: Vintage, 1969), 53–56; Kopytoff, *Preface to Modern Nigeria,* 10–23; Michael Mullin, ed., *American Negro Slavery: A Documentary History* (New York: Harper and Row, 1976), 42–44; Lloyd, *Political Development of Yoruba Kingdoms,* 4–8.

95. Faloba, interviewed at Ile-Ife, Nigeria, July 1981.

96. For historical documentation on which such interpretations are based, see S. Johnson, *History of the Yorubas,* chap. 1; see also R. Smith, *Kingdoms of the Yoruba,* 12.

97. Belasco, *Entrepreneur,* 38.

98. A. A. Smith, "African Religion in the Americas," 38.

99. Hoch-Smith and Pichardo, "Having Thrown a Stone," 19.

100. Raboteau, *Slave Religion,* 6. For the missionary work in Nigeria by these Christianized slaves, see Kopytoff, *Preface to Modern Nigeria.*

101. This influence is reflected in Paul V.A. Williams, "Exu: The Master and the Slave in Afro-Brazilian Religion," in *The Fool and the Trickster: Studies in Honour of Enid Welsford,* ed. Paul V.A. Williams (Cambridge, England: D. S. Brewer, 1979). Some of Exu's stories in New World interpretation also suggest this; for example, "The King of Congo had three sons, Xango, Ogun and Exu, . . ." ibid., 114.

102. D. V. Trotman, "The Yoruba and Orisha worship in Trinidad and British Guiana, 1838–70," *African Studies Review* 19, no. 2 (1976): 1–17.

103. See Walker, "African Gods in the Americas."

104. See P. Williams, "Exu," 109–111; also Hoch-Smith and Pichardo, "Having Thrown a Stone."

105. Mechal Sobel, *Trabelin' On: The Slave Journey to Afro-Baptist Faith* (Westport, Conn.: Greenwood Press, 1979), esp. 38–39.

106. For a short commentary on the classical Western conception of the black, see George, "Civilized West Looks at Primitive Africa," 62–72. On the inhuman treatment of slaves from capture through the Atlantic crossing to the enslavement on the plantations, see Blassingame, *Slave Community,* chap. 1; see chap. 6 in the same work on the white masters' perception of black slaves. Other sources in American slavery include Franklin, *From Slavery to Freedom;* Genovese, *Roll, Jordan, Roll;* Anne Loveland, *Southern Evangelicals and the Social Order, 1800–1860* (Baton Rouge: Louisiana State University Press, 1980); Thomas V. Peterson, *Ham and Japheth: The Mythic World of Whites in the Antebellum South* (Metuchen, N.J.: Scarecrow Press and American Theological Library Association, 1978).

107. Some of the objectives of Christian missions are reflected in Kopytoff, *Preface to Modern Nigeria,* part 1.

108. "Mary Slessor," *Nigerian Magazine* 58 (1958); 207. For the attitude toward slavery, see Raboteau, *Slave Religion,* 65–67; see also Loveland, *Southern Evangelicals.*

109. Sources on proslavery arguments include E. L. McKitrick, *Slavery Defended: The Views of the Old South* (N.J.: Englewood Cliffs, N.J.: Prentice-Hall, 1963); W. S. Jenkins, *Proslavery Thought in the Old South* (Chapel Hill: University of North Carolina Press, 1935); Drew G. Faust, "Evangelism and the Meaning of the Proslavery Argument," *Virginia Magazine of History and Biography* 85, no. 1 (1977): 3–17; R. F. Morrow, "The Proslavery Argument Revisited," *Mississippi Valley Historical Review* 47 (1961): 79–94.

110. See Peterson, *Ham and Japheth.*

111. See George, "Civilized West Looks at Primitive Africa"; for a general but more detailed study of classical writers' comments about Africans, see William L. Hansberry, *Africa and Africans as Seen by Classical Writers: The William Leo Hansberry African History Notebook* vol. 2, ed. Joseph E. Harris (Washington, D.C: Howard University Press, 1977); for a detailed study of Africans in the Greco-Roman world, see Frank Snowden, *Blacks in Antiquity: Ethiopians in the Greco-Roman Experience* (Cambridge, Mass.: Harvard University Press, 1970).

112. Henry L. Gates, Jr., "Introduction" to Wole Soyinka's "The Mask of Blackness," unpublished pilot script for projected television documentary series "The Image

of the Black in Western Imagination,'' 1981, 40–45. The project has since been abandoned.

113. For an attempt to contrast the traditional African way of life and life on the plantations, see Blassingame, *Slave Community,* chap. 1; also Franklin, *From Slavery to Freedom,* chaps. 3, 4. For documented views on the subject, see Mullin, *American Negro Slavery,* part 1a.

114. For the concept of paternalism, see Fred Siegel, ''The Paternalist Thesis: Virginia as a Test Case,'' *Civil War History* 35, no. 1 (1979): 246–261. For various views on the subject, see Peterson, *Ham and Japheth,* 56; Eugene D. Genovese, *The World the Slaveholders Made* (New York: Pantheon Books, 1969); Genovese, *Roll, Jordan, Roll;* George Fredrickson, ''Master and Mudsills: The Role of Race in the Planter Ideology of South Carolina,'' *South Atlantic Urban Studies* 2 (1978): 34–48.

115. For the views of proslavery advocates like Governor James Hammond (''mudsills of society''), Chancellor William Harper (''perpetual child''), Josiah C. Nott, George Fitzhugh, Rev. Thornton Stringfellow, etc., see Drew G. Faust, *The Ideology of Slavery: Proslavery Thought in Antebellum South, 1830–1860* (Baton Rouge: Louisiana State University Press, 1981); Peterson, *Ham and Japheth;* Morrow, ''Proslavery Argument Revisited''; Drew G. Faust, ''A Southern Stewardship: The Intellectual and the Proslavery Argument,'' *Virginia Magazine* 85 (1977): 3–17; Jenkins, *Proslavery Thought in the Old South.*

116. On the treatment of slaves and the subsequent reaction, see Blassingame, *Slave Community,* chap. 5; on evangelism in the plantation South, see Loveland, *Southern Evangelicals.*

117. Newbell N. Puckett, *Folk Beliefs of the Southern Negro* (Montclair, N.J.: Patterson Smith, 1968) 548. See also Haskins, *Witchcraft, Mysticism and Magic,* 51.

118. Genovese, *Roll, Jordan, Roll,* 217.

119. Part of an American Negro folk song. Quoted in Fela Sowande, *Ifa* (Oja, Nigeria: Forward Press, 1965), 13.

120. Henry Gates, Jr., has attempted to find a definition for black literary criticism through Esu; see ''The 'Blackness of Blackness': A Critique of the Sign and the Signifying Monkey,'' *Critical Inquiry* 9 (1983): 685–723; a more elaborate work on this by Gates is *The Signifying Monkey: A Theory of Afro-American Literary Criticism* (New York: Oxford University Press, 1988).

121. George P. Rawick, *From Sundown to Sunup: The Making of the Black Community* (Westport, Conn.: Greenwood Press, 1972), 47; see also Simpson, *Black Religions in the New World,* 217.

122. Various studies that have tried to explore slave personality types on the plantations include Blassingame, *Slave Community,* esp. chaps. 6 and 8; Eugene Genovese, ''Rebellion and Docility in the Negro Slave,'' *Civil War History* 13, no. 4 (1967): 293–314; Kenneth Stampp, ''Rebels and Sambos: The Search for the Negro's Personality in Slavery,'' *The Journal of Southern History* 37, 3 (August 1971): 367–392.

123. For a general account of the insurrections, see Blassingame, *Slave Community,* chap. 6. For documentary views on the insurrections of Denmark Vesey and Nat Turner, see Mullin, *American Negro Slavery,* 227–241. For quote on Sarah, see Blassingame, *Slave Community,* 206.

124. On possible factors promoting internalization, see Blassingame, *Slave Community,* 284–290.

125. See ibid., chap. 6. Also documented in Mullin, *American Negro Slavery*, 81–100.

126. Translation of "Gbirari" in Ogundipe, *Esu Elegbara*, 2:10, lines 21-23.

127. See Blassingame, *Slave Community*, chap. 6.

128. Stanley M. Elkins, *Slavery: A Problem in American Institutional and Intellectual Life* (Chicago: University of Chicago Press, 1959). For a criticism of Elkins' theory, see Genovese, "Rebelliousness and Docility."

129. Genovese, *Roll, Jordan, Roll.*

130. Blassingame, *Slave Community;* Stampp, "Rebels and Sambos."

131. David B. Davis, *The Problem of Slavery in Western Culture* (Ithaca, N.Y.: Cornell University Press, 1966), 59–60.

132. D. L. Dillard notes the different derivations of the word in Hausa and other West African communities in *Black English* (New York: Vintage Books, 1973), 130–132; see also Peter Wood, *Black Majority* (New York: Alfred A. Knopf, 1974), 185.

133. Alvin Shuster, "British Debating 'Black Sambo,' " *New York Times*, May 1, 1972, p. 2.

134. Mark Miller, "Bring Back Amos 'n' Andy," *Evening Sun* (Baltimore), April 3, 1986, p. A9.

135. Joseph Boskin, *Sambo: The Rise and Demise of an American Jester* (New York: Oxford University Press, 1986).

136. Stampp, "Rebels and Sambos," 392.

137. See, for instance, the story of the crimson parrot feather in Juana Elbein dos Santos, *Os Nago E A Morte*, 171–181; see also Thompson's comment on the story in *Flash of the Spirit*, 18; for other stories about Esu as the most powerful of the gods, see Bascom, Sixteen Cowries, 101–102; verse A.18; Ogundipe, *Esu Elegbara*, vol. 2, tale 42.

138. See Wescott, "Sculpture and Myths."

139. Chief Ojeyemi, interviewed at Ikirun, Nigeria, July 1981.

140. See Pelton, *Trickster in West Africa*, esp. 80–88.

141. Stampp, "Rebels and Sambos," 384.

142. Blassingame, *Slave Community*, 272–273.

143. See Bascom, "Eighteenth Century Slaves."

144. For arguments on what led to the Civil War, see Eric Foner, *Free Soil, Free Labor, Free Men: The Ideology of the Republican Party Before the Civil War* (New York: Oxford University Press, 1970). For a general historical view, see Franklin, *From Slavery to Freedom*, chaps. 13–16. For religious arguments, see Loveland, *Southern Evangelicals.*

145. Studies and texts relating to the image include James W. Johnson, *Black Manhattan* (New York: Alfred A. Knopf, 1930); Sterling Brown, "Negro Character as Seen by White Authors," *Journal of Negro Education* 2, no. 1 (1938): 180–203; Stanley J. Lemons, "Black Stereotypes as Reflected in Popular Culture, 1880–1920," *American Quarterly* 29, no. 1 (1977): 102–116; Charles E. Burch "Negro Characters in the Novels of William Gilmore Simms," *Southern Workman* 52 (April 1923), 192–195; Alexander Saxton, "Blackface Minstrelsy and Jacksonian Ideology," *American Quarterly* 27, no. 1 (1975): 3–28; Robert C. Toll, *Blacking Up: The Minstrel Show in Nineteenth Century America* (New York: Oxford University Press, 1974); Harriet Beecher Stowe, *Uncle Tom's Cabin* (New York: Modern Library, 1948); *Samboe, The African Boy* (London: Harvey and Darton, 1923).

146. For similar comments on this Sambo, see Blassingame, *Slave Community*, 225.

147. See Elkins, *Slavery*.

148. See Blassingame, *Slave Community*, 204–206.

149. For a detailed analysis of these Sambo types on the stage, see Alfonso Sherman, *The Diversity of Treatment of the Negro Character in American Drama, Prior to 1860* (Ann Arbor: UMI, 1965).

150. See John Murdock, Triumphs of Love; or Happy Reconciliation (Folwell, Philadelphia, 1795), see Readex Microprint collection, edition of Early American Imprints, no. 29129.

151. For comments on this play, see Sherman, *Diversity of Treatment*, 47–51, 235–236.

152. See excerpt of Henry Clay Bruce's narrative in Blassingame, *Slave Community*, 291.

153. See Charles C. Bishop, "The Pro-slavery Argument Reconsidered: James Henley Thornwell (1812–1862), Millennial Abolitionist," *South Carolina Historical Magazine* 73, no. 1 (1972): 18–26; also Loveland, *Southern Evangelicals*, 205–207.

154. For such manipulation in the so-called Tom Shows, see Toll, *Blacking Up*, 88–97.

155. Stowe, *Uncle Tom's Cabin*, 295–296.

156. On blackface minstrelsy, see Toll, *Blacking Up*; Saxton, "Blackface Minstrelsy and Jacksonian Ideology"; Carl Wittke, *Tambo and Bones* (Durham, N.C.: Duke University Press, 1930); Hans Nathan, *Dan Emmett and the Rise of Early Minstrelsy* (Norman: University of Oklahoma Press, 1962); Alan W.C. Green, " 'Jim Crow,' 'Zip Coon': The Northern Origins of Negro Minstrelsy," *Massachusetts Review* 11 (Spring 1970): 385–397.

157. Blassingame, *Slave Community*, 219.

158. Stampp, "Rebels and Sambos," 391.

159. See Franklin, *From Slavery to Freedom*, 205–209, esp. 208.

160. See Faust, "Southern Stewardship."

161. Quoted in Blassingame, *Slave Community*, 205. For other advertisements, see Bascom, "Eighteenth Century Slaves."

162. See Blassingame, *Slave Community*, 217–221.

163. Ibid., 205.

164. For a study of the development, see J.D.Y. Peel, *Aladura: A Religious Movement* (London: Oxford University Press for International African Institute, 1968). For a review of the study, see Robin Horton, "African Conversion," *Africa* 41, no. 2 (1971): 85–108. See also Parrinder, *Religion in an African City*, which also reflects the syncretism.

165. See Raboteau, *Slave Religion*, 24–25.

166. Ibid., 4–5.

167. Stampp, "Rebels and Sambos," 392.

4

Drama of Epidemic

Ultimately, the satiric concept of Esu, within the framework of formal drama, emerges as an aesthetic concept of theatre. This I have called the "Drama of Epidemic," and, as has been suggested, it is a concept that should be useful in assessing plays that constitute black theatre. While this implies that every black drama has a potential for satire, since satire is an inevitable and essential factor of survival, the concept nevertheless seeks to establish its satiric process as a theatrical device that significantly identifies the black dramatic expression. Consequently, the plays discussed in this chapter as illustration are chosen at random, although the selection has been made with the "epidemic" content in mind. Before turning to the plays, however, it seems imperative to have a clear understanding of the epidemic factor and process. I shall start by relating the concept in broad terms to the African and the Afro-American worlds. This, in fact, is a continuation of what was begun in the last chapter, locating the satiric concept in African and Afro-American realities. Here the dramatic and theatrical evolution of the concept will first be sought in the Yoruba context and then suggested as an aesthetic concept which later identifies the New World expression.

Through Esu-Elegbara, the Drama of Epidemic primarily seeks to legitimate satire in the black tradition. Its salient dramatic force of expression is the ritual, and through this its theatrical features become evident. For ritual, whether in its traditional aspects or in its more aesthetic expression, localizes a crisis which, like an epidemic, becomes a cause for concern and must be brought under control. Like an epidemic, it can destroy. Yet, again like an epidemic, the necessary control is never attained until some kind of purgation by destruction has occurred, through which a cathartic therapy or cure is experienced. The destruction, symbolized by a sacrificial offering (human, animal or object), represents direct or indirect capitulation of and control over the hostile influences that have caused the crisis.[1] In this respect, on a less religious but more realistic note, an analogy may be made with what has become a ritual in modern Africa—the military coup. Like a ritual epidemic, a coup often destroys in order to restore sanity in a political crisis that has reached epidemic proportions. The crisis is felt or seen to be destroying, or to have destroyed, sanity.

The analogy in fact leads conveniently to the concept of epidemic as a satiric expression. In satire, as in the coup, the destructive aspect serves as or is effected through an indictment, an imprecation, or the castigation of the human vice and folly that have brought about the disorder or the crisis. This indictment, or its impact, anticipates better and sanative prospects which, together with the destructive, evoke the satiric catharsis.[2] As we shall see, the drama of the black which constitutes the Drama of Epidemic reflects these features, although the features are by no means peculiar to the black—since satire, and epidemic for that matter, are universal processes. What, however, makes this subject a black concern are certain aspects which manifest the resonance and the prevalence of satire, aspects which are conditioned by the history and fate of the black people.

Dwelling further on the coup d'etat analogy of satire and epidemic we may, in anticipation of my analysis, look at a play whose subject and dramatic action unintentionally seem to fuse the ritual, the satiric and the artistic processes of epidemic drama. When, in Soyinka's *A Play of Giants*,[3] Professor Batey, the new speechwriter of President Kamini, finally reveals to the other African leaders inside the Bugaran Embassy the maddening news that has driven Kamini out of the room—that there has been a coup in Bugara—President Kasco immediately wonders, "Is it an epidemic beginning you imagine?"[4] For the coup, in Africa, is now a ritual that has itself become an epidemic concern.

As explained, a coup in its objective has affinities with an epidemic process. It wishes to destroy the old, corrupt system so that sanity can be restored. But then this objective is heavily laden with a festering irony—the frequency of the coup is of epidemic concern, which implicates it as a destructive and counterproductive endeavor. This much is implicit in Batey's outburst on the ignorance of Africans as the gulls and puppets of the superpowers, whom he also indicts as the brains behind all coups.[5] The dramatic irony is unmistakable, for Kamini, centrally, as well as the other African leaders, is being revealed by the play's subtle action as a dangerous, power-drunk, power-corrupted sadist and assassin. With such satiric indictment and counterindictment, there is no sanative prospect in view, and the play ends with this catatonic ambiguity: while the Bugaran exiles and rebels outside are storming the embassy with stones, and the Bugaran artillery inside has opened fire in a counterassault, Soyinka freezes the picture with Kamini aiming his gun at his European diplomatic hostages.

The illustration given here should put the processes of the epidemic drama in perspective. As implied, the concept is at once a ritualistic, satiric and artistic expression. In *A Play of Giants* we get a feeling that the dramatic process has been conditioned by colonial and political experiences in Africa, and therefore the indictment on Kamini is primarily motivated by the effects of such influences on the shaping of modern Africa. However, apart from this surface conditioning, there seem to be other sources for the satiric potential of the black, sources that can be traced in black cultural history and in the development of black theatre. For instance, in a brilliant attempt to document the origins of the Yoruba theatre in Nigeria, J. A. Adedeji has studied the Alarinjo, the traditional Yoruba travelling theatre, from its possible evolution from the Egungun, the masqueraders' cult of the Yorubas, to its development in the nineteenth century and its influences on modern Yoruba travelling theatre companies.[6] The evolution, in fact, introduces directly the satiric power of the Egungun, what is to be the main strength of the theatre.

According to Adedeji, the theatrical venture started with a Yoruba king in exile whose caucus of councillors wanted to frustrate his yearning and efforts to return to the original royal settlement. The caucus, therefore, through the expertise of the Egungun cult, of which they were members, devised some grotesque masks with which they frightened and sent packing the king's emissaries to the old capital. The ruse was later discovered, and in a dramatic turn, after the weekly religious gathering with his councillors, the king secretly organized a repeat performance of the ''ghost mummers.'' The show succeeded in its objective, which was to shock the unsuspecting councillors out of their wits. Adedeji then follows the development of this band of entertainers into the travelling theatre in the nineteenth century and as we know it today. But the king's dramatic turn is unmistakably a satiric venture, to punish, exhort and deride as well as entertain.

Apart from the symbolic and ritual use of the masks in the Egungun society,[7] itself a cult of satiric overtures[8] (and Esu devotees are found in the cult, like my informant at Ikirun),[9] we have in this episode a satiric conflict of interest. There was in the plot an attempt to frustrate the emotional concerns of the king—his longings and interests—as a crisis that had to be abated. He got wind of it through a loyal member of his household, rounded up the mummers and redirected the satiric onslaught at his councillors. It was a case of the satiric boomerang in which the satirist becomes satirized. But it also described, dramatized and set in motion the satiric art of the black tradition. Not only did the masks become a permanent feature of the Alarinjo and its other names, but they also projected the dramatic art of deception and satire that could be said to form the basis of black theatre. Adedeji records some of these artistic trends and some actual cases when the deception and satire hit home, resulting in performances of plays or playlets being banned.[10] There are also many plays, especially in the Yoruba travelling theatre repertoire, for instance those of Moses Olaiya, alias Baba Sala, in which trickery or dissembling is a central feature of the action.[11] Referring to the character Baba Sala as the ''anti-heroic hero of Olaiya's plays,'' Biodun Jeyifo sums up this dissembling role as ''a braggart, a coward, a liar, a cheat, a glutton and quite often, a generous felon."[12] In such roles it is easy to link the fate of the character and his fatal but humorous escapades with Esu, the fate god and master dissembler.

Making a wide leap across to the Americas—and it is only natural that the "art" crossed with the slaves—we can take up another case of the satiric potential of the black. The stereotyped image of the black not only contributed to the development of the American theatre in colonial and antebellum America, but has also been the basis of black theatre. At its most exploitative and prolific stage, the image, as explained in the last chapter, was the central feature of blackface minstrelsy. It was at this stage that the blacks also tried to develop their art, taking their cue from the popularity of stereotyped and grotesque images and the economic opportunities it provided.[13] For when they took over minstrelsy, not without setbacks and frustrations, they seem to have legitimized rather than corrected the image, and in fact for a while they applied the burnt-cork makeup of the white artists.[14]

On the surface, this adoption of the white's conception of the black would appear to be a treacherous letdown of the black race. But it is necessary to understand why this occurred. Reasons have been suggested why blacks, in spite of the racial difficulties that minstrelsy posed for them, leapt at the opportunity to become minstrels.[15] Viewed in terms of survival, we may in fact find that the reasons reflect similarities with those that propagated the image of Sambo on the plantations. Minstrelsy gave black artists a chance to improve their financial condition and a chance to see another world, since they travelled extensively in America and in Europe. More than anything else, at a time when freedom from slavery offered only the "slavery" of serfdom, it was a chance to be somebody, as some of the black minstrels acknowledged.[16] In other words, minstrelsy was a way of establishing the black identity in American culture, and in this sense was a type of reaction to slavery similar to the reaction of the rebel slave. The adoption of the feature of "blackface" by the black should, therefore, be seen beyond the question of stereotypes; the acceptance of the roles was a ruse by which it was possible to take all the risks involved in venturing into the white-dominated, discriminatory business world of theatre.

But then, the perpetration of the caricatures may be regarded as an indirect indictment, and therefore a satiric action through the black art of dissembling. The grotesque "masks" of blackface were the way white America conceived of the black on the slave plantations. As far as the white artists were concerned, and they had full support of the white audience, these images were authentic.[17] This criterion for their representation had been established long before blacks took over the minstrel stage, and to resist it there and then would obviously have produced some unnecessary and disastrous results. For one thing, the white patrons, the audience and company owners, who were responsible in large part for the success of the show, would have reacted, and perhaps opportunities for black participation would have been curtailed, as the experience of some defiant black artists shows.[18] At any rate, there is evidence that some changes were in fact made in the black stereotypes, but these were probably too subtle to have been taken seriously by the white audience or too coded in the black lingo and art to have made any significant impact on the white conception. Otherwise, the black audience to which black minstrelsy later owed its collaborative support would not have been drawn in large numbers to the shows. However, music, an integral part of the shows, and one that really established the black culture, did appear to help modify the caricatures.[19] In fact, this would seem to endorse the subtle art of deception of the black. For visual modification of minstrelsy would not be to their interest, whereas aural and sensual modification, which only the cultural sensibilities of the black could assess, would establish what it was essential to assert, that is, black identity. Hence, it would be wrong to assume that black minstrelsy did not do much to question the stereotyped image of the black at that early stage.

A more recent analogy of the satiric ruse of black art can be made using Melvin Van Peebles' *Aint Supposed to Die a Natural Death*. When the *New York Times Magazine* critic acclaims Van Peebles as "the first black man in show business to beat the white man at his own game,"[20] it is doubtful whether he is merely thinking of the artistic merits of the musical. For the black author eventually reveals himself as a shrewd and subtle satirist, more so than he at first appears. Having painted with satiric humor, for most of the play, the various black types of the world of the ghetto, and also having made them seemingly slave-bound to the white culture, he finally launches a vociferous indictment of white America. We find also that the stereotypic characters were created precisely to give his imprecations such impact. In fact, in terms of the aesthetic concept of the musical, we could say that the author has created a crisis, or an epidemic, of stereotypes (as the image of the black) with which he is able to satirize the culture that has generated and tolerated such a pathetic existence. This is the province of the Drama of Epidemic, and we can go further to take a satiric stance by illustrating its objective—that is, its destructive and restorative processes.

Antebellum minstrelsy not only involved Afro-American culture, it presented a crisis to that culture by stereotyping blacks as grotesque creatures of the slave plantations. The crisis, or the violation of the image, need not have been so crucial were it not for the fact of its assertion as an authentic image of the black. As a violation of the survival and identity of the black, it needed to be challenged and the stereotyped image destroyed and redefined. As we have seen, the indictment of the white violator by the black artist against this representation had taken many forms outside the theatre. It had been expressed through running away, insurrection, suicide and, by far the most subtle, through the art of dissembling. In the world of minstrelsy, the indictment had, quite appropriately, taken the form of that subtle art. It was the beginning of the satiric confrontation and of the restorative process that was to span many years to the modern theatre.

By propagating the caricature of blackface, black artists became the authentic and legitimate wearers of the grotesque "masks." As established, there was no way to take over minstrelsy effectively other than by at least seeming to accept the stereotype. But by doing this, blacks indirectly were indicting and satirizing the outrageous illegitimacy or the false claims of the white wearers. For the black artists took over not only because it was their right to participate in an entertainment that was supposed to depict them authentically, but because the whites had hitherto been the sole claimants of its economic advantages. The takeover therefore assumes an indictment of the illegal white dominance and exploitation of the black's blackness, an exploitation that can, in fact, be construed as synonymous with slavery. In this regard, the "black mask" was made a satiric vehicle of the ridiculous conception of the white artists and, by extension, of the supportive white audience. The satire becomes sharper, placed against the fact that these caricatures exposed black minstrels to all the opportunities they had so far been denied or that had not come easily to them— geographic, social and economic mobility and a chance to become somebody. Therefore, more than being a commercial popularization of black stereotypes or a masochistic or ignorant perpetration of them by the black supporting audience, black minstrelsy was a subtle and indirect protest, ridiculing the white conception of the black. What looked like masochism may be seen, with a cathartic perception, as a therapy for exorcising the maligning of blacks by whites. It is the restorative aspect of the epidemic process. In fact, it was the beginning of a long process of redefinition and rediscovery of black identity. The process was to span through the civil rights movement in America in the 1960s, when the protests and the satiric indictment were more direct, and the movement to define black expression in the theatre was more pronounced.

The plays that will be discussed to illustrate the concept of the Drama of Epidemic describe the various facets of its expression in Africa and in the Americas. As noted, this expression relates to the survival of the black, which inevitably employs a satiric action because of the nature of the process of survival, that is, its obstacles, its struggles and its consequences. In the African dramas, for instance, the expression has been explored within its four main genres—the ritual, the historical, the political and the literary. In the Americas, however, the Afro-American plays reflect, within any of the genres, the black experience and the struggle to establish a black identity in a culturally different white society. From yet another dimension, the South American and the Caribbean plays focus on the drama that has sought a meaning in the New World from African survivals. Significantly, all the plays, whether specifically or incidentally, have a common source from which they draw their artistic, satiric content. This is the fate of the black man as ritually described by the concept of Esu-Elegbara, the archetype of the black satire and satirist.

THE AFRICAN EXPRESSION

The satiric process of the Drama of Epidemic in plays by African authors will be considered in four categories: ritual, historical, political and literary.

However, these categories are by no means definitive or clear-cut, since a play can easily fit into more than one genre, as will be seen. More important, the classification should serve to demonstrate the basic fact that various kinds of plays can be analyzed with, or can achieve their aesthetic value and clarity through, the concept.

Perhaps no play can better illustrate the ritual genre than a play which dramatizes the very idea of the Drama of Epidemic—that is, a play about Esu-Elegbara, which ritualizes the fate of its central character. I hasten to say, however, that there are plays about Esu-Elegbara that are difficult to use in this sense, for example, Wale Ogunyemi's *Eshu Elegbara* or Dipo Kalejaiye's *The Creator and the Disrupter,* both of which seem to have a Christian bias by posing Esu as a fallen god who is downright evil.[21] I have not tried to analyze Esu from this very untraditional conception. Obotunde Ijimere's *The Imprisonment of Obatala,* on the other hand, can serve as a good introduction to the subject, as can its Brazilian counterpart, *The Story of Oxala,* which will be discussed later in the chapter.[22]

Indeed, in *The Imprisonment,* Esu as god of fate, unlike in the other two plays, is the central power in control of the fates of the other characters, also gods in their own right. Obatala, the creation sculptor and principle of endurance, under the influence of fate, insists on setting out on a journey to visit his impulsive and irrational friend, Shango, god of thunder and lightning. Crucial to this will of fate is the inevitable retribution for Obatala's cosmic crime—for even the gods err and are accountable for their faults or crimes. In the case of Obatala, he was once, while molding the human form, given to the excesses of palm wine—no doubt the will of fate, or of Esu. The intoxication that resulted from this license prevented him from creating perfect human forms; instead he created deformities such as cripples, hunchbacks, albinos, and so on. His crime or fatal weakness, therefore, is his compulsively naive drive, which gets him into trouble again during the play, for which he must suffer. The whole action, his suffering, is an indictment of fate, his fate. He encounters Eshu twice on the journey, and each time he is put to the test by Eshu, who provokes his anger with satiric attacks. These challenges of fate culminate in a third and most critical action—his imprisonment at the hands of his quick-tempered and irrational friend, Shango. However, Obatala, with a recognition of fate's indictment, comes to terms with all the satiric overtures. His reactions, in fact, have restorative consequences.

Obatala's characteristic patience and endurance are survival attributes that save him from catastrophic fatalities. For fate, we may say, has ritually satirized Obatala into a deeper understanding of himself. But the experience also induces a spiritual therapy in the communicant-audience or -reader, whose sense of patience and endurance is renewed. Incidentally, Shango's irrational temper is also satirized in the play. Although this is not central to the action, his own self-knowledge, through the destructive consequences of his impulsiveness, essentially contributes to the restorative process. We learn that his irrational casting of Obatala into imprisonment is symbolic of, and consequential to, an epidemic of barrenness and famine which ravages his kingdom. It is only through his self-knowledge and subsequent reordering of his temper and of events (the release of Obatala from imprisonment) that calm is restored. The epidemic process is complete.

The ritual theme of the fate of man and its satiric action is also central to plays like Ola Rotimi's *The Gods Are Not to Blame*, Duro Ladipo's *Oba Koso*, and Wole Soyinka's *A Dance of the Forests* and *Death and the King's Horseman.*[23] In *The Gods*, Rotimi's adaptation of *Oedipus Rex*, the satire of fate is directed through an oracle of a curse by which the action of the drama is developed from a crisis to a catastrophic self-knowledge. There is a kind of impulsive drive, reminiscent of Shango's, in Odewale, the new king of Kutuje, who is faced with finding the cause and cure for the epidemic devastating his town. Odewale's compulsive fatal weakness, of which he is accused and indicted by the seer, Baba Fakunle, is the cause of his crisis. Actually, the crisis is an indictment of fate that Odewale must eventually acknowledge. It is the process to this knowledge that the action of the play describes as it develops from one impulsive move to another—Odewale's pursuit and determination to find the cause and prove his accusers wrong. This drive carries with it an irony-laden oath and curse uttered by Odewale as a just punishment for the murderer of the old king, the criminal that has brought on the town's epidemic. The oath, of course, is a curse on himself, the same indictment of fate that the seer has pronounced on Odewale's irascible, impulsive temper. The grotesque, satiric consequence of this indictment is Odewale's brutal gouging out of his own eyes—the catastrophic self-knowledge of the indictment. But it is this savage "sacrifice" that ritually restores life to the town, thus completing the epidemic process or the satiric cycle of fate—that is, the destructive and sanative processes.

In *The Imprisonment* and Duro Ladipo's *Oba Koso,* a folk opera, this ritual cycle is expressed as cosmic. Eshu, in *The Imprisonment,* is emphatic on this, contrasting the attributes of Obatala, principle of peace, with Ogun, the god of war and principle of aggression:

> Now they are happy.
> Obatala rests in the sky like a swarm of bees,
> He watches the world in silence.
> Ogun has retired to the dark forest of Ekiti.
>
> . . . .
>
> [But] The time will come when the owner of
>   Heaven
> Will send me back to confuse the heads of men.
> Then Ogun will burst out of his forest
> To cool his parched throat with blood.
> Then the father of laughter will be driven
>   from the city.
> And the rule of iron returns.

. . . .
For the owner of the world has interlocked
   creation and death
Inseparably like mating gods.[24]

In *Oba Koso,* we see this cycle through the suicide and the eventual deification
of Sango, actions marked by his aggressive, impulsive and irrational nature. It
is easy to see that his intrigues against his war generals, of which he is a
victim, emanated from his own fatal weakness, his vacillating quick temper
and decisions which result in his irrevocable catastrophe. But, more important,
this fatality of his nature, even after his self-knowledge, does not die with him;
rather, it becomes a creative device of apotheosis. It is transformed into the
cosmic, fatal power of lightning and thunder, which is a potential satiric device
to punish whoever deserves such an action. In fact, this cosmic action, or the
awareness of this levelling justice, is a spiritual therapy for communicants and
audience alike.

When we come to plays like Soyinka's *A Dance of the Forests* and *Death
and the King's Horseman,* we encounter what a modern literary dramatist has
done with the epidemic components of ritual. In fact, the destructive and restorative cycle is seen more in human terms than cosmic ones, even though the
process is based on a traditional concept.

Soyinka's own concept of the artist (actor, dramatist, plastic artist, etc.) has
been fully described, as earlier stated, in "The Fourth Stage."[25] It is based on
his concept of Ogun, the creative principle who is described as the archetype
of the tragic actor, the destructive and creative potential of his artist-descen-
dants. The introduction explains how Esu-Elegba is basically instrumental to
this potential. Elsewhere, I have argued how Soyinka's major characters, artists
in their own right, have described this complementarity.[26] In terms of the Drama
of Epidemic, it can also be argued that this characteristic of the artist, which
really is an epidemic process, has ritual and satiric overtones for the individual
in Soyinka's plays. *A Play of Giants* was used earlier to illustrate the epidemic
process itself. In this play, Kamini, along with what he represents, the archi-
tect-artist of corrupted power, may be said to be satirized by his own rituals of
corrupt power. However, we will benefit more by considering the play in terms
of its political and literary emphasis, to be discussed later in this section.

In *A Dance of the Forests,* Demoke, the carver-artist, is driven by the guilt
of his crime through the action of the play. He has destroyed his apprentice,
Oremole, through his fatal weakness—for he is "slave, alas, to height, and the
tapered end / Of the silk-cotton tree."[27] The apprentice, carving the totem for
the national festival way above the reaches of his master on the silk-cotton
tree, was struck down with spite. This crime cries out to be avenged, and from
it Demoke must absolve himself in order to discover his artistic potential. For
it is only by such restorative processes that he can mature as a true artist.
Through a long, "searing" night in the forest, and through a shattering dance

of the forest spirits, who indict him, he suffers the dissolution of self and comes out alive with a mature knowledge of himself.[28] The whole ritual experience is a satiric process, and the visions of guilt, or the tantalizing spectacle of the forest spirits that dazzles and torments his psyche, can be seen as a satirist's or satiric scourging. His expiation, therefore, is the restorative complement of the destructive process. But *A Dance* is littered with a number of complex ideas, part of Soyinka's attempt to work out a Yoruba concept of tragedy, an exploration that seems to have been firmly resolved, with an artistic maturity, by *Death and the King's Horseman.*

Significantly, also, in *Death and the King's Horseman,* the ritual and satiric processes of the epidemic concept are more sharply drawn. Here again dance is a central device of satire. Perhaps Elesin Oba, the central character, has every intention of going through with the demands tradition imposes on him—the ritual sacrifice he must perform in order to accompany the dead king (who is waiting at heaven's gate). According to tradition, an Elesin Oba, the king's horseman and favorite companion, must die a month after the death of the king, as part of the burial observances, in order to ensure the king's smooth passage into the world of the ancestors. The ritual demand is also to ascertain the continuity of tradition and the well-being of the community. However, this Elesin has a fatal weakness that eventually obstructs the ritual process—his rather indulgent sexual appetite. In the play, he exploits this weakness, taking advantage of his imminent self-sacrifice by untraditionally consummating a marriage to a woman who is already betrothed to another man. At first, his argument for this violation, as also considered by Iyaloja, head of market women and a traditionalist, seems reasonable. It would be an unusual but opportune experience, for the issue from this union or consummation may help realize a traditional questing—that of the "numinous passage" of experience, here the metaphysical link between the worlds of the unborn, the living, and the dead—a link that tradition believes exists.[29] Incidentally, this questing also describes the author's aesthetic concept.[30]

As it happens, the unnatural act proves a fatal obstacle to the ritual sacrifice, as he later realizes.[31] In his ritual dance of death by which he is expected to cross to the other world, he readily welcomes the interruption of the British District Officer, Pilkings, thereby committing, as he puts it later, "the awful treachery of relief," or "the blasphemy of thought."[32] For the ritual process is stopped, and continuity of tradition is at stake; honor is disgraced and violated. Elesin Oba, the instrument of the violation, is consequently the curse of tradition. Iyaloja, the staunch representative of tradition, is full of contempt for this: "I warned you, if you must leave a seed behind, be sure it is not tainted with the curses of the world. Who are you to open a new life when you dared not open the door to a new existence? I say who are you to make so bold?"[33] We realize in this speech that Elesin has committed a crime against tradition and consequently has been indicted. As such, Elesin's dance of death may be looked at from an ironic perspective. For his dance steps eventually run counter to the rhythm of the drumming and of the traditional world view. The stage direction at the end of scene 3 seems to prepare us for this. We see the traditional vision through the eyes of Olohuniyo, the praise-singer. Intoning a recitative dirge-chant, he has hitherto been on the same emotional level with Elesin Oba's transitional dance. The stage direction then takes over: "He [Olohuniyo] appears to break down. ELESIN dances on, completely in a trance. The dirge wells up louder and stronger. ELESIN'S dance does not lose its elasticity but his gestures become, if possible, even more weighty."[34]

It is almost impossible to appreciate the visual effect on the printed page. In the premiere performance of the play, the director (Soyinka himself) used a traditional Yoruba dirge-chant as a counterpoint to Olohuniyo's recitative. Olohuniyo's vocal breakdown, the trailing off of his chant, anticipates Elesin's own faltering. The dirge that "wells up louder and stronger" is traditional insistence on continuity, which Elesin, however, fails to sustain. His weighty gestures are signalling toward this moment of failure, which happens outside the scene. But Olohuniyo's breakdown has anticipated this ironic limitation of the will.

The satirizing of Elesin by his will, through dance, is focused and made more emphatic by the juxtaposing travesty of the following scene, the colonial fancy-dress ball, in which Pilkings and his wife desecrate tradition. They don, for the frivolous ball, the sacred traditional costume and mask of the Egungun masquerader's cult.

The efficacy of Elesin's satire on himself and the restorative process are not unlike Ogun's floundering in the "transitional abyss" and the combative will that rescues him from annihilation.[35] He flounders in the gulf of transition, suffering dishonor, and the traditional, which he represents, is at the point of destruction—which calamity results in his son's, Olunde's, sacrificial and substitute death. For the honor of tradition and family must be restored. Yet, it is this act of selfless will that summons Elesin's own restorative energies, perhaps too late, to his eventual and less honorable suicide. I will come back to these two Soyinka plays.

So far, the individual satirized by his own fate in the epidemic process is essentially fictional, conceived within a mythical or metaphysical context. The individual is drawn into a ritual fate process in which he becomes satirized, and through which the restorative prospects of satire are realized or felt. In plays based on or motivated by a historical idea, or plays that raise a political perspective, we move from the fictional individual in a ritual process to a fictionalized figure in history or factual life. The individual is indicted and satirized, through a historical process, by his fate more as a fact of history than as a metaphysical entity. Furthermore, perhaps more realistically here than in ritual, the community or society is not only implicated but may also be affected by the satiric action.

In plays that emanated from the francophone countries in Africa, we encounter, perhaps as nowhere else in the European colonized societies on the African continent, a penchant for the historical past. This is, however, hardly surprising, what with the influence of the William Ponty School, which encouraged such dramas from the beginning of its theatrical tradition.[36] It is also a tradition which is strongly rooted in French classical tragedy and Aristotle's tragic principles, and therefore requires a personality of noble birth or an illustrious "son" for its tragic heroism. The result, within the traditional African background, is the proliferation in African drama of the African chief, whose various roles in colonial history apparently lent themselves to a heroism that was often tragic.[37] The dramatized ventures attempt to evoke an African sense of pride and identity with the past, with that moment in history which has more than any other provoked a reassessment of such attributes. Thus, we have represented in the drama of the French-African expression nation builders like Chaka (there are many versions), Beatrice in *Beatrice du Congo,* Lumumba in *Une Saison de Congo,* or Christophe in *La Tragedie du Roi Christophe.* They represent historical personages who, one way or another, tried to resist colonial incursion and power, an action that often resolved itself in tragedy.[38]

On the one hand, some of these characters and plays satisfy the objectives of Negritude for which they were written—that is, the glorification of the African past and the demoralized or lost black attributes of blackness, self-pride and dignity.[39] On the other hand, these plays describe the tragedy of the human will, and it is when one considers the causes of the downfall of the characters that one relates their drama with aspects of the epidemic concept. For their tragedy is brought about by a weakness of their individual fates, such as intransigence, vainglorious pride, overconfidence or tyrannic power. Preoccupied with the fate of their people, they are often lost in their far-sightedness between national interest and personal ambition, on account of which they are satirized by their own fate.

In *The Tragedy of King Christophe,* Christophe, who is actually a Haitian African by slave descent, seems to have captured this satiric consequence when he says, his paralytic downfall staring him in the face, "Envious fortune has struck me down."[40] For a man of his unyielding will, which refuses to submit to any obstacle in his path, he is quite in character with the rationalizing conscience suggested by the translation. But it is precisely because of his intransigence and despotic will that he is inevitably brought down. This is the deeper meaning of his rationale, conveyed more directly in another translation as an "outrage of fate."[41] Discussion of *The Tragedy of King Christophe* belongs more appropriately to the second section of this chapter. But the play relates very well to the states emerging from colonialism in Africa as well as to the states freed from slavery in the New World, where it is set. On the one hand, the play describes an ideal leadership and the dynamism that African states require to stand on their own feet and face the world in their own right, as Christophe himself expresses throughout the play. It is a requirement that demands "too much of men. But not enough of black men."[42] It is also a requirement whose process and work ethic convey a paradox. For the "paths of freedom and of slavery are identical'' (or so it seems), and it is conceivable that Christophe "employs the means of slavery to attain the ends of freedom," as two upper-class ladies try to reason out with one of his aides.[43] On the other hand, however, Rome was not built in a day, and Christophe does go too far. Intoxicated with his vision of a free black city, he becomes and symbolizes the worst satiric victim of his own vision as he falls, paralyzed from his hallucination or by the psychotic images of that terror.

In spite of his megalomania, Christophe is a consistent and positive character, and one cannot help but admire his heroism, which transposes satiric action into the tragic. His blowing up of himself with a gun is characteristic of his combative will and his uncompromising determination—both of which, again, are reminiscent of Ogun's. He does it not because of any guilt or shame, since he believes in himself and in his vision to the last, but because, as he puts it in what is apparently a Congo proverb, "When you see an arrow that's not going to miss you, throw out your chest and meet it head on."[44] It is a tragic will that challenges the status quo of being a man.

We will not find this resoluteness or the sterner stuff of tragedy in a historical figure like Ovonramwen, at least the way Ola Rotimi depicts him.[45] Wishing to reconstruct what he calls a biased portrayal of the character by colonial historians, Rotimi sets out to describe "a man more sinned against than he ever sinned."[46] The original outcry of King Lear is "I am a man more sinned against than sinning."[47] In the attempt to revise the portrayal of Ovonramwen as an "abominable sadist" of colonial history, who would as such have deserved a satiric whipping of fate, Rotimi depicts a weak-minded king who is too cautious and is so calculating that he does not wish to take responsibility for his actions. As it turns out, he, far from Rotimi's intention, in fact deserves the satiric whipping of fate. Caught within the satiric web because of his fatal weakness, he lacks the tragic defiance that King Lear poses against the fatal elements, and that wins him the cathartic admiration of his audience. In contrast, Ovonramwen deserves what he gets. His caution and his inability to make a crucial decision when troubled by oracular predictions result in a senseless war-provoking massacre of an ambushed expedition of British officers. In the ensuing confrontation, Ovonramwen allows himself to be caught and, worse, humiliated as a king. Since tragedy, in the real sense, does not exist in this play, although it is intended, there can be no tragic catharsis. And as for satiric catharsis, if it exists, it is misevoked. For it is the British who seem to hold the satiric sway and therefore have the last laugh. Ovonramwen, having been captured and humiliated, runs away and hides, only to be recaptured through an informant, one of his men, and this time he is shackled. Ovonramwen's treatment by the British is justified by General Moor: "Welcome Overami. It is now quite clear that you are not prepared to work with me in the interest of and for the peace of this land."[48] Admittedly the restorative condition is an exploitative one, the mission of British capitalism under the guise of peace. But Ovonramwen's last statement, his sarcastic message to Queen Victoria, is really quite harmless and, if anything, ludicrously out of place: "Tell Queen Victoria that at last the big pot of corn has toppled; now mother hen and her children may rejoice."[49] The pathetic remark cannot fail to receive a sneering chuckle from Moor and the other British officers on stage, and, by extension, from the audience. Rotimi, however, tries to force the satiric catharsis and the audience's sympathy through other means.

The action that provokes Ovonramwen's overcaution and indecision was really a ritual condition—the curse from the chiefs he has executed at the beginning of the play for being rebellious; and the message from an oracle predicting an imminent act of violence.[50] Ovonramwen is disturbed by the likely efficacy of both pronouncements. Consequently, it can be argued that he is tormented into inaction in the attempt to avert the seemingly unjust and destructive hands of fate. And in this sense, our sympathy might be aroused—although Ovonramwen should have stood as uncompromisingly high as his deed, which involved the fates of the executed chiefs. However, from the premise of ritual satire, fate's satiric humiliation is conditioned by character and will. Ovonramwen, rather than striving to maintain his stance by being consistently in control, cunningly places the fate of his nation in the hands of his lieutenant, Ologbosere. This culminates in his humiliation, an act which, as stated, is unintentionally effected for Pax Britannica. Because of this flaw in the writing and in Ovonramwen's character, a whole nation has been satirically thwarted, and this undeservedly. Furthermore, the restorative process, from the viewpoint of the black, is not in evidence. As if to emphasize this lack, the epilogue concludes with chants of lament, "symbolic representations of enshacklement," encouraging "fate [to] laugh on."[51]

For reasons probably obvious, political drama has a potential for producing good and more direct satire. Matthew Hodgart writes, "Satire is not only the commonest form of political literature but insofar as it tries to influence public behavior, it is the most political part of literature."[52] It seems to be a natural vehicle for a direct indictment of the social, economic and political injustices in a society or nation, and to call for change or revolutionary action. In the introduction to his essay on satiric tendencies in the works of Nigerian writers, which also relates to the African scene in general, James Ngugi implies the same motives when he says that, in "discussing any satirist . . . we must see him in his social and political setting."[53] Again, colonialism, as Ngugi also argues in terms of the works he discusses, seems to be the source of conflict and satire in this genre of African drama. For the political impact and its dramatic expression, I would like to consider plays from East and South African countries where colonialism has most vividly demonstrated its oppressive tendencies. Incidentally, contrary to this East and South African experience, what we gather at the end of Ngugi's essay is that the satirical impact is weak in some of the Nigerian works he discusses—precisely, I think, because the oppressive nature of colonialism in Nigeria or other West African countries was less active and less felt. I do not, however, share his opinion that the satiric picture in West African literature, for example in Soyinka's works, is static,[54] for reasons already explored in the epidemic processes in Soyinka's plays.

Indeed, because of the strong impact of colonialism in East and South Africa, most plays from these countries deal, one way or another, with the theme of oppression arising directly or indirectly from the exploits of colonial rule. The plays thus present a confrontation between oppressors and the oppressed. For instance, in Ebrahim Hussein's *Kinjeketile,* we have a confrontation of the Wamatunbi tribe with their German colonial masters.[55] Ngugi Wa Thiong'o and Micere Mugo's *The Trial of Dedan Kimathi* dramatizes a conflict between the forces of imperialism and the African rebels constituting the Mau-Mau organization.[56] And dealing with the oppression of apartheid, we have plays like Lewis Nkosi's *The Rhythm of Violence,* Athol Fugard, John Kani and Winston Ntshona's *Sizwe Bansi Is Dead,* and Percy Mtwa, Mbongeni Ngema and Barney Simon's *Woza Albert.*[57] But there are other forms of oppression, albeit rooted in or paralleling the colonial, since the evil of exploitation continues during and after the independence of these African states or among the Africans themselves. Some of these forms are expressed in Mukotani Rugyendo's *The Barbed Wire* or Peniah Mukando's *Tambueni Haki Zetus,* which deal with the oppression of the weaker by the stronger.[58] There is also the oppression of women, as dramatized in *The Scar* by Rebecca Njau.[59]

Looking at some of these plays from the point of view of the concept of the Drama of Epidemic, one can naturally expect the playwright to identify with the oppressed, and therefore conclude that the satiric thrust will probably be aimed at the oppressor. But such a supposition, even where the oppressed are supposed to have gained victory or freedom, is not necessarily consistent with the concept. For instance, in *The Barbed Wire,* the oppressed of the play, the villagers whose fertile farmland is robbed from them by the cunning of a rich man from the city, finally win their case against him. There is even an indictment, backed by the weapons of the villagers (spears, picks, staves, etc.), for a possible satiric action against the approaching tractors of the rich man.[60] But the confrontational action is dissipated by the choices the playwright makes. Rwambura, the rich man, recalls his tractors and calls the police who arrest the poor peasants. The peasants, who spent one night in the cold and under guard outside the District Commissioner's office, are released after their fines have been paid. They then present their case legally and win it. What the play lacks, however, is a strong dramatic action, verbal or physical, through which the characters could be well defined and the political nature of their oppression starkly perceived and felt. Without this, the satiric process of the epidemic drama is not focused and is obscure. For in the political arena of the concept, the indictment launches an incisive action, or an invective, against a strongly felt issue. The epidemic efficacy of this indictment, in this regard, depends on the grotesquery of the "evil" and the dire need to oppose and eradicate it. It is an action that may destroy its object, or, indeed, its subject, either of which evokes a catharsis. And the action is satiric precisely because of the human errors or fatal weaknesses which tend to play tricks on us, or make our actions look purposeful yet, sometimes, ridiculous.

This satiric action is well expressed, for instance, in *Kinjeketile* and *The Rhythm of Violence*. The Magi-Magi uprising against the German colonialist regime in *Kinjeketile* builds its action on the cause of the oppression (German brutality, forced labor and taxes, rape, etc.). However, the battle for freedom from oppression is catastrophic for the oppressed peasants and, superficially, for their cause, because of their ignorant choice of weapons for waging a modern war—they believe in the traditional protective power of magic, intended to counter modern technology. But the epidemic implications of the action and its efficacy are seen in total through the brain behind all this, Kinjeketile, the seer whose vision, after all, is shattered helplessly and satirically. After uniting the tribes through the miraculous powers of the Magi-water so that they can be strong enough to rebel against German oppression, Kinjeketile begins to doubt the reality and practicality of his vision. It is precisely at this point that the conviction of the mobilized tribes is at a climax, the conviction that they can win the attack against the Germans since, according to the vision, the water with which they are "baptized" will give them immunity from being killed by bullets. Heedless of the warnings and advice of Kinjeketile to wait until they are technically fit to attack, the tribes, with no defense, launch a foray into the barrage of machine guns awaiting them. On Kinjeketile's head, therefore, lies the catastrophic fate that befalls his people. He has raised their hopes for a better future, and this bold effort has eventually gotten out of hand and misfired. He realizes the ironies of this effort, hence the recurrent pricking of his thoughts: "A man gives birth to a . . . word. And the word . . . grows . . . it grows bigger and bigger. Finally, it becomes bigger than the man who gave it birth."[61]

The physical manifestation of this satiric thought is the senseless massacre into which the tribes throw themselves. But through this grotesque expression, through this destructive aspect of satire or of the epidemic process, comes the restorative—the hope for the future, the hope of eventual freedom. Kinjeketile refuses to renounce the efficacy of the Magi-water, insisting, conclusively: "A word has been born. Our children will tell their children about this word. Our great grand children will hear of it. One day the word will cease to be a dream, it will be a reality!"[62] Actually, it is the cathartic evocation of the dialectic of thought and the satiric indictment and turbulence he has been experiencing in his mind. It is the kind of catharsis evoked, for instance, at the end of *The Trial of Dedan Kimathi*, which elicits the freedom song and dance from the crowd of workers and peasants, suggesting that the struggle continues. It is also the case with *Woza Albert* when at the finale of the intense expression of apartheid, the dead black activists against apartheid, following the example of Moreno's (Christ's) resurrection, are ritually invoked as heroes. The catharsis is, of course, shared by the audience.

In *The Rhythm of Violence*, on the other hand, such a restorative evocation is not possible because the whole satiric action or the validity of its grotesque, destructive expression is in question. The rebel movement against the apartheid regime is waiting for a time bomb to explode that will destroy the central image of the institution. The action is to be the beginning of the letting out of the pent-up frustrations of the oppressed and the humiliated. Into this expectation, as tension builds regarding the possibility of its success, is thrown a dream of compromise—the honest relationship of love that is developing between Tula, brother to the leader of the black movement, and Sarie, the daughter of an active but decamping member of the apartheid regime. When Tula finds out that Sarie's father is about to be blown up along with the others in City Hall, the objective of the black movement, the efficacy of its indictment, becomes a questionable action. The clear-sighted justification of the movement's action is thrown into disarray. There are, consequently, frantic attempts to rescue Sarie's father, and the final, impulsively desperate attempt of Tula is too late. The bomb explodes on time and Tula, of course, goes along with it. It is as if Time, a device of fate, has satirized the satirizing subject, that is, the satirist black. The grotesquery of Tula's shattered body (he "tried to stop time") placed against a background of the grotesquery of the blown-up symbol of apartheid, the image with which we are left at the end, sustains the question posed on violence. Even though we are certain that compromise between the apartheid regime and the oppressed black is inconceivable, and there is nothing suggesting an end to the oppression in the future, we are still left with the idea that violence cannot resolve it. Sarie, kneeling over Tula's body, explodes in exasperation: "Brutes! All of you! A whole pack of murderers! All of you. Black and white and yellow! It doesn't make a damn bit of difference! You're all killers! Murderers!"[63] Actually, she is to make a statement to the police, and we can be sure that all the black movement leaders will eventually be rounded up. There is hardly a breather in sight for the oppressor and the oppressed, the indicted and the indicter, the satirized and the satirist. The restorative aspect of the epidemic process is left hanging.

The last genre of plays from Africa to be considered here is the literary, which emphasizes stylistic qualities. As these plays not only include some of those already discussed, but also repeat most of the distinctions already made, it is not necessary to examine them at length.

Style normally should complement or reinforce the theme and the dramatic action and content in a play. Therefore, in dealing with an idea or concept of theatre, the stylistic components of a play expressing that idea should logically reinforce the components of that idea. A ready example is the play just discussed. In *The Rhythm of Violence*, Time, which is an integral aspect of fate and therefore has a potential for both destructive and restorative processes, is evoked to satirize the forces of oppression of the apartheid regime.[64] The dramatic device used to activate this is a time bomb. For its dramatic as well as its epidemic quality lies in its timing. As a mechanical device, it might go off or not, it might be early or late; so, in fact, it can be as unpredictable as its abstract counterpart, Time. Also, like Time, either its detonation or its silence can be both destructive and restorative, depending on the purpose for which it is used. On the one hand, its successful detonation can bring the restorative rewards of freedom, or so its users think and hope. On the other hand, its silence or deactivation can destroy the cause for which it is activated in the first place, but can also bring mental relief and perhaps the beginning of peaceful negotiation toward a positive black and white relationship such as that demonstrated by Tula and Sarie. These are some of the fleeting considerations that cause nervous tension—unrest, sensitiveness, irascibleness—but also mixed with them are tenderness, sexuality, expansiveness, etc., all of which characterize the dialogue and action in the black movement's gathering.[65] All of these characteristics are conditioned by and directed toward the timing of the bomb. To register this confusion in the air caused by Time, there are beats and strains of black music—jazz. As noted, the destructive aspect of Time is realized, but in this play the restorative aspect is out of focus, and there is no healing in sight. Consistent with this fact, the "slow blues number" that ends the play has a "harsh, violent, discordant melody."

Similarly, *Kinjeketile* has some stylistic features that complement its epidemic process. Myth, the narrative of ritual,[66] is its central device. Here, in fact, is the case of myth and history, manifestations of illusion and reality, forming a nondescript unity to describe the dialectical state of mind of Kinjeketile. On the one hand is the literal interpretation of the myth of Magi used historically as a force that is detrimental to the urgent needs of revolt and to the survival of the tribes. On the other hand is the metaphorical usage, a symbol of unity needed to begin to develop the physical and technical strength, a long process, that could effectively match German military expertise and eventually liberate the tribes. What then develops is that the reality of the myth, its ineffectiveness and destructiveness on the tribes, is recreated into a restorative and functional historical truth—for myth, categorically refuted as a lie, should serve as a symbol of solidarity in the struggle toward eventual freedom. The episodic scenes of the play, in their Brechtian epic theatre style, are also functional in terms of the dialectical argument. For they should encourage the audience to observe, to consider the various levels, to allow no lingering or long-lasting emotional involvement with the character; yet the ideas and the action they generate are thought-provoking, rousing the audience and forcing them to make decisions.[67] But then, more importantly, such a perception and response on the part of the audience is consistent with the cathartic evocation of the Drama of Epidemic, a satiric catharsis meant to incite an audience to mental or physical action.

We will find a similar dialectic of thought and functionality in *The Trial of Dedan Kimathi,* dramatized by the flashbacks of Kimathi's background, which sensitively prod his mind and raise a conflict between giving in to the white lure of compromises and continuing the guerrilla struggle for black freedom. These trials of his mind, set against the court trial occurring during the play, are a direct result of forces that are trying to destroy the cause and black solidarity—forces including, importantly, blacks used by whites to deflate the effectiveness of a just satiric assault. In *Woza Albert,* however, the dialectic is posed by the fact (or myth?) of Christ used to dramatize the seemingly unreal and outrageous fact of apartheid—revealing the ironies of South Africa's supposedly Christian apartheid regime. For the play builds with a succession of contrasting vignettes depicting various reactions to Christ's second coming in South Africa. The satiric irony and paradox that punctuate and deflate the grotesque fact of apartheid are the dramatization of the nonproductivity of apartheid in terms of the Christian doctrine and the functionality of that doctrine in terms of the black struggle for freedom.

While on the subject of the political objective of the epidemic process, I would like to make a qualification on its cathartic quality in African political plays, especially ones that profess to have adopted the Brechtian epic idea and style. A case in point is *Sizwe Bansi Is Dead* by Athol Fugard, the well-known South African playwright, coauthored by John Kani and Winston Nrshona, a play which, like some of the other Fugard plays, attempts to express a strong concern against apartheid. An article by Fugard discusses the reception, in a black township in South Africa, of the first performance of *Sizwe Bansi.*[68] He talks about how the performance was interrupted by the participation of the audience in a heated debate on a moral and political issue concerning the bane of every black South African's existence, the Passbook Book. In the play, Sizwe Bansi by force of circumstance has been drawn into the criminal act of relinquishing his invalidated passbook in order to assume the name and active employment status of a dead man. This chance of a lifetime promises him a small though precarious hope of minimal survival as opposed to dearth and destitution. The choice between total destitution and earning a minimal livelihood by criminal means is pregnant with frustrating, pathetic irony, since neither really offers relief in terms of human rights. Equally pathetic in this regard is any debate on the choice between the two dehumanizing, satiric conditions of survival, a choice which totally frustrates Sizwe, a tragic expression of the powerlessness of "unaccommodated" man. All of this should make political agitation for freedom from the strictures of apartheid very crucial and immediate.

Fugard's article, principally because of that debate by the audience, claims a Brechtian approach and significance which I have always questioned for reasons not exactly relevant here. But in terms of the restorative process of the Drama of Epidemic and the political objective of such plays, one distinction remains obvious.

The play is powerful in its own right as an evocation of the evils of apartheid—and one must not forget that the play evolved with Fugard's two black South African actors and coauthors. But the power is weakened by the argument that the play poses at the end. Sizwe rounds off the play with the conclusion of the letter to his wife, accounting for his fortunate choice for survival:

"So Nowetu, for the time being my troubles are over. . . . Spend the money I am sending you carefully. If all goes well I will send some more each week." The feeling we get is that the apartheid problem, though abated momentarily for Sizwe, in fact continues—and this is demonstrated actively at various levels of the play. On the surface, there is nothing wrong with this idea; but the crucial question, surely, is whether this is in the best interest of the majority of South African blacks who, contrarily, seek total freedom from apartheid. For them, it is a struggle for freedom that continues, and, as has been suggested, this is the restorative commitment of plays like the East African *Trial of Dedan Kimathi* and the South African *Woza Albert*. Expressive of this commitment are the song and dance at the end of these plays, which reflect and parallel the forward, pulsing movement of hope that we see often on the streets of South Africa by the agitating, persistent crowd. All this seems to make Fugard's idea somewhat limited and ineffective, and therefore renders his audience's argument on the Reference Book abortive on account of the restorative hope for the blacks who, rather unjustifiably, face satiric destruction from the whites. For the black writer, that kind of satire must necessarily be challenged, indicted and destroyed, out of which destruction must be seen the objective of his or her fatal imprecation—a restorative hope to freedom.

Much more favorably conceived works, in terms of their stylistic consistency with the idea of epidemic processes, are the works by Soyinka already discussed. For these plays are the dramatic expressions of his concept of Yoruba tragedy, based on Ogun's myth. As established in the introduction, this concept, which introduces Ogun as the first actor, argues that the artist has a potential for both destructive and creative action. This potential is expressed by Demoke, the carver in *A Dance of the Forests,* and more successfully by Elesin Oba, the artist of poetry, dance and metaphysics in *Death and the King's Horseman.* But we also have such features in the Professor, another artist of metaphysics as regards death, in *The Road,* and in the character of Old Man, the artist of the philosophy of the system "As" in *Madmen and Specialists.*[69] In both *A Dance* and *Death* Soyinka, as stated, uses dance as the evocative satiric vehicle for the epidemic processes.

But of Soyinka's plays to date, one in which style is subtle and yet probably most emphatic is *A Play of Giants,* and, perhaps because of this, the play is unusually static. In the whole of Part 1, we read or listen to the "shit" (power corruption) of Kamini, in all forms of expression, as described or pontificated by him and all the other African heads of state around him. For instance, Benefacio Gunema expresses this power by Voodoo,[70] while General Bara Tuboum does it by cannibalism.[71] But Kamini is by far the most demonstrative, as the "sound of the emptying cistern" that persists throughout the scene consistently reminds us. For that sound describes one of the sadistic tortures he inflicts on his victims. In this scene, he inflicts punishment on the Chairman for being blatantly realistic about the Bugaran "national currency," which is "not worth its size in toilet paper"; in other words, it is not worth "shit." The constant, ritual flushing of the cistern on the head of the Chairman in the toilet bowl culminates in the actual burying of his head in Kamini's real shit.[72]

In the second part, the "shit" or fatal power of Kamini becomes more elaborately demonstrative when the news comes of his overthrow and the Bugaran Embassy building is under siege outside—that is, when the restorative, out of the destruction or the destructive prospects of Kamini, is in sight. As his embassy is thus besieged by rebels, he forces the representatives of white power (Russian and American diplomatic officials sent to him) into a corner and holds them at gun point as hostages. The picture we get, as explained earlier, is ironic—a satire on Kamini who, however, launches a counter-satiric thrust on his own victims. We almost do not know where Soyinka stands at this point, and it is possible that he is fascinated by the grotesque figure of Kamini and his grotesque actions. However, regarding this, we must not lose track of what the play is about in terms of style and the epidemic process. It is an indictment on Kamini's fatal "shit," which the playwright paints grotesquely and satirically. If the restorative process that should arise or that is seen to materialize from the momentary overthrow of Kamini does seem abortive, may it not be because such criminals as Kamini remain loose, roaming the universe, unabatable? Or perhaps, on a more global basis, the satiric thrust is aimed at both Kamini and the Western and Eastern powers who are the creators of corrupt powers such as Kamini. The restorative aspect of the epidemic process is horrifyingly questioned and held pessimistically suspended, as the final picture suggests: "Guns and rocket launchers open up everywhere. . . . The sound of the crowd [outside] in panicked retreat. . . . KAMINI swings back into the room, his gun aimed directly at the HOSTAGES. Their horror-stricken faces in various postures—freeze. The SCULPTOR works on in slow motion. Slow fade."[73] Consistent with Soyinka's "artists," Kamini stands as an architect of recurrent destructive power. The satiric capitulation of such a power, in an African context, is monumental and cannot be taken at face value, Soyinka seems to acknowledge. For its indictment must be seen and measured against the sum total of the destructive forces that have generated its existence.

THE NEW WORLD EXPRESSION

In its attempt to establish a black identity, the drama in black America, with regard to the concept of the Drama of Epidemic, expresses in general, and like the African political plays, an indictment on the oppressor by the oppressed. The indictment, evoking an image of the pervading oppression, seeks not only to rid the oppressed of the oppression's grotesque manifestations, its "ugliness," but also seeks an ameliorating change. The need is not so much for a separatist nationalism, although there is a plea for national black solidarity, as for a rediscovery of self as a black person. However, an arm of the civil rights movement in North America favored separatism, and this is reflected in plays like Leroi Jones' *The Slave*. The attempt to rediscover black identity, despite stereotypes and the inevitable acculturation of white values and concepts, in fact began in American drama when blacks started to write plays. Apparently the first play by a black man, *King Shotaway* (1820–1821), was about insurrection.[74] Since then, there have been various expressions of this struggle to rescue the black identity from an oppressive culture. Such plays include, for instance, *The Black Doctor* (1847) by the great black tragedian Ira Aldridge, about the struggles of a black ("handsome Mulatto") doctor for recognition in a white society;[75] William Wells Brown's *The Escape* (1858), about slave life and the struggle to escape from the corrupted power of the white slave masters;[76] Theodore Ward's *Our Lan'* (1946), about black resistance and rebellion;[77] Langston Hughes' satiric drama on black religiosity as influenced by white religion, *Tambourines to Glory;*[78] and Lorraine Hansberry's *A Raisin in the Sun* (1959), which will be discussed below. In the struggle to rediscover the black identity, some plays, like *The Black Doctor,* because of the nature of acculturation, have of course been attracted by the characteristics of white culture, which have been conceived as human, therefore black, characteristics. This in itself is not necessarily an unrealistic perception; on the contrary, it is useful as a process toward a better understanding of the black self.

But it seems to me that, in terms of the epidemic concept, the attempt of rediscovery has its clearest and strongest expression in the black arts movement of the 1960s.[79] And by far the finest exponent of the ideas of the movement for black theatre is Leroi Jones (Amiri Baraka). Consequently, his works will serve primarily to illustrate the affinities of the black arts movement and the concept of the Drama of Epidemic. But I must hastily say that the beginnings of this movement, its positive strides toward establishing a black theatre, can be located in Lorraine Hansberry's drama prior to the sixties, as exemplified by *A Raisin in the Sun.*

The demands for the rediscovery of self or of blackness, as set out in Jones' "The Revolutionary Theatre," are "epidemic" demands, for it also expresses the destructive and restorative processes of the concept. It is a theatre about black people, with black people and for black people, a radical alternative to the hitherto existent American theatre, and it is imbued with the black power with which to indict and to change:

The Revolutionary Theatre should force change: it should be change. (All their faces turned into the lights at having seen the ugliness. And if the beautiful see themselves, they will love themselves). . . . Our theatre will show victims, so that their brother in the audience will be better able to understand that they are brothers of victims, and that they themselves are victims if they are blood brothers.[80]

It is a call to the theatre for a satiric action that empowers and provokes through its satiric catharsis. For the brothers of the victims "will find themselves tensed and clenched, even ready to die. We will scream and cry, murder, run through the streets in agony, if it means some soul will be moved, moved to actual life understanding of what the world is, and what it ought to be."[81]

To argue that the action is hardly satiric or cathartic or restorative is to misunderstand the aesthetic factor or the epidemic symptom of the black revolutionary theatre. Interpreting this aesthetic, Larry Neal identifies the oppression that is confronting the Third World and Black America as a condition under the direct influence of "European American cultural sensibility. This sensibility, antihuman in nature, has, until recently, dominated the psyche of most Black artists and intellectuals; it must be destroyed before the Black creative artist can have a meaningful role in the transformation of society."[82] What Leroi Jones' revolutionary theatre tried to do was just that—provoke its audience with its satiric power to such an extent that the power makes them wish to destroy their white cultural sensibility (which is, indirectly, under indictment) in order for them to be able to effectively assimilate their own. For "culture is the basis of all ideas, images and actions. To move is to move culturally, i.e. by a set of values given to you and your culture."[83]

Prior to Leroi Jones, Lorraine Hansberry dramatizes this epidemic idea in *A Raisin in the Sun*.[84] Walter Lee Younger is obsessed by the exploitative values of white culture. Naturally so, since he and his family, in a Southside Chicago black ghetto, are victims of white oppression. The background set that Hansberry gives us is clearly emphatic about this:

THE YOUNGER living room would be a comfortable and well-ordered room if it were not for a number of indestructible contradictions to this state of being. . . . Weariness has, in fact, won in this room. Everything has been polished, washed, sat on, used, scrubbed too often. All pretences but living itself have long since vanished from the very atmosphere to this room.[85]

Hence, in terms of survival, there seems no alternative other than to entertain dreams of getting out of the black condition. Walter's dream, to become a businessman by investing in a liquor store, is prompted and intoxicated by the expectation of insurance money owed to his mother on account of his father's death. This dream is in conflict with the standards of the black family. As Mama, the head of the family, says: "We ain't no business people. . . . We just plain working folks."[86] The risk that investment in the liquor store involves does not augur well for establishing black identity; it is in conflict with black cultural values of pride and dignity. These values, on the other hand, are in consonance with Mama's dream—to invest in a house of their own and save the rest of the money for Beneatha's education and family funds. Contrary to Walter's, this dream is devoid of speculation or uncertainties; it is a more productive and surer way to becoming somebody. However, the money entrusted to Walter Lee to save finds its way to satisfying his dream, which dies when the horrible truth is discovered—Walter's business partner has absconded with the money. Mama's fears have been realized, and the pride and dignity of the family are in danger of being destroyed, not only by this but also by Walter's desperate consideration of another scheme. The white neighborhood in which Mama has invested in a house does not want a black family and is willing to buy off the Youngers with an amount greater than the down payment. Walter, in desperation, calls for the white representative, whom they had earlier derided, to come and make a deal. The satirized family, through Walter, is in need of a restorative action to save it, and Walter again is going about it the wrong way. It takes the initiative and mind-prodding foresight and reasoning of Mama to arrive at the positive, thus restoring the highly prized values of the black. For the house-move must take place at all costs. It is the restorative aspect of the epidemic concept that cannot fail to relate to black people as a whole, a satiric catharsis that calls for a determination to fight oppression by the only weapon available to the black race—respect for cultural values.

Leroi Jones dramatizes these ideas more directly in his plays. For instance, Clay in *Dutchman* and Walker Vessels in *The Slave* are, like Walter, satirized victims of the white cultural sensibility.[87] In *Dutchman,* Clay, a middle-class black, allows himself to be taunted by "the seductive white thing" and into hoping to get a little action (really a ridiculous and fatal notion) from its representation, Lula, a beautiful white woman, perhaps an epitome of all that is evil in white cultural sensibility—noting the apple images and connotations. He is provoked into finally letting out the truth from his black oppressed conscience in a verbal assault on white America that seems to be leading to a physical assault. Realizing the imminent "murder"—and perhaps this is her strategy all along—Lula kills Clay, who is too liberal-minded to kill her anyway.

In terms of Jones' revolutionary theatre of "victims" and the concept of the Drama of Epidemic, the satiric objective and resolution are fulfilled. It is a satire on the white-culture-corrupted black psyche which seeks to acquire power by accommodating white values and expectations.[88] Clay wakes up too late to what he should do, what "crazy niggers turning their back on sanity," as he himself calls them, should do, "that simple act. Just murder." An act that would "make us all sane."[89] This proposal, which as I said Clay is too liberal-conscious to effect and because of which he is a satiric victim, is the satire's cathartic projection on the black audience.

Walker Vessels, the revolutionary in *The Slave,* on the contrary takes up the challenge of the proposal for his sanity by attempting to destroy his white past, which involved, crucially, a white wife and two children. For it is, as rightly interpreted by James Hatch, a "ritual drama of decolonization wherein not only is the colonizer killed, but his powerful spirit that possessed the colonized is ripped out and destroyed."[90] Against a background reality of ongoing explosions by the black liberation forces, Walker confronts the physical and psychological forces that have paralyzed his capabilities and those of his people. These forces are represented socially by Grace, his former white wife, and intellectually by Easley, her present husband/companion, a pretentious white liberal. In the process of ridding himself of these ties, he (an experienced Clay) kills the resisting husband and encourages his wife and children to die. Exhausted and emotionally drained by the whole liberation process, he, the ritual satirist, drags himself out to rejoin the black liberating, satiric force.

The play touches on an important trait of satiric power, later developed in *Jello*. This is the ability of the satirist to dissemble. I argued earlier that this is a cultural trait linking black people to the satirist archetype, Esu-Elegbara. Also, it is a characteristic that enables us to perceive Sambo, the white conception of the image of the black, from a more productive perspective—productive in contrast to the humiliating, corrupted idea of antebellum literature. For he is not merely the endearing cultural entertainer of all times on the American stage, as Joseph Boskin's thesis rightly claims,[91] but also the chameleon satirist archetype of Afro-American culture. Walker Vessels, whose real character, intentions and actions have never really been understood and have been grossly misinterpreted by Grace and Easley (he is "liar," "hoodlum," "hypocritical idealist nigger," "murderer," etc.), confuses his victims all the more. Faced with the possibility of Walker killing her and her husband, Grace says: "He's lying again, Brad. Really most times he's not to be taken seriously. He was making metaphor before . . . one of those ritual metaphors. . . ."[92] Walker also confuses Grace as to his intentions toward his children—whether or not he is going to take them away. But emblematic of the "metaphor" is another exploitative twist of the black potential, the insignia of Walker's army: apparently a "red-lipped" grinning "minstrel."[93] The recalled image of Sambo and blackface minstrelsy immediately assumes a radical and pragmatic usage.

This twisting and inversion is a characteristic bound up with the satiric power itself, which Jones fully utilizes in the character of Rochester in *Jello*.[94] Rochester, modelled on the Uncle Tom clown character (Rochester of the Jack Benny show on television; Jack Benny assumes his own character here also) has been inverted, in the black arts, into a revolutionary figure. In fact, what we have in this play is a satiric boomerang, already described as functional in the use by blacks of blackface; the link with minstrelsy is unmistakable. Jack Benny, the comedian and exploiter-promoter of the black stereotype, is caught in his own satiric web. Rochester, his chauffeur and dissembling avenger, with dexterity and humor cleans him out to the last penny and then murders him—and nobody would take all Benny's efforts at protesting seriously. The other actors on the show, as they come in, think Benny's skinning by Rochester, and his protests, are all a big joke and part of a new television script.

Significantly, as a trickster and master of understatement, Rochester is a satirist descendant of Sambo and Esu-Elegba. Larry Neal rightly makes similar parallels with the trickster figures in Afro-American tradition: Signifying Monkey, Shine and Stagolee.[95] Incidentally, a play that, most ambitiously, links all these types in its epic journey into the Afro-American pedigree and spirituality is *The Great MacDaddy* by Paul Carter Harrison.[96] In fact, in this play and in *Jello,* the fusion of ritual satire and the theatrical makes both, like *A Play of Giants,* classic examples of the aesthetics of the Drama of Epidemic. In this regard, Leroi Jones' revolutionary theatre must be taken beyond its literal con-

sideration as a "theatre of assault." For the revolutionary ideas are clearly
bound up with the destructive and restorative processes of the epidemic concept, that is, the ritual destruction of the white image and white values, and
the cathartic satisfaction and "sane" orientation of the black audience and the
black race as a whole.[97]

The satiric power, the fatal potential of black power with all its epidemic
implications—the aesthetic power of the black arts that assaults, murders, and
provokes kindred spirits into action—is the subject of Jones' *A Black Mass*.[98]
Here, also, by an inversion of white cultural sensibility, we perceive a creation
myth (therefore a creative power) through the eyes of blacks, as opposed to,
say, the biblical creation and its influences on white aesthetics. Three black
magicians (conjure men, gods?) have been endowed with the power to create
black values and aesthetics as an alternative to the white ones, like Time, which
must be destroyed along with those who have created them. Ironically, Jacoub,
the third magician, cannot seem to get away from white values. And since we
are looking at creation from the black point of view, Time, which has been
banished to alien climes—the cold North as opposed to the warm (black) South—
is acknowledged as Jacoub's creation. Thus, he creates another alien and evil
sensibility, a white devil, an uncontrollable monster which attacks and destroys
everything black, including the magicians. Jacoub, before he dies, manages to
banish the beast, once again, to the alien cold North.

Here, again, is the case of the satirist being satirized but with a focus on the
power itself, represented by the three magicians. Regarding this, Jones perhaps
achieves his theme—that the alien sensibility which informs and destroys black
cultural values must itself be destroyed before a black aesthetic can be established. However, the confusion arises in finding what exactly constitutes a black
aesthetic. We only feel it in the play as a product of black values; but what it
is, or what these values actually are, we are not told. If Jacoub has been de-
luded into creating alien concepts and values, which he presumes to be black,
neither of the other two magicians have given specific alternatives, even though
they disagree with Jacoub.[99] Hence, it is possible to see the destruction of all
three as cultural victims of a fatal weakness, thus recalling the wealth pacts
and the epidemic satirizing of society, en masse, described in the last chapter.

But the Drama of Epidemic specifically acknowledges a black aesthetic which
is based on the Yoruba concept of good and evil. As opposed to the biblical
concept, both forces form complementary units embodied in Esu-Elegba, the
trickster, god of fate, satire and satirist. This relationship of the forces seems
to have evaded Jacoub and his associates, or their counterparts in the real world.
However, Leroi Jones' conclusion, as an objective of the black arts movement,
is consistent with the sanative prospects of the epidemic concept. The Holy
War, or Jihad, declared at the end against the Beasts roaming the world is
supposed to be a war of the conscience toward cultural freedom, toward the
spiritual release that should establish the much needed black aesthetic.

I have dwelt on Leroi Jones as the chief exponent of the black arts movement and revolutionary theatre, the ideas of which, I have argued, fall in place with the concept of the Drama of Epidemic. Hence his plays provide excellent illustrations of the concept. However, there are other playwrights, directly or indirectly connected with the movement, whose theories and plays can also relate to the epidemic concept.[100] This is so especially since the concept addresses black survival, and since the struggle to survive being black and to locate a black identity is prior to, and is continued after, Jones' deliberate and conscious expression of it. Some of the plays that could relate the movement and concept were mentioned earlier. Others include Jimmy Garrett's *And We Own the Night*,[101] Ron Milner's *Who's Got His Own*,[102] and Adrienne Kennedy's *Funny House of a Negro*[103]—all of whose characters are also victims of white sensibility and express the general mood of the black arts movement. Sometimes emphasis on the idea of blackness in these plays is more consciously satirical, as in the case of Ben Caldwell's satirized black minister in *Prayer Meeting; or, The First Militant Minister*,[104] the deflation of Sister Agnes' religiosity in James Baldwin's *The Amen Corner*,[105] and the tour de force of blackness in Douglas Turner Ward's *Day of Absence*, which reverses blackface to whiteface and thus satirizes white America's assumed conception of its black residents.[106]

More recently, this satirizing tour de force has been explored, with all its spiritual, social and historical manifestations, in works of perhaps the most prolific black playwright at present, August Wilson. For instance, in *Joe Turner's Come and Gone*, in a desperate call for the search for and recognition of black identity, Wilson succeeds in dramatizing and fusing the ritual, satiric and theatrical components of the epidemic concept.[107] Loomis, the main character, whom fate (the fate of blackness) has satirized through forced labor, seeks a restorative impulse, his missing wife. Yet this palpable impulse is, in itself, a red herring, since Loomis (the image of the black) is spiritually paralyzed and needs must regain his identity through a spiritual confrontation with that identity (his "song"). This is the dramatic center that is ritualized and theatricalized concretely on the stage. It is the center that also satirizes the impotence of every black man and forces him to reach out for sanative measures to recover the wholesomeness of his missing and corrupted "song." Apparently this all-powerful center was not well focused in the original script.[108] This, in fact, would seem to make a case for the concept of the Drama of Epidemic as an important aesthetic factor to be used in assessing the quality of a drama like *Joe Turner*. Indeed, the concept should apply critically to many black American plays because much of black American writing deals with black survival, and the epidemic factor is the destructive and restorative processes experienced with that survival. However, as my analysis has so far shown, the application cannot be assumed as always straightforward.

Moving, finally, into South America and the Caribbean, we will focus, from yet another dimension, on plays that directly relate to the African past, or which find their expression in the African world view as a motivation for establishing their own ideals. As these plays, directly or indirectly, are influenced by African rituals, we are back in fact at the source of the Drama of Epidemic and within traceable history. What then may be of interest are the differences, if any, in belief and concept of ritual, and how these differences have affected thought, social interaction and expression; also, how this interaction informs the epidemic concept. Of the first two directions of inquiry, the concern here is with only a brief historical perspective. We are still within the world the slaves made and where, when the slaves were transported from Africa, they brought their gods. Hence, African religion has been a continuous process, especially in South America and in the Caribbean. Also of considerable influence and dominance has been the Yoruba religion, as evidenced by the orisa cults in Brazil (Candomble and Macumba), Cuba (Santeria), Haiti (Voodoo) and Trinidad (Shango). The process of continuity, however, has not been easy, and not without some obstacles, since it had to survive within Western religious precepts. And precisely because of this contact, African religion as practiced in South America and the Caribbean has a syncretic existence with Christianity. This is important since, for instance, the gods have moved their abode from palpable terrestrial boundaries to amorphous, celestial or ethereal reaches.[109] Consequently, the perspectives of ritual have also changed—from a localized identification with a specific god and his attributes, to a wider identification with a collective unit of gods.[110] In the Candomble, or Voodoo, for instance, the gods are worshipped under one roof even though each has a specific ritual function. In this regard, attributes tend to overlap more consciously than in the Yoruba locality of origin in Nigeria.

Along with this change in perspective, and consistent with the syncretism of religious values, is the modification in aesthetics. Dramatizing the qualities of some of these African gods, centrally those of Obatala, and in an effort to make a racial identification and definition, Zora Seljam in her play *Oxala* explains the syncretic significance of Obatala's drama. According to her, it is related to the captivity of the Christianized Yoruba slaves in Brazil, whose suffering in slavery embodies a "new idea of Christ's passion." She continues:

In the process of being catechized the Yoruba slaves from Nigeria and Dahomey, today Benin, embodied the new idea of Christ's Passion, with their ancestral memory of Oxala's captivity. . . . In a sort of penance, and echoing customs whose origins were buried in time, the uncomplicated piety of the Brazilian Negroes induced in them a desire to expiate a racial burden. It was as if they wanted to relive the sorrow of their deity, a sort of compensation and restitution of his figure to its former majesty and dignity.[111]

It is easy to appreciate the sensitivity of the effort to make parallels between Obatala's suffering and that of the slave, and also to equate this suffering with that of Christ. But, on closer scrutiny, the new syncretic idea, in the long run, would seem to conflict with itself by the very fact of the components of the syncretism. Indeed, we are at a loss as to how to construe the "racial burden" in terms of the individual characteristics of the slave, Obatala and Christ all in one. For expiating a "racial burden" in order to regain the black's dignity suggests, with regard to Christ and Christian thought, a quietistic act of resignation to fate, which is hardly in consonance with the historical fact of the overall attitude of the slave to slavery. And it is hardly, for that matter, consistent with the Yoruba world view of Obatala's "passion" as represented, for instance, in myth and in Ijimere's *The Imprisonment of Obatala,* discussed earlier. The story, we recall, is that Obatala sets out on a journey he has been forewarned not to make. True to the premonition, his journey is beset with fateful and fatal encounters which cost him very dearly but out of which, through a quintessential patience and endurance, he regains his dignity. Although in the Yoruba myth and the play Obatala encounters fate and endures its assaults with an exemplary patience, his endurance of suffering does not quite describe a simple and "uncomplicated" character, since we find that behind the seemingly quiet spirit lies a strong and determined will that puts fate to task, the same determined will that launches him on his journey, in spite of warnings, to visit Shango. At any rate, his burden is not, like Christ's, the sins of the world but is conditioned by his own wilful, intoxicated and indulgent act, which led him to mold deformities. All these characteristics, we will find, are redefined, true to Zora Seljam's premise, in *The Story of Oxala.*

But the "uncomplicated piety of the Brazilian Negroes" in expiating a "racial burden," whatever that may be, is also not in tune with the character of the slave, nor with the image of the black being hitherto redefined. In fact, it would seem to support the antebellum white American representation of the image of the black, that stereotyped conception of Sambo as a docile and noble slave.

The clue to these incongruities may be found, I think, in the Christian concept of good and evil that has influenced Western and subsequently New World black aesthetics. It is a concept which perceives evil as an outside, malevolent influence, and which continually attempts to sever and to exorcise such influences from man's basic goodness. Often used against the slave, the concept condemned the slave's rebellious temperament as savage and devil-willed, a nature considered to be detrimental to the good will of plantation life and of the slave masters, a sinful spirit which the Christian evangelism to the plantations made it its responsibility to exorcise.[112]

This Christian-biased concept, which is the basis of *Oxala,* is a far cry from the Yoruba cultural world view as dramatized in *The Imprisonment of Obatala.* It is antithetical to the good and evil complementarity in "black" aesthetics, as conceptualized in the Drama of Epidemic, which implies Esu-Elegbara as the tour de force of the concept. Indeed, the two plays offer us remarkable contrasts in the concept of Esu, and a brief analysis should give us an insight into the aesthetic foundations of the Epidemic Drama in the New World.

Esu, in *The Imprisonment,* is the controlling retributive power that initiates the ritual and satiric action on Obatala for his unforgotten crimes—his molding of deformities under the influence of the intoxicating palm wine. In *Oxala,* it seems that "deformities" are conceived as sin-provoking, and that it is these that are being expiated, not Obatala's "sins." Consequently, Exu (Esu) is described as a physically grotesque child of Oxala (Obatala). Although, quite curiously, he is hardly implicated for the main criminal act on Oxala, which Xango's servants inflicted, he in fact is mischievous and is capable of evil. In a rather unsuccessful effort to associate him with fate, he is described as a spirit impartial to either good or evil.[113] His fatal action on Oxala, however, is hardly satiric. It is a kind of unmotivated, mischievous action that is reminiscent of Hermes' ironies on Apollo, discussed in chapter 2. At best, it smacks of self-justification for being born ugly and mischievous. As the background story in *Oxala* goes, Oxala gave (molded for) his wife Nanan Burucu two horrible-looking sons, Omolu and Exu. They are deliberately conceived as such, it seems, to complement their moral beauty or their geniuses—one, skilled in the curative arts, and the other, a "blind executor" of the proclamations of Destiny.[114] And perhaps there is an influential Christian moral behind these creations: All that glitters is not gold.

Nanan, who prefers physical beauty to moral goodness, or would rather have moral ugliness, gets angry and leaves Oxala, finding refuge in Xango's domain. Thus, it is love and the longing for Nanan that present the motivation for Oxala's journey to Xango. Furthermore, with regard to Oxala's deliberate creation of deformities (Exu and Omolu and, by extension, all deformed creatures), he is above any crime and is blameless. He is, in fact, implied as the dispenser of destiny, and the subsequent beating he receives from Xango's servants and his imprisonment are designed to portray him as an epitome of Christian goodness and sacrifice in the midst of world's evil and tribulations. Where then, one must eventually ask, is the epidemic impulse of the play?

As noted, we are back with the ritual emphasis of the concept in which the individual, because of his fatal weakness, is satirized. However, regarding the main thrust of ritual, there is a shift in perspective. It seems that the long years of acculturation in a different locality have inevitably distanced and clouded the memory of the archetypal ritual. And even though the orisha images constituting its enactment, now syncretized with the Catholic saints, are still physically present, the actual experience of the ritual can no longer be felt physically but psychically. In other words, although the images are still described by the physical elements of enactment, such as dance, chants, dialogue, etc., these are superficially perceived as felt experiences in the sense that Wole Soyinka, for instance, contrasts their imagery with that in the Yoruba locality of origin:

The Yoruba gods in the Brazilian version do not copulate. . . . What we encounter in their place is the transcendental essence, the commencement of the attenuation of terrestrialism. In plays from the original source, the gods are conceived more in the imagery of peat, chalk, oil, kernels, blood, heartwood and tuber, and the active metaphors of human social preoccupations. When ritual archetypes acquire new aesthetics, we may expect re-adjustments of moral imperatives that brought them into existence in the first place.[115]

The readjustment, as explained, is from physical to psychical. Therefore, in terms of the Drama of Epidemic, what is being ritualized in a satiric expression is not the individual's fate, but fate as a collective entity of a race of humans. In the process, as exemplified in *Oxala,* there is confusion with regard to attribution of fate, perhaps a result of the present general worship of the gods. For instance, Oxala is conceived as the dispenser of fate and the creator of Exu whose own attribution, however, is actively amorphous.

It is in the abstract and nonspecific sense that we may regard Seljam's representation of Oxala's sacrifice as an epidemic expression. Since he is presented as blameless and with no crime, unlike his Yoruba counterpart, Obatala, the action of Exu and, principally, that of the servants of Xango cannot come across as satiric. But then we are told that, by these actions, he carries a "racial burden" which is expiated. If we see these actions, especially his imprisonment, as an attempt to express the fate of the black in slavery, then the burden that is being expiated is the white slavers' sins of enslavement, the deformity and the grotesquery that is being indicted and chastised. The restorative aspect, the restitution of Oxala to his former majesty and dignity, is the affirmation of black identity and social justice of the race, the reordering of the fate˜ of the black race. In fact, to jump back a little, it is this expiation and reordering that August Wilson seems to have ritualized in his plays, notably in *Joe Turner,* with this added insight—now that "Joe Turner" is gone (or "slavery" is over), let the black race recognize his "song" (dignity) and hold on to it.

Another example may be made of the Cuban play *Shango de Ima* by Pepe Carril.[116] Here, also, a ritual archetype describes new aesthetics through a definition of the black condition and the quality of survival in a new environment. Again, and perhaps more so here than in *Oxala,* the process of definition is achieved through a confusion of ideas and attributes and through a change of "moral imperatives" as a result of acculturation and the difficulties of survival in a different locality. Therefore, comparisons with the attributes of the god in the culture of origin should yield some useful interpretation. In the Yoruba folk drama *Oba Koso* by Duro Ladipo, we see Sango, though powerful with the magic of emitting fire from his mouth, as an impulsive, fiery, rash, but weak and vacillating king. Ill-advised by his chiefs and subjects, and with no mind of his own, he is a victim of his own intrigues against his war generals. Losing control of his power, his fire-magic extinguished by the overpowering satiric general, Gbonka, he commits suicide by hanging himself from a tree. However, his loyal chiefs will not accept such a demeaning end for their formerly revered king, so they manipulate his deification. It is a deliberate effort to maintain and perpetuate the myth of Sango, an effort perhaps reminiscent of Kinjeketile's refusal to renounce the Magi myth, earlier described. Ritually, and consistent with Yoruba belief, this deification of a king can be seen as a transference of energies from the mortal world to the ancestral; but the drama is about Sango, who is satirized by his own human folly or, as Soyinka puts it, "the human unit that constitutes the chorus of his downfall."[117]

In *Shango de Ima,* this "human unit" is generalized and abstracted to represent a communal, racial identity. As the introduction to the play explains, "Shango typifies man and his struggle to gain mastery of himself." As a Yoruba god that has survived New World slavery, he typifies the black man and his struggle to establish himself in a world of survival. His gift of fire has in this play become a symbol of his sexual prowess. His weakness is his sensitivity and nonchalance, an attitude that causes him not to question the fact of his lies and boasts. But then, on the other hand, placed against the intrigues of women around him, it is possible to regard this attitude as the characteristic feature of his struggle to survive. Significantly, his mother, Obatala, calls herself "the woman or the lie, and Shango the man or the question."[118] (In this play Obatala, following some myths, is characterized as a woman.)

However, with this characteristic, Shango's road, or his fate of doom has been mapped out. He seduces and uses his women with impunity, even his adopted mother, Yemaya, in whose house he takes refuge from the indictment of the women—"coquettish Oshun, tyrannical Oya, faithful Obba"—and from the ongoing battle with Ogun.[119] The agent of his punishment is the satirist Iku, who emerges now and again from the cemetery to confront Shango with his destiny. Actually Iku has been given the function of Elegua (Esu), who is not personified in the play but is suggested as an everpresent force throughout the action of the play.[120] Shango's punishment, the efficacy of the satiric action, is inevitable, as Obatala states from her seat of justice. For "Man's punishment will be found in his own condition."[121] As in the drama of origin, the restorative complements the destructive in the cosmic cycle of "death and light." But further to this, as in these ritual dramas from the New World, the restorative evokes the approbation of the survival of the black race.

Sortilege (Black Mystery) by Abdias do Nascimento is more experimental and adventurous with its use of transatlantic ritual of the gods to express the social and political consciousness in Brazil.[122] It does not attempt to personify the gods; rather, the author gives them an aesthetic and contemplative distance through their intermittent and pantomimic appearances, and through the chorus and chant of the devotees that endure the length of the drama. But since the subject concerns destiny itself, the destiny of the black, or of blackness, in the New World, Exu and his concept are used deliberately as the officiating principle of satiric judgment. Or, as the playwright describes him in the glossary, he is the basis for dialectical interchange.

The aesthetic and dialectical argument posed by the drama is this: Racial harmony or democracy, as ideologized, is a fraud which is destroying the aesthetic and creative possibilities of acculturation. In the present reality of fraud, acculturation, according to the playwright, is turning blacks white inside, and assimilation is turning blacks white in appearance.[123] The only way to come to terms with this fraud is to denounce and destroy its precepts by upholding the theory of blackness. For being black is destiny itself, from which no black person can escape.

Dramatizing this argument is Dr. Emanuel, a black lawyer who has been indicted and is being judged by destiny, that is, Exu, blackness and the black race represented by Exu's devotees, the Filha De Santos.[124] But he is also judged by the name he represents. For Emanuel cries and is to die, as the chorus of devotees hint, for "the divided human race."[125] Emanuel's crime is the slighting of destiny, denying the dignity of blackness by perverting black culture. Actually, his past black experience, like the present action of the play, has been a series of denials and what may be termed dialectical conflicts. He loved a black woman who gradually allowed herself to be prostituted by whites. Then he married a white woman who became unfaithful to him by attracting black lovers. He went to jail for defending or protecting both. Now on the run and in hiding in the hills at the shrine of Exu, he is haunted by the death and the accusations of both women. As he recollects these experiences, trapped, as it were, by destiny, he relives the ironies of his crime, desecrating but also getting intoxicated by blackness. It is a conflict of acculturation and assimilation and the regenerative process he has to go through. It culminates in the only choice left to him for salvation or total freedom—death, and the total destruction of the white thing, his self-deception. Significantly, Emanuel confesses at last: "I killed Margarida. I'm a free black man."[126] His death is a dramatic example of what has been described much earlier—the self-propagation of satiric grotesquery. Emanuel's denial of destiny, of the grotesque image of Exu, is in fact the slighting of his own image, which at the end he comes to terms with and accepts by the grotesque sacrifice he experiences at the hands (lance) of destiny, that is, the final assault of destiny (blackness and the black race).

A similar exorcism and severance, this time from the white lure and confusion, occurs at the end of the Caribbean play *Dream on Monkey Mountain* by Derek Walcott.[127] In fact, the strain of the difficult severance, in order to achieve liberation, is echoed in both *Sortilege* and *Dream*. Removing his kingly robes and lifting the sword of blackness, Makak in *Dream* says, "Now, O God, now I am free."[128] Thus Makak, the old peasant and charcoal burner, painfully strips and severs himself from his drunken vision. It is the vision of the underdog seeing himself as somebody and subsequently reclaiming his dignity. The playwright describes the play as "the West Indian search for identity and the damage that the colonial spirit has done to the soul."[129] The vision is all part of the disastrous colonial upbringing that made blacks reject blackness and see inspiration and superiority in whiteness. However, it is a false vision, emanating from the false education of colonialism, which projects a sense of nobility in the civilized image of blacks amid the savagery and barbarism of their African past. The reaction to this false vision differs, from Makak through Moustique to Lestrade.

With Corporal Lestrade, the white-aping prison guard, it is, as with Emanuel, a rejection of everything black. With Moustique, the companion of Makak, it is the exploitation of the vision of black power and dignity. With Makak, it is a total belief in the vision and the wish to realize it, consequently his intoxicated desire to return to Africa where, he believes, he comes from a line of kings. All these traits, however, are false to the idea of being black, and each receives its just satiric levelling.

The main experience is Makak's; it is the least dangerous although the most complex, since the fatality of the other two derives from it and consequently is woven into his vision. Makak's experience, induced by intoxication and marijuana, is a searing adventure to Africa. The identity crisis, itself a state of anguish, is nurtured by an escapist but rather harmless dream of the eventual dignity and freedom of blackness. However, this dream-journey is buffeted by opportunists and exploiters, by Moustique and power-mongers, and by the haters of blackness like Lestrade, all of them characters that Makak knew in the real world. Both Moustique's and Lestrade's expectations are also deflated by the satirist character in Makak's Caribbean folk narratives, Le Baron Samedi or, as he is called here, Basil the carpenter and coffin maker. He is a representation of the ever-present fate and symbol of death. Actually, having a similar habitat at the crossroads and in the marketplace, Basil is a Caribbean version of Esu-Elegba. Moustique meets his death by his own allergic aversion to common spiders, and Lestrade is stripped naked of his white-complex, out in the cold and in the maddening euphoria of forest noises.

But the main vision must also be relieved of its inspiration and impulse, although not before the indictment of all the personalities and collaborators, for which the impulse serves as a symbol—all the enemies of black progress and black identity. This indictment has had to take place, so that when the dream is deflated into the reality of the present everybody is therapeutically, or restoratively, calmer and happier, and the prison of life seems a better place to live in. In the morning, after the searing night, Moustique comes to collect Makak from prison, Lestrade is happy to release him, and the chorus jubilates from the "Church of Revelation." It is a contrasting chorus of the restorative process to the one in the beginning of the play—which cautions against the destructive process that occurs in jail, against which the prisoner's mother should "band the belly." Apparently the notion is from a Caribbean belief: "In the weakness of misfortune, an unprotected abdomen is believed to permit the entrance of the Devil."[130]

The orisa worship in the New World is also known as Voodoo, especially where slaves from Dahomey in West Africa settled, such as Haiti and New Orleans. Interestingly, both the present Dahomey (now the Republic of Benin) and some of these areas in the Americas were French settlements in the colonial period, and therefore betray French influences in their black cultures and literature. However, I must hastily say that in the case of the Americas there were other influences through the various countries that participated in the slave trade, such as Spain, Portugal and Britain. We may further note that Voodoo has some Yoruba gods in common with Santeria, Macumba and the Candomble, and Esu-Elegba is known as Legba.

An important characteristic in drama common to the African cultures of the French expression has already been discussed—the proud and keen sense of the historical and therefore an attempt to dramatize the heroic deeds of chiefs and noblemen in African history who proved themselves as nation builders. This also seems to be the emphasis in some of the Caribbean plays, and there is an important figure in Caribbean history that has been of interest to many dramatists. This is Toussaint L'Ouverture, the hero of the slave insurrection for freedom in Haiti (San Domingo) in the eighteenth century. For instance, he is the central figure in C.L.R James' *The Black Jacobins* and Edouard Glissant's *Monsieur Toussaint*.[131] He is also the background inspiration in Aime Cesaire's *The Tragedy of King Christophe*. However, we are concerned here with the survival of the African gods and culture, particularly with the fateful and fatal impulses that produce the satirical.

Because of the historical factor, these impulses are naturally linked with the historical personage, and sometimes a satiric figure, in its mythic or human form, is represented one way or another. For instance, in *King Christophe*, discussed earlier, some of the songs provide the satiric overtones of the plays' idea—the tragic but noble fate of King Christophe as he tries to build a nation devoid of destructive colonial ties. The first song, for example, sung by the market women, establishes a satiric vengeance of fate on the arm of the law, that is, the royal colonial police representing the French law:

> In the sea
> It wasn't me
> Who sank the skiff
> With the police
>
> In the sea
> It wasn't you
> Who sank the skiff
> With the police
>
> In the sea
> The Devil did that
> For you and me.
>
> Yes, Satan
> Sank the skiff
> Police and all.[132]

The "Devil" or "Satan" who accomplishes the action of vengeance, sinking the skiff with "police and all," must be noted as fate, and hardly as the Christian downright evil one. For he did the job for the good of all; hence his affinities with Esu-Elegba, the embodiment of good and evil and lord of the marketplace, can be argued. The action, in fact, is reminiscent of the story told by the devotee of Esu in Iworo (Badagry, Nigeria), referred to in chapter 3, about the sinking of a skiff along with the white exploiters that try to get away with Esu's cowries, the nation's wealth, which the exploiters found in the marketplace. Songs such as the one quoted are scattered through *King Christophe,* some of them sung by the real satiric figure of the play, Hugonin, who at the end rightly reveals himself as "Baron Saturday." [133]

Hugonin, described as "a combination of parasite, buffoon and political agent," indeed strikes one as the satiric agent of Christophe's fate. As the market women are singing the song of the sunken skiff in the background, he manipulates the crowd into accepting Christophe as king. [134] At the height of Christophe's intoxicated work ethic for the national Citadel being built, which demands the labor service of "everybody, the women and children," Christophe makes Hugonin the Minister-controller of "public morality." Hugonin, no doubt making an ironic throaty chortle, answers: "Oh, thank you, your Majesty. Coming from my Prince, nothing could touch me so deeply as such homage to my character, my morals, my virtue." [135] He then warms up to performing Christophe's megalomaniacal wishes—implementing forced marriages, because he thinks the family unit as a solid foundation of the state will improve work efficiency. And at the end, as Christophe heroically shoots himself after losing the support of his people, Hugonin reveals himself as Baron Samedi.

In Glissant's *Monsieur Toussaint,* however, Legba is invoked and remains throughout at the crossroads as the spirit of revolution. Against this background are the characterized figures of "The Dead" from the world of ancestors, making appearances from time to time and serving as Toussaint's satiric mind-prodders. They not only advise and admonish, but also foretell and establish Toussaint's fatal, although heroic, weakness—his inability to trust anyone, and his gift of Sambo's art of dissembling. Actually, the dialogue with "The Dead" is characteristic of African religion and Voodoo—the constant communication with the ancestral world and with the gods through ritual. It is these ancestors, evoked in and out of the celluloid back wall, or mind of Toussaint, who orchestrate Glissant's "prophetic vision of the past." [136] Seeing his own misunderstood vision clearly with Mackandal (a heroic fugitive slave who had been executed by burning, and the persistent prophetic voice and mind-prodder), Toussaint rises, and he too disappears into the world of the ancestors—Africa.

It is fitting and purposeful that the world of the ancestors should be thought of as Africa. [137] As has been continually expressed throughout the play, Haiti's freedom is linked with the fated Atlantic crossing of the slaves from Africa, to which eventually freed souls must return to prepare "an army for the deliverance of our brothers" all over the slave world. [138] For the purposes of this book, we have come full circle to where the satiric thrust of the Drama of Epidemic has been invoked. We are back to the origins of the ritual of fate and Esu-Elegbara, a ritual that has described satire, satirists and satiric victims in the black world and theatre.

NOTES

1. On this as a theatrical force in African theatre, see J. C. de Graft, "Roots in African Drama and Theatre," in *African Literature Today,* no. 8, ed. Eldred D. Jones (London: Heinemann Educational Books, 1976), 1–25.

2. For a theory and analysis of satiric catharsis, see introduction to Birney, *Satiric Catharsis in Shakespeare.*

3. Wole Soyinka, *A Play of Giants* (London: Methuen, 1984).

4. Ibid., 52.

5. Ibid., 52–53.

6. J. A. Adedeji, "The Alarinjo Theatre: The Study of a Yoruba Theatrical Art from Its Earliest Beginning to the Present Times," Ph.D. diss., University of Ibadan, 1969. For an abridged version, see J. A. Adedeji, "Alarinjo: The Traditional Yoruba Travelling Theatre," in *Drama and Theatre in Nigeria,* ed. Yemi Ogunbiyi (Lagos: Nigeria Magazine, 1981).

7. See B. Lawal, "The Living Dead: Art and Immortality Among the Yoruba of Nigeria," *Africa* 47, no. 1 (1977): 50–61.

8. See J. A. Adedeji, "Traditional Yoruba Theatre," *African Arts* 3, no. 1 (1969): 60–63; J. A. Adedeji, "Form and Function of Satire in Yoruba Drama," *Odu* 4, no. 1 (1969): 61–72.

9. Chief Ojeyemi, head of the Egungun cult in Ikirun. One of his names, Esulani (Esu is what we have), identifies him.

10. See Adedeji, "Alarinjo Theatre"; also Adedeji, "Form and Function of Satire."

11. For a detailed analysis of the theatrical operations of the Yoruba travelling theatre troupes, see Biodun Jeyifo, *The Yoruba Popular Travelling Theatre of Nigeria* (Lagos: Nigeria Magazine, 1984).

12. Ibid., 109.

13. See Toll, *Blacking Up,* chap. 7.

14. Ibid.

15. Ibid., 219–229.

16. Ibid.

17. Ibid., 42–47, and 66–97; see also Wittke, *Tambo and Bones;* Green, " 'Jim Crow,' 'Zip Coon' "; Nathan, *Dan Emmett.*

18. See Toll, *Blacking Up,* 221–222.

19. Ibid., 228.

20. Quoted in Melvin Van Peebles, *Aint Supposed to Die a Natural Death* (New York: Bantam Books, 1973).

21. Wale Ogunyemi, *Eshu Elegbara* (Ibadan, Nigeria: Orisun Acting Editions, n.d.); Dipo Kalejaiye, *The Creator and the Disrupter* (Calabar, Nigeria: Centaur Press, 1982).

22. Ijimere, *The Imprisonment of Obatala;* Zora Seljam, *The Story of Oxala: The Feast of Bomfim* (London: Rex Collings, 1978).

23. Ola Rotimi, *The Gods Are Not to Blame* (London: Oxford University Press, 1971); Duro Ladipo, *Oba Koso* (The King Did Not Hang), in *Three Yoruba Plays,*

trans. Ulli Beier (Ibadan, Nigeria: Mbari Publications, 1964); Wole Soyinka, *A Dance of the Forests* (London: Oxford University Press, 1973); Wole Soyinka, *Death and the King's Horseman* (London: Eyre Methuen, 1975).

24. Ijimere, *The Imprisonment*, 42–44.

25. Soyinka, *Myth, Literature*, 140–160.

26. Femi Euba, "Soyinka's Artists," unpublished.

27. Soyinka, in *Collected Plays*, vol. 1, 26–27.

28. Contrast Ogun's experience in Soyinka, *Myth, Literature*, 140–160; also see both Demoke and Ogun compared in James Gibbs, "The Origins of 'A Dance of the Forests,' " in Jones, *African Literature Today*, 66–71.

29. Soyinka, *Death and the King's Horseman*, 20–22.

30. Ibid., see "Author's Note."

31. Ibid., 65 (with Pilkings); 67–70 (with Iyaloja).

32. Ibid., 69.

33. Ibid., 67.

34. Ibid., 45.

35. See Soyinka, *Myth, Literature*, 149–150.

36. On the William Ponty School and the development of the African theatre in French, see Bakary Traore, *The Black African Theatre and Its Social Functions*, trans. Dapo Adelugba (Ibadan, Nigeria: Ibadan University Press, 1972), esp. chap. 2.

37. See Colin Granderson, "The Chief in Contemporary Black African Theatre of French Expression," in *Theatre in Africa*, ed. Oyin Ogunba and Abiola Irele (Ibadan, Nigeria: University of Ibadan Press, 1978), 73–89. Quotation from p. 74.

38. For commentary on these and other plays, see Granderson, "Chief in Contemporary Black African Theatre."

39. See ibid., 83–84.

40. Aime Cesaire, *The Tragedy of King Christophe*, trans. R. Manheim (New York: Grove Press, 1969), 81.

41. Granderson, "Chief in Contemporary Black African Theatre," 80.

42. Cesaire, *King Christophe* (Manheim translation), 41.

43. Ibid., 52–53.

44. Ibid., 88.

45. Ola Rotimi, *Ovonramwen Nogbaisi* (Benin, Nigeria: Ethiope Publishing; Ibadan, Nigeria: Oxford University Press, 1974).

46. Ibid., xi.

47. William Shakespeare, *King Lear*, Act 3, sc. 2, lines 53–54.

48. Rotimi, *Ovonramwen*, 77.

49. Ibid., 78.

50. Ibid., sc. 4, p. 37.

51. Ibid., 78–79.

52. Hodgart, *Satire*, 33.

53. Ngugi, "Satire in Nigeria," 56. For the development of political satire through the ages, see Hodgart, *Satire*, chap. 2.

54. See Ngugi, "Satire in Nigeria," 69.

55. Ebrahim Hussein, *Kinjeketile* (Dar-es-Salaam: Oxford University Press, 1969).

56. Ngugi wa Thiong'o and Micere Mugo, *The Trial of Dedan Kimathi* (London: Heinemann Educational Books, 1976).

57. Lewis Nkosi, *The Rhythm of Violence*, in *Plays from Black Africa*, ed. Fredric M. Litto (New York: Hill and Wang, 1968); Athol Fugard, J. Kani and W. Ntshona, *Sizwe Bansi Is Dead*, in *Sizwe Bansi Is Dead and The Island* (New York: The Viking-Penguin, 1976); Percy Mtwa, Mbongeni Ngema, and Barney Simon, *Woza Albert*, in *Woza Afrika!*, ed. Duma Ndlovu (New York: George Braziller, 1986), 3–53.

58. Mukotani Rugyendo, *The Barbed Wire and Other Plays* (London: Heinemann Educational Books, 1977); Peniah Mukando, *Tambueni Haki Zetus*, trans. L. A. Mbugbuni (Dar-es-Salaam: Tanzania Publishing House, 1973).

59. Rebecca Njau, *The Scar* (Nairobi: Kibo Art Gallery, 1965). For a discussion of these and other plays, see L. A. Mbughuni, "Old and New Drama from East Africa," in Jones, *African Literature Today*, 85–98.

60. Rugyendo, *Barbed Wire and Other Plays*, 15–17.

61. Hussein, *Kinjeketile*, 30.

62. Ibid., 53.

63. Nkosi, *Rhythm of Violence*, 69.

64. On Time as an aesthetic device by South African writers, see E. O. Apronti, "The Tyranny of Time: The Theme of Time in the Artistic Consciousness of South African Writers," in Jones, *African Literature Today*, 106–114.

65. Nkosi, *Rhythm of Violence*, Act 2.

66. See Frye, *Anatomy of Criticism*, 106–108.

67. For a summary of Brecht's theory of epic theatre, see Richard Gilman, *The Making of Modern Drama* (New York: Farrar, Straus and Giroux, 1972), 213–223.

68. Athol Fugard, "Sizwe Bansi," in *A Night at the Theatre*, ed. Ronald Harwood (London: Methuen, 1982), 26–32.

69. Wole Soyinka, *Collected Plays*, 2 vols. (London: Oxford University Press, 1973), 1:147–232; ibid., 2:215–276. On these characters as extensions of Ogun, see F. Euba, "Soyinka's Artists."

70. Soyinka, *A Play of Giants*, 21, 26.

71. Ibid., 19–20.

72. Ibid., 32–34.

73. Ibid., 69.

74. See James V. Hatch, "A White Folk's Guide to 200 Years of Drama," *Drama Review* 16, no. 4 (December 1972): 22. See also Errol Hill, "The Revolutionary Tradition in Black Drama," *Theatre Journal* 38, no. 4 (1986): 409.

75. An adaptation by Ira Aldridge, from the original by Anicet-Bourgeois. See introduction to the play in *Black Theatre U.S.A.*, ed. James V. Hatch (New York: The Free Press, 1974).

76. In Hatch, *Black Theatre U.S.A.*

77. On Ward's problems with and revisions of *Our Lan'*, see Owen C. Brady, "Theodore Ward's *Our Lan'*: From Slavery of Melodrama to the Freedom of Tragedy," *Callaloo* 7, no. 2 (1984): 40–54.

78. In *Five Plays by Langston Hughes*, ed. W. Smalley (Bloomington: University of Indiana Press, 1968).

79. For a summary of this movement, see Larry Neal, "The Black Arts Movement," *Drama Review* 12, no. 4 (1968): 29–39. For a short survey of the plays that developed from the movement, see A. Peter Bailey, "A Look at the Contemporary Black Theatre Movement," *Black American Literature Forum* 17, no. 1 (1983): 19–21. On the artistic

quality and direction of the plays, see Kimberly W. Benston, "The Aesthetics of Modern Black Drama: From Mimesis to Methexis," in Hill, *Theatre of Black Americans,* 1:61–78.

80. Baraka, "Revolutionary Theatre," 130–133. On Baraka, see Kimberly Benston, *Baraka: The Renegade and the Mask* (New Haven: Yale University Press, 1976).

81. Baraka, "Revolutionary Theatre," 131.

82. Neal, "Black Arts Movement," 30.

83. Maulana Karenga, quoted in ibid., 33.

84. Lorraine Hansberry, *A Raisin in the Sun* (New York: Random House, Inc./ Alfred A. Knopf, 1966).

85. Ibid., 11–12.

86. Ibid., 30.

87. Leroi Jones [Amiri Baraka], *Two Plays by Leroi Jones: Dutchman and The Slave* (New York: Morrow Quill Paperbacks, 1964).

88. See Larry Neal's interpretation of the play in "Black Arts Movement," 34; also, for a fuller analysis, see Benston, *Baraka,* 149–173. On the structure of *Dutchman,* see Andrzej Ceynowa, "The Dramatic Structure of *Dutchman,*" *Black American Literature Forum* 17, no. 1 (1983): 15–21.

89. Jones, *Two Plays,* 35.

90. Hatch, *Black Theatre, U.S.A.,* 812.

91. Boskin, *Sambo.*

92. Jones, *Two Plays,* 70.

93. See Baraka, "Revolutionary Theatre," 312.

94. Amiri Baraka, *Jello* (Chicago: Third World Press, 1970).

95. Neal, "Black Arts Movement," 36.

96. Paul Carter Harrison, *The Great MacDaddy,* in *Kunta Drama,* ed. P. C. Harrison (New York: Grove Press, 1974).

97. Kim Benston seems to have distinguished between Baraka's "theatre of assault" and Paul C. Harrison's "ritual theatre"; see "Aesthetics of Modern Black Drama," 74–75.

98. Leroi Jones [Amiri Baraka], *A Black Mass,* in *Four Revolutionary Plays* (Indianapolis: Bobbs-Merrill, 1969).

99. On this delusion and Jones' reaction to it, see Jones, "Negro Theater Pimps Get Big off Nationalism," introduction to *Jello,* 5–8.

100. For example, Ed Bullins, "The So-Called Western Avant-Garde Drama," in *Black Expression,* ed. Addison Gayle (New York: Weybright and Talley, 1969); K. William Kgositsile, "Toward Our Theatre: A Definitive Act," in Gayle, *Black Expression;* Ron Milner, "Black Theatre—Go Home," in Gayle, *Black Aesthetic;* P. C. Harrison, *Drama of Nommo.* See also various essays in Hill, *Theatre of Black Americans,* vol. 1, esp. sec. 1.

101. Jimmy Garrett, *And We Own the Night,* in *Drama Review* 12, no. 4 (Summer 1968): 62–69.

102. For commentary on this and Garrett's *And We Own the Night,* etc., see Neal, "Black Arts Movement."

103. Adrienne Kennedy, *Funny House of a Negro,* in *Contemporary Black Drama,* ed. Clinton C. Oliver (New York: Charles Scribner's Sons, 1971).

104. Ben Caldwell, *Prayer Meeting; or, The First Militant Minister,* in *A Black Quartet* (New York: New American Library, 1970), 27–36.

105. James Baldwin, *The Amen Corner,* in Patterson, *Black Theater,* 519–588.

106. Douglas Turner Ward, *Day of Absence,* in Hatch, *Black Theater U.S.A.,* 695–710; also in Douglas Turner Ward, *Two Plays* (New York: William Morrow, 1970).

107. August Wilson, *Joe Turner's Come and Gone* (New York: New American Library, 1988).

108. See Dena Kleiman, " 'Joe Turner,' The Spirit of Synergy," *New York Times,* May 1986, 19, sec. C, p. 11.

109. On this, with Seljam's *Oxala* and Ijimere's *The Imprisonment* compared, see Soyinka, *Myth, Literature,* esp. 22–25.

110. See Deren, *Divine Horsemen.*

111. See "Explanation" in Seljam, *Story of Oxala.*

112. See Loveland, *Southern Evangelicals.*

113. Seljam, *Story of Oxala,* 6.

114. Ibid., 5–6.

115. Soyinka, *Myth, Literature,* 24–25.

116. Pepe Carril, *Shango de Ima* (New York: Doubleday, 1970).

117. Soyinka, *Myth, Literature,* 11.

118. Carril, *Shango de Ima,* 51.

119. Ibid., 85–86.

120. Ibid., 47n.

121. Ibid., 88–89.

122. Abidias do Nascimento, *Sortilege* (Black Mystery), trans. Peter Lownds (Chicago: Third World Press, 1978).

123. Ibid., vii. For Nascimento's views on racial harmony in Brazil, see Abdias do Nascimento, *"Racial Democracy" in Brazil: Myth or Reality?* trans. Elisa Larkin do Nascimento. (Ibadan, Nigeria: Sketch Publishing, 1977).

124. Nascimento, *Sortilege;* see their first speeches, 4–11.

125. Ibid., 38–39.

126. Ibid., 51.

127. Derek Walcott, *Dream on Monkey Mountain and Other Plays* (New York: Farrar, Straus and Giroux, 1970).

128. Ibid., 320.

129. See "The Talk of the Town," *New Yorker* (June 26, 1971), 30.

130. Quoted in a review of the 1976 production in *Hartford (Conn.) Times,* April 11, 1976, p. 36.

131. C.L.R. James, *The Black Jacobins,* in *A Time . . . and a Season: Eight Caribbean Plays,* ed. Errol Hill (Trinidad: University of West Indies Extramural Studies Unit, 1976); Edouard Glissant, *Monsieur Toussaint,* trans. J. G. Foster and B. A. Franklin (Washington, D.C.: Three Continents Press, 1981).

132. Cesaire, *King Christophe,* 15.

133. Ibid., 92–93.

134. Ibid., 15–19.

135. Ibid., 56.

136. Glissant, *Monsieur Toussaint,* 17.

137. See Cesaire, *King Christophe,* 88, 90; Glissant, *Monsieur Toussaint,* 3, 86, 97. See also D. Roediger, "The Meaning of Africa for the American Slave," *Journal of Ethnic Studies* 4, no. 4 (1977): 1–15.

138. Glissant, *Monsieur Toussaint,* 86.

Conclusion

An attempt has been made in the preceding chapters to come to terms with a concept of satire in the light of concepts of ritual and fate in the black tradition. Specifically, I have used as a model for my construct the versatile Yoruba traditional deity, Esu-Elegbara, whose ritual and attributes of fate, both in Africa and in the New World, not only illustrate the satirical but also describe the belief and character of his people, and therefore commit them dramatically to a satiric process. In the development of this idea, a concept of theatre termed the Drama of Epidemic has been explored. It is in fact a concept which expresses at once ritual, dramatic and satiric processes, and which is argued to characterize the generality of works by black dramatists both in Africa and in the New World.

The idea of satire that derives from Esu-Elegbara, and which formulates the Drama of Epidemic, is necessarily construed in terms of the ritual origins of satire, which assumes a fatalistic power of the word and a strong belief in ritual efficacies. In this regard, the nature of satire takes a sardonic, sometimes tragic edge, more than a witty and comical one. Although the arguments that develop the thesis are somewhat tentative, satire is seen as a fate indictment, and its victims as victims of fate. This functional view of fate establishes the efficacious power of satire, in fact the "epidemic" factor, as both destructive and restorative. Relating this factor and its process to the drama of the black, the concept demonstrates its applicability in the fateful and fatal interactions and survival patterns as expressed within the black cultures of Africa and the New World.

The overall perspective of the Drama of Epidemic suggests, through its models and dramatic illustrations, that satire, that is, ritual satire, is prevalent in black drama. In this regard, the concept offers a new direction in assessing black drama. This should be readily seen as an important contribution when one considers the fact that there is, as yet, no clear and distinctive approach regarding the evaluation of black drama, which has hitherto suffered from the analytic strictures of Western criteria and critical practice. Saying this is, of course, taking into consideration the recent work of Henry Gates, Jr., *The Signifying Monkey,* which attempts to set the Afro-American critical theory in place. While Gates' work and mine basically derive from the same source, that is, from Esu-Elegbara, his more deliberately structuralist construct focuses more on the Afro-American literature and language through the Esu-Signifying Monkey metaphor, and my own more traditional and analytic approach explores specifically a theory for black drama through the Esu-fate-satire vehicle. A view that both works may share is the fact that what Gates' theory sees more as signifying tropes my own concept sees more as satiric thrusts which, because of their ritual and dramatic identifications, I have called "epidemic." Although the epidemic concept, as it stands, does not pretend to have exhausted its subject, it nevertheless establishes, like Gates' theory of blackness, a daring and provocative direction toward positive and more productive measures of evaluation.

But then, my concept, by its definitions and constructs of ritual and satire, should also be informative to theatre scholarship in general. As it happens, the processes of ritual and satire in modern times have gradually become estranged from their origins through developments in cultural and aesthetic perceptions. Consequently, scholarship, especially Western scholarship, on subjects in relation to the ritual origins of theatre, even when supported with evidence, has often on the whole tended to be too abstractly conceived. And, at any rate, in the working out of their theories, Western scholars have had to look for their concrete models in the modern societies, such as those in Africa, that are closer still to their traditional origins. Since the Drama of Epidemic derives from the ritual and satiric manifestations of Esu-Elegbara, it should serve as an eye-opener in terms of taking satire back to the roots, and in its fusion of the ritual, the satiric and the theatrical as an epidemic process. As stated in the introduction, Esu appears to have effected a clear link between ritual and drama.

If my concept establishes an approach to evaluating black drama with a view to opening up other significant perspectives, an area that may need immediate attention for research along the same lines could be the actual theatre performance. Using the concept of the Drama of Epidemic as a theoretical base, the researcher could investigate the theatrical practice and the performance style existent in black theatres. Such theatres would include not only the traditional, dramatic expressions and folk dramas, but also the actual interpretative idea or the tour de force behind and within productions of plays by modern black writers, such as those that came under discussion in the explication of my concept. In the relentless effort to assess and redefine the image of the black and to establish the characteristic features of black theatre, one can only hope that the satiric concept of Esu-Elegbara will help to justify and make affirmative positive structures and "signifiers" that may come out of such a quest.

Appendix: List of Informants

Babalola Fatoogun, an Ifa priest from Ilobu, near Osogbo, Oyo State, Nigeria. Interviewed at the University of Ife, August 4, 1981, January, 1986, and August 18, 1986.

Chief "Esulani" Ojeyemi, "Elesu" and Head of the Egungun Cult in Ikirun, Oyo State, Nigeria. Interviewed in his house, at Ikirun, July 21, 1981, and July 1986.

Joseph Oyediran, Oba Arojomo, the Oniworo of Iworo, Badagry, Lagos State, Nigeria. Interviewed in his palace, at Iworo, August 22, 1981, and April 1983.

Chief Ojomo Josiah Apata, a household chief of Oniworo of Iworo, Badagry, Lagos State. Interviewed at the Oba's palace, August 22, 1981.

Babalawo Faloba, "Elesu" and Ifa priest in Ile-Ife, Oyo State, Nigeria. Interviewed in his house, with a group of other "elesus," July 1981.

Madam Osunponmile, an "Elesu" at Iragbiji, Oyo State, Nigeria. Interviewed on a hill outside Muraina Oyelami's house, in Iragbiji, July 1981.

Some interviews were also conducted in December 1982 in Oyo, Oyo State, by my research assistants, Adisa Taiwo and Tunji Ojeyemi, members of the University of Ife Theatre Company.

Glossary: Yoruba Tones in Words, Phrases, and Sentences

The three main tones used are:

Low   : `
Middle : - (where this occurs, the vowelled syllable is left unaccented)
High   : ´

INTRODUCTION

Ògún
Èṣù Ẹlẹ́gbára [or, Ẹlẹ́gbá(a)] ("e" with a mark under sounds as in "fete," but without a mark sounds closer to "ai"; "gb" is sounded together as a combination of labial and guttural). Èṣù is sometimes spelled "Eshu," for the "ṣ" sound.
Ìpín ("p" sounds like "kp" together)
Kádàrá
Àyànmọ́ or Àyọ̀nmọ́n ("o" with a mark under sounds like "aw")
Orí
B'Ọ́lọ́run bá ńṣere, àá ló ńṣebi ("s" with a mark under = "sh")
Èrò
Ròwáyé
Oníbodè
Adúrógbònà
Yangí
Ṣàngó (sometimes spelled "Shango," for the "ṣ" sound)
Ọbàtálá

CHAPTER 1

Ajá
Ẹlẹ́dẹ̀

Òrúkọ
Ìgbẹ̀tì
Ọ̀fà Ilé
Ifẹ̀ Wàrà
Kétu
Èṣù-oríta
Èṣù-ọ̀nà
Èṣù-ọjà
Àlìjọ́nú
Èfúùfú
Ẹ̀gbá
Òde Ìṣálọ̀run
Odùduwà
Èṣù Ọbasin
Olódùmarè
Aláwọ̀ agẹmọ
Òjìji fírífírí
Àbá tí alágẹmo bá ti dá, òun ni òrìsà òkè ńgbà
Òrìsàńlá
Ìjẹ̀bú
Elésù
Àṣẹ
Àdó-ìran (a magical vessel of visions)
Lógẹmọ ọ̀run
Alágẹmọ
Ọlójà

Ìwà nìkan ló ṣòro o
Orí kan kì(í) burú l'ótù(ú) Ifẹ̀

Ẹ mà fi t'Èṣù ṣe è

Eeèéè, t'Èṣù Òdàrà
Ló sòro o
Bákeré ò j'àdí o
Aráà 'Lodè
Ayé rèé o

Àdí
Ìwà

Èṣù o, Èṣù mi, Èṣù mi
Èṣù dákun má bì(í)nú Èṣù mi
Ayé t'áwa ní tìrẹ ni
Aya t'áwa ní tìrẹ ni
Ilé t'áwa kọ́ tìrẹ ni

Ojúbọ
Àdó-àsúre (a magical vessel of blessings)
Ọlọ́run
Òrúnmìlà

Ẹlẹ́rì(í)-ìpín
Òrìṣà (sometimes spelled "orisha," for the "ṣ" sound)
Enìà
Ara
Ẹ̀mí
Ẹlẹ́dà(á)
Ìpònrí
Àjàlá
Òjìji

Àní ẹjẹ́ Bara ó wọlé
Ẹ̀ yin òwo kùmọ̀ tí Lá(a)róyè, tó gbé lọ́wọ́
Gan-gan-gan
Látopa èrẹ́ kọlọbọ, èrẹ́

Orí ẹni ní ńgba ni
Ohun orí(i) wá ṣẹ́ / kò mà ní ṣ'aláì ṣẹ o
Ẹni t'ó gbọ́n / Orí ẹ̀ ló ní ó gbọ́n
Ẹ̀èyàn tí ò gbọ́n / Orí(i) rẹ̀ ló ní ó gọ̀ j'uṣu lọ

Ìyèròsùn
Ìròsùn
Odù-Ifá
Ifá
A tóó bọ bí Orí
Oníbodè-légi
Olúlànà
Ọ̀ṣẹtùá
Ọ̀sun
Ìyánlá
Àṣẹtùwá
Èwó
Ọ(ò)ni
Wọlè
Ìbọrí (ìbọ-orí)
Orí mi gbà mí o
Olórí burúkú
Má kòó tì ẹ bá mi
Má jẹẹ́ k'órí mi mú ẹ
Orí mi á jẹ́ ko pàdánù
Èṣù má ṣemí ẹlòmíràn ni o ṣe

CHAPTER 2

Òòòṣà tí ò lólúa láiyé
Béẹ̀ni ò ní lọ́run
Akọrii-gbájẹ̀ tíí so láàárín àpáta
Ọ̀wàrà òjò tíí ba ońlé ọgbà lẹ́rù
Òkúùṣẹ́ ò báráiye nú

Alagbalúgbú ọbẹ̀ tíí yọpin lẹ́nu
Alagbalúgbú ọbẹ̀ tíí ró kọ̀mùkọ̀mù
Yèèpè ò ní bi táàá gbáa mú;
Gbogbo ara níí fií jóni.
Ọ̀tàkìtì pọ́nwọ́ lá
Ò bomi ẹ́nu fẹ́ná jò

Fìrí ò, ojú àláá ò
Olówó aiyé l'èmi ó mọ̀mọ̀ sìn
Alákétu èré jà ju'wọ̀ lọ
Èpè a já j'oògùn
Èṣù l'ọmọ èréelé
Ọmọ èré òde
Ọmọ òkunlẹ̀-l'ógùngùn
Èré mo kúnlẹ̀ l'ógùnbẹ̀rẹ̀
Èré mo kúnlẹ̀ ngò r'ẹ́léjó
Ẹléjó ti gb'ẹ̀bi, ó bá tìrẹ̀ lọ

Kùmọ̀
Igbá Odù
Igbá Ìwà
Wèrèpè
Ọ̀tẹ̀ẹ́kóyàdé
Aṣorebíẹ́ńgò

CHAPTER 3

Aiyé l'ọjà, ọjà l'aiyé
Owólẹwà
Ìwàlẹwà
Olórí rere
Ṣẹ́ṣó owó
A kìí l'áhun, ká n'íyì
Òòṣa tí gb'ọ̀lẹ, kò sí
Ọ̀kánjúwà àti olè, déédé ni wọ́njẹ́
Àgbẹ́kòyà
Ọmọge
Jésù o ṣeun
Ẹ yé bínú Orí
Ìgbẹ̀hìn a dùn
Ìwà
Ìwàpẹ̀lẹ́
Sùúrù ni Baba Ìwà
Ìgbà laiyé; Fẹ̀sò jaiyé; Má ṣèkà ọ̀rẹ́ mi
Ẹsinmi ìbàjẹ́
Sélèkẹ̀ (?)
Oníkòyí
Bọ́lèkájà
Olúwọlé

Òkú-Èkó
Dánfó
Olórí Eléṣù

CHAPTER 4

Alárìnjò
Egúngún
Ọba Kòso
Kùtùjé
Ọdẹ́wálé
Ẹlẹ́ṣin-Ọba
Olóhùn-iyọ̀
Olú(ù)ńdé

Selected Bibliography

ESU-ELEGBARA

Dos Santos, Juana Elbein, and Deoscoredes M. dos Santos. *Esu Bara Laroye*. Institute of African Studies. University of Nigeria, Ibadan, Nigeria: 1971.

————. "Esu Bara, Principle of Individual Life in the Nago System." In *Colloque International sur la Nation de Personne en Afrique Noire*. Paris Centre National de la Recherche Scientifique, 1971.

Dos Santos, Juana Elbein. *Os Nago E A Morte: Pade Asesse e o Culto Egun na Bahia*. Petropolis: Editora Vozes, 1976.

Euba, Akin. "Ilu Esu (Drumming for Esu): Analysis of Dundun Performance." In *Essays for a Humanist: An Offering to Klaus Wachsmann*. K.W.P. Festschrift Committee. New York: Town House, 1977.

Hoch-Smith, Judith, and Ernesto Pichardo. "Having Thrown a Stone Today Eshu Kills a Bird of Yesterday." *Caribbean Review* 7, no. 4 (1978): 16–20.

Leurquin-Tefnin, Anne. "Eshu l'insaisissable: le 'Trickster' dans la pensee religieuse des Yoruba du Nigeria." *Art d'Afrique Noire* 36 (1980): 26–37.

Ogundipe, Ayodele. *Esu Elegbara, the Yoruba God of Chance and Uncertainty: A Study in Yoruba Mythology*. 2 vols. Ann Arbor: UMI, 1978. 7900410.

Pelton, Robert D. *The Trickster in West Africa: A Study of Mythic Irony and Sacred Delight*. Los Angeles: University of California Press, 1980.

Pemberton, John. "Eshu-Elegba: The Yoruba Trickster God." *African Arts* 9 (1975): 20–27, 66–70, 90–92.

Wescott, Joan. "The Sculpture and Myths of Eshu-Elegba, the Yoruba Trickster." *Africa* 32, no. 4 (1962): 336–353.

Williams, Paul V.A. "Exu: The Master and the Slave in Afro-Brazilian Religion." In *The Fool and the Trickster: Studies in Honour of Enid Welsford*, edited by Paul V.A. Williams. Cambridge, England: D. S. Brewer, 1979.

FATE

Abimbola, Wande. *Sixteen Great Poems of Ifa*. New York: UNESCO, 1975.

————. "Iwapele: The Concept of Good Character in Ifa Literary Corpus." In *Yoruba Oral Tradition: Poetry in Music, Dance and Drama,* edited by Wande Abimbola. Ile-Ife, Nigeria: University of Ife, 1975, 389–420.

————. *Ifa: An Exposition of Ifa Literary Corpus*. Ibadan, Nigeria: Oxford University Press, 1976.

————. *Ifa Divination Poetry*. New York: Nok Publishers, 1977.

Armstrong, Robert, et al., trans. and eds. *Iyere Ifa: The Deep Chants of Ifa*. Ibadan, Nigeria: University of Ibadan, Institute of African Studies, 1978.

Awolalu, J. O. "The Concept of Death and Hereafter in Yoruba Traditional Religion." *West African Religion* 17, no. 2 (1978): 35–47.

Bascom, W. R. "Yoruba Concepts of Soul." In *Men and Cultures,* edited by A.F.C. Wallace. Pittsburgh: University of Pennsylvania Press, 1960.

————. *Ifa Divination: Communication Between Gods and Men in Africa*. Bloomington: Indiana University Press, 1969.

————. *Sixteen Cowries: Yoruba Divination from Africa to the New World*. Bloomington: Indiana University Press, 1980.

Beier, H. U. *The Origin of Life and Death*. London: Heinemann Educational Books, 1966.

Bell, Robert E., ed. *Dictionary of Classical Myth*. Santa Barbara, Calif. ABC-Clio, 1982.

Beyioku, O. A. Fagbenro. *Ifa: Its Worship and Prayers*. Lagos, Nigeria: Salako Press, 1971.

Brandon, S.G.F., ed. *A Dictionary of Comparative Religion*. New York: Charles Scribner's Sons, 1970.

Edwards, Paul, ed. *Encyclopedia of Philosophy*. 8 vols. New York: The Free Press, 1967.

Eliade, Mircea, ed. *The Encyclopedia of Religion*. 16 vols. New York: Macmillan, 1987.

Fortes, Meyer. *Oedipus and Job in West African Religion*. Cambridge, England: Cambridge University Press, 1959.

Gleason, Judith. *A Recitation of Ifa, Oracle of the Yoruba*. New York: Grossman, 1973.

Hammond, N.G.L., and H. H. Scullard, eds. *Oxford Classical Dictionary*. 2nd ed. Oxford: Clarendon Press, 1970.

Horton, Robin. "Destiny and the Unconscious in West Africa." *Africa* 31, no. 2 (1961): 110–116.

Morakinyo, O., and A. Akiwowo. "The Yoruba Ontology of Personality and Motivation: A Multidisciplinary Approach." *Journal of Social Biological Structure* 4 (1981): 19–38.

Thompson, Robert F. *Black Gods and Kings*. Los Angeles: University of California Press, 1971.

SATIRE

Adedeji, J. A. "Form and Function of Satire in Yoruba Drama." *Odu* 4, no. 1 (1967): 61–72.

Birney, Alice L. *Satiric Catharsis in Shakespeare: A Theory of Dramatic Structure.* Los Angeles: University of California Press, 1973.

Bloom, Edward, and Lillian Bloom. *Satire's Persuasive Voice.* Ithaca, N.Y.: Cornell University Press, 1979.

Campbell, O. J. *Comicall Satyre and Shakespeare's Troilus and Cressida.* San Marino, Calif.: Huntington Library Publications, 1965.

Clark, John, and A. Motto, eds. *Satire: That Blasted Art.* New York: G. P. Putnam's Sons, 1973.

Dennis, John. "To Matthew Prior, Esq.; Upon the Roman Satirists." In *The Critical Works of John Dennis,* vols. 2 Edited by Edward N. Hooker. Baltimore: Johns Hopkins University Press, 1943, 2:218–220.

Edmonds, J. M., trans. *The Greek Bucolic Poets.* London: Heinemann, 1912. Reprint. Cambridge, Mass.: Harvard University Press, 1928.

———, ed. and trans. *Lyra Graeca.* 3 vols. London: Heinemann; New York: G. P. Putnam's Sons, 1926–1928.

———, ed. and trans. *Elegy and Iambus.* 2 vols. London Heinemann; New York: G. P. Putnam's Sons, 1931.

Elliott, Robert C. *The Power of Satire: Magic, Ritual, Art.* Princeton, N.J.: Princeton University Press, 1960.

———. "The Definition of Satire: A Note on Method." *Yearbook of Comparative and General Literature* 11 (1962): 19–23.

Fairclough, H. Rushton, trans. *Horace: Satires, Epistles and Ars Poetica.* Cambridge, Mass.: Harvard University Press, 1932.

Feinberg, Leonard. *The Satirist: His Temperament, Motivation, and Influence.* Dubuque: Iowa State University Press, 1963.

Fox, W. Sherwood. "Cursing as a Fine Art." *Sewanee Review Quarterly* 27 (1919): 460–477.

Frye, Northrop. "The Nature of Satire." *University of Toronto Quarterly* 14 (1944–45): 75–89.

Hendrickson, George L. "The Dramatic Satura and the Old Comedy at Rome." *American Journal of Philology* 15, no. 1 (1894): 1–30.

———. "Archilochus and Catullus." *Classical Philology* 20 (1925): 155–157.

———. "Archilochus and the Victims of His Iambics." *American Journal of Philology* 56 (1925): 101–127.

———. "Satura Tota Nostra Est." In *Satire: Modern Essays in Criticism.* Edited by R. Paulson. Englewood Cliffs, N.J.: Prentice-Hall, 1971.

Highet, Gilbert. *The Anatomy of Satire.* Princeton, N.J.: Princeton University Press, 1962.

Hodgart, Matthew. *Satire.* New York: McGraw-Hill, 1969.

Jonson, Ben. *Peotaster.* Vol. 4 of *Ben Jonson.* 11 vols. Edited by C. H. Hereford and Percy Simpson. Oxford: Clarendon Press, 1932.

Kiley, Frederick, and J. M. Shuttleworth, eds. *Satire: From Aesop to Buchwald.* New York: Odyssey Press, 1971.

Lattimore, Richard, ed. and trans. *Greek Lyrics.* Chicago: University of Chicago Press, 1955.

Lewis, Wyndham. "The Greatest Satire is Nonmoral." In *Satire: Modern Essays in Criticism.* Edited by R. Paulson. Englewood Cliffs, N.J.: Prentice-Hall, 1971.

Leyburn, Ellen D. *Satiric Allegory: Mirror of Man*. New Haven: Yale University Press, 1956.

Ngugi, James. "Satire in Nigeria." In *Protest and Conflict in African Literature*. Edited by Cosmo Pieterse. London: Heinemann, 1969.

Paton, W. R., trans. *The Greek Anthology*. 5 vols. London: Heinemann; New York: G. P. Putnam's Sons, 1915–1919.

Paulson, Ronald. *The Fictions of Satire*. Baltimore: Johns Hopkins University Press, 1967.

———. *Satire: Modern Essays in Criticism*. Englewood Cliffs, N.J.: Prentice-Hall, 1971.

Petro, Peter. *Modern Satire: Four Studies*. Berlin: Mouton, 1982.

Ramage, Edwin S., et al. *Roman Satirists and Their Satire: A Fine Art of Criticism in Ancient Rome*. Park Ridge, N.J.: Noyes Press, 1974.

Ramsay, G. G., trans. *Juvenal and Persius*. London: Heinemann; New York: G. P. Putnam's Sons, 1918.

Randolph, Mary C. "The Medical Concept in English Renaissance Satiric Theory: Its Possible Relationships and Implications." *Studies in Philology* 38, no. 2 (1941): 125–157.

———. "The Structural Design of the Formal Verse Satire." *Philological Quarterly* 21, no. 4 (1942): 368–384.

Randolph, Thomas. "The Muses' Looking Glass." In *Poetical and Dramatic Works*. London: Reeves and Turner, 1875, 176–226.

Seidel, Michael. *Satiric Inheritance: Rabelais to Sterne*. Princeton, N.J.: Princeton University Press, 1979.

Thomson, James. *Satires and Profanities*. London: Progressive Publishing, 1884.

Ullman, B. L. "Satura and Satire." *Classical Philology* 8 (1913): 172–194.

Valle-Killeen, Suzanne D. *The Satiric Perspective: A Structural Analysis of Late Medieval, Early Renaissance Satiric Treatises*. New York: Senda Naeva de Ediciones, 1980.

Will, Frederic. *Archilochus*. New York: Twayne, 1969.

Worcester, David. *The Art of Satire*. Cambridge, Mass.: Harvard University Press, 1940.

THE BLACK

Image

Barker, Anthony J. *The African Link*. Totowa, N.J.: Frank Cass, 1978.

Bascom, W. R. "Eighteenth Century Slaves as Advertised by Their Masters." *Journal of Negro History* 1 (1916): 165–216.

Blassingame, John. *Slave Testimony*. Baton Rouge: Louisiana State University Press, 1976.

———. *The Slave Community*. Rev. and enl. ed. New York: Oxford University Press, 1979.

Bogle, D. *Toms, Coons, Mulattoes, Mammies and Bucks*. New York: Viking Press, 1973.

Boskin, Joseph. *Sambo: The Rise and Demise of an American Jester*. New York: Oxford University Press, 1986.

Brown, Sterling. "The Negro as Seen by White Authors." *Journal of Negro Education* 2, no. 1 (1938): 180–203.

Burch, Charles E. "Negro Characters in the Novels of William Simms." *Southern Workman* 52 (1923): 192–195.

Butcher, Margaret. *The Negro in American Culture*. New York: Alfred A. Knopf, 1956.

Cline, Julia. "The Rise of the American Stage Negro." *Drama* 21, no. 4 (1931): 9–10, 14.

Cripps, Thomas. *Slow Fade to Black: The Negro in American Film*. New York: Oxford University Press, 1977.

———. *Black Film as Genre*. Bloomington: Indiana University Press, 1978.

Davis, Charles T., and Henry L. Gates, Jr. *The Slave's Narrative*. New York: Oxford University Press, 1985.

Day, Charles H. *Fun in Black, or Sketches of Minstrel Life*. New York: De Witt, 1874.

DuBois, W.E.B. *The Souls of Black Folk*. New York: A. C. McClurg, 1903.

Fredrickson, George. "Master and Mudsills: The Role of Race in the Planter Ideology of South Carolina." *South Atlantic Studies* 2 (1978): 34–48.

Gates, Henry L., Jr. "The 'Blackness of Blackness': A Critique of the Sign and the Signifying Monkey." *Critical Inquiry* 9 (1983): 685–723.

———. *The Signifying Monkey: A Theory of Afro-American Literary Criticism*. New York: Oxford University Press, 1988.

Genovese, Eugene. "Rebellion and Docility in the Negro Slave." *Civil War History* 13, no. 4 (1967): 293–314.

George, Katharine. "The Civilized West Looks at Primitive Africa, 1400–1800." *The Concept of the Primitive*. Edited by A. Montagu. New York: Free Press, 1968.

Green, Alan W.C. " 'Jim Crow,' 'Zip Coon': The Northern Origins of Negro Minstrelsy." *Massachusetts Review* (Spring 1970): 385–397.

Harris, Joseph E., ed. *Africa and Africans as Seen by Classical Writers: The William Leo Hansberry African History Notebook*. Washington, D.C.: Howard University Press, 1977.

Henries, A. Doris Banks. "Black African Cultural Identity." *Presence Africaine* 101–102 (1977): 119–128.

Herskovits, M. *The American Negro: A Study in Racial Crossing*. New York: Alfred A. Knopf, 1928.

Lemons, Stanley J. "Black Stereotypes as Reflected in Popular Culture, 1880–1920." *American Quarterly* 29, no. 1 (1977): 102–116.

Linneham, Edward G. "We Wear Mask: The Use of Negro Life and Character in American Drama." Ph.D. diss., University of Pennsylvania, 1948.

Miller, Mark. "Bring Back Amos 'n' Andy." *Evening Sun* (Baltimore), April 3, 1986, p. A9.

Murdock, John. *Triumphs of Love; or, Happy Reconciliation*. Philadelphia: Folwell, 1795. Readex Microprint edition of Early American Imprints, no. 29129.

Muffett, D. J. "Uncle Remus Was a Hausa-man?" *Southern Folklore Quarterly* 39 (1975): 151–166.

Peterson, Thomas V. *Ham and Japheth: The Mythic World of Whites in the Antebellum South*. Metuchen, N.J.: Scarecrow Press and American Theological Library Association, 1978.

Rawick, George P. *From Sundown to Sunup: The Making of the Black Community*.

Vol. 1 of *The American Slave: A Composite Autobiography*. Westport, Conn.: Greenwood Press, 1972.

Read, Allen W. "The Speech of Negroes in Colonial America." *Journal of Negro History* 24 (July 1934): 247–258.

Rice, Edward Leroy. *Monarchs of Minstrelsy from Daddy Rice to Date*. New York: Kenny, 1911.

———. *Samboe, The African Boy*. London: Harvey and Darton, 1923.

Saxton, Alexander. "Blackface Minstrelsy and Jacksonian Ideology." *American Quarterly* 27, no. 1 (March 1975): 3–28.

Scott, Freda L. "Black Drama and the Harlem Renaissance." *Theatre Journal* 37, no. 4 (1985): 426–439.

Sherman, Alfonso. *The Diversity of Treatment of the Negro Character in American Drama, Prior to 1860*. Ann Arbor: UMI, 1965. 65–03518.

Shuster, Alvin. "British Debating 'Black Sambo.' " *New York Times*, May 1, 1972, p. 2.

Snowden, Frank. *Blacks in Antiquity: Ethiopians in the Greco-Roman Experience*. Cambridge, Mass.: Harvard University Press, 1970.

Soyinka, Wole. "The Mask of Blackness." Pilot script for projected television documentary series, "The Image of the Black in Western Imagination" (1981). Introduction by Henry L. Gates, Jr.

Stampp, Kenneth. "Rebels and Sambos: The Search for the Negro's Personality in Slavery." *The Journal of Southern History* 37, 3 (August 1971): 367–392.

Stoddard, Albert H. "Origin, Dialect, Beliefs and Characteristics of the Negroes of the South Carolina and Georgia Coasts." *Georgia Historical Quarterly* 28 (1944): 87–95.

Stowe, Harriet Beecher. *Uncle Tom's Cabin*. New York: Modern Library, 1948.

Toll, Robert C. *Blacking Up: The Minstrel Show in Nineteenth Century America*. New York: Oxford University Press, 1974.

Vercoutter, J. L., et al. *The Image of the Black in Western Art*. 2 vols. New York: William Morrow, 1976.

Wittke, Carl. *Tambo and Bones: A History of the American Minstrel Stage*. Durham, N.C.: Duke University Press, 1930.

Zins, Henryk. "Africa and the Africans in English Eyes of the Renaissance." *Kwartalnik Neofilologiczny* 25 (1978): 151–166.

Theatre

Adedeji, J. A. "The Alarinjo Theatre: The Study of a Yoruba Theatrical Art from Its Earliest Beginning to the Present Times." Ph.D. diss., University of Ibadan, 1969.

———. "Traditional Yoruba Theatre." *African Arts* 3, no. 1 (1969): 60–63.

———. "The Poetry of the Yoruba Masque Theatre." *African Arts* 11, no. 3 (1978): 62–64, 100.

Agovi, J. "Of Actors, Performers and Audience in Traditional African Drama." *Presence Africaine* 116 (1980): 141–158.

Bailey, A. Peter. "A Look at the Contemporary Black Theatre Movement." *Black American Literature Forum* 17, no. 1 (1983): 19–21.

Baraka, Amiri [Leroi Jones]. *Home and Social Essays*. New York: William Morrow, 1966.

———. "Negro Theater Pimps Get Big Off Nationalism." Introduction to *Jello*. Chicago: Third World Press, 1970.

———. "Black (Art) Drama Is the Same as Black Life." *Ebony* 26, no. 4 (1971): 74–82.

———. "Selected Plays and Prose of Amiri Baraka/Leroi Jones. New York: William Morrow, 1979.

Benston, Kimberly. *Baraka: The Renegade and the Mask*. New Haven: Yale University Press, 1976.

———. "The Aesthetics of Modern Black Drama: From Mimesis to Methexis." In *The Theater of Black Americans*. 2 vols. Edited by Errol Hill. Englewood Cliffs, N.J.: Prentice-Hall, 1980, 1:61–78.

Brady, Owen C. "Theodore Ward's *Our Lan'*: From Slavery of Melodrama to the Freedom of Tragedy." *Calaloo* 7, no. 2 (1984): 40–54.

Brown, Sterling. "Negro Poetry and Drama." *Bronze Booklet No. 7*. Washington, D.C.: Associates in Negro Folk Education, 1937.

Ceynowa, Andrzej. "The Dramatic Structure of *Dutchman*." *Black American Literature Forum* 17, no. 1 (1983): 15–21.

Clarke, W. H. *Travels and Explorations in Yorubaland (1856–58)*. Ibadan, Nigeria: University of Ibadan Press, 1972.

De Graft, J. C. "Roots in African Drama and Theatre." In *African Literature Today*, no. 8. Edited by Eldred D. Jones. London: Heinemann Educational Books, 1976.

Echeruo, M. J. "The Dramatic Limits of Igbo Ritual." *Research in African Literature* 4, no. 1 (1973): 21–31.

Elam, Harry J., Jr. "Ritual Theory and Political Theatre: 'Quinta Temporada' and 'Slave Ship.' " *Theatre Journal* 38, no. 4 (1986): 463–472.

Euba, Femi. "Manifestations of Eshu Elegba, the Yoruba Trickster Figure." M.A. thesis, Yale University, 1973.

———. "Of Masks and Men." Unpublished paper for seminar on "The Interrelationship of the Arts in Nigeria." University of Lagos, Centre for Cultural Studies, 1978.

Gayle, Addison, ed. *The Black Aesthetic*. New York: Doubleday, 1971.

———, ed. *Black Expression*. New York: Weybright and Talley, 1969.

Gotrick, Kacke. *Apidan Theatre and Modern Drama: A Study in a Traditional Yoruba Theatre and Its Influence on Modern Drama by Yoruba Playwrights*. Stockholm, Sweden: Almqvist and Wiksell International, 1984.

Granderson, Colin. "The Chief in Contemporary Black African Theatre of French Expression." In *Theatre in Africa*, edited by Oyin Ogunba and Abiola Irele. Ibadan, Nigeria: University of Ibadan Press, 1978.

Harrison, Paul Carter. *The Drama of Nommo*. New York: Grove Press, 1972.

Hatch, James V. "A White Folks Guide to 200 Years of Black and White Drama." *Drama Review* 16, no. 4 (1972): 5–24.

———, ed. *Black Theater U.S.A.: Forty-five Plays by Black Americans, 1867–1974*. New York: The Free Press, 1974.

Hill, Errol, ed. *The Theater of Black Americans: A Collection of Critical Essays*. 2 vols. Englewood Cliffs, N.J.: Prentice-Hall, 1980.

———. "The Revolutionary Tradition in Black Drama." *Theatre Journal* 38, no. 4 (1986): 408–426.

Hoch-Smith, Judith. "Yoruba Theatre in Ibadan: Performance and Urban Social Process." Ph.D. diss., McGill University, 1975.

Isaacs, Edith J.R. *The Negro in the Theatre*. New York: Theatre Arts, 1947.

Jeyifo, Biodun. *The Yoruba Popular Travelling Theatre of Nigeria*. Lagos, Nigeria: Nigeria Magazine, 1984.

Johnson, James W. *Black Manhattan*. New York: Alfred A. Knopf, 1930.

Jones, Eldred D., ed. *African Literature Today*. No. 8. London: Heinemann Educational Books, 1976.

Kirby, E. T. "Indigenous African Theatre." *Drama Review* 18 (December 1974): 22–35.

Mahood, M. M. "Drama in Newborn States." *Presence Africaine* (English ed.) 31, no. 60 (1966): 23–29.

Neal, Larry. "The Black Arts Movement." *Drama Review* 12, no. 4 (1968): 29–39.

Ogunba, Oyin, and Abiola Irele. *Theatre in Africa*. Ibadan, Nigeria: University of Ibadan Press, 1978.

Ogunbiyi, Yemi, ed. *Drama and Theatre in Nigeria*. Lagos, Nigeria: Nigeria Magazine, 1981.

Osofisan, B. A. "The Origins of Drama in West Africa: A Study of the Development of Drama from the Traditional Forms to Modern Theatre in English and French." Ph.D. dissertation. University of Ibadan, 1973.

Owomeyela, Oyekan. "Folklore and the Rise of Theatre Among the Yoruba." Ph.D. dissertation, UCLA.

Traore, Bakary. *The Black African Theatre and Its Social Functions*. Translated by Dapo Adelugba. Ibadan, Nigeria: University of Ibadan Press, 1972.

RELATED STUDIES

Books

Abimbola, Wande, ed. *Yoruba Oral Tradition: Poetry in Music, Dance and Drama*. Ile-Ife, Nigeria: University of Ife, 1975.

Abraham, R. C. *Dictionary of Modern Yoruba*. London: University of London Press, 1958.

Abrahams, Roger D. *Deep Down in the Jungle. . . : Negro Narrative Folklore from the Streets of Philadelphia*. Rev. ed. Chicago: Aldine, 1970.

Armstrong, Robert P. *The Powers of Presence: Consciousness, Myth, and Affecting Presence*. Philadelphia: University of Pennsylvania Press, 1981.

Artaud, Antonin. *The Theatre and Its Double*. Translated by M. C. Richard. New York: Grove Press, 1958.

Avery, Catherine B., ed. *New Century Classical Handbook*. New York: Appleton-Century-Crofts, 1962.

Awolalu, J. O. *Yoruba Beliefs and Sacrificial Rites*. London: Longman, 1979.

Babalola, S. A. *The Content and Form of Yoruba Ijala*. London: Oxford University Press, 1966.

Baraka, Amiri [LeRoi Jones]. *Blues People: Negro Music in White America*. New York: William Morrow, 1963.

Bascom, W. R. *Shango in the New World*. Austin, Tex.: African and Afro-American Research Institute, 1972.

———. *The Sociological Role of the Yoruba Cult Group. Memoirs of the American Anthropological Association* 46 (January 1944).

————. *The Yoruba of Southwestern Nigeria*. Prospect Heights, Ill.: Waveland Press, 1984.

Bastide, Roger. *The African Religions of Brazil*. Translated by Helen Sebba. Baltimore: Johns Hopkins University Press, 1978.

Baudin, M. *Fetishism and Fetish Worshippers*. New York: Benzinger Brothers, 1885.

Beattie, John, and John Middleton, eds. *Spirit Mediumship and Society in Africa*. London: Routledge and Kegan Paul, 1969.

Beier, H. U. *Yoruba Poetry*. London: Cambridge University Press, 1970.

————. *Yoruba Myths*. New York: Cambridge University Press, 1980.

Beier, H. U., and B. Gbadamosi, trans. *Yoruba Poetry*. Ibadan, Nigeria: Ministry of Education, 1959.

Belasco, Bernard. *The Entrepreneur as Culture Hero: Preadaptations on Nigeria Economic Development*. New York: J. F. Bergin, 1980.

Blassingame, John. *Black New Orleans*. Chicago: University of Chicago Press, 1973.

Boas, Franz, ed. *General Anthropology*. Boston: D. C. Heath, 1938.

Booth, Newell S., Jr., ed. *African Religions: A Symposium*. New York: Nok, 1977.

Bourke, V. J. *Ethics: A Textbook in Moral Philosophy*. New York: Macmillan, 1966.

Bramly, Serge. *Macumba*. Translated by Meg Bogin. New York: St. Martin's Press, 1977.

Brockett, Oscar. *History of the Theatre*. Boston: Allyn and Bacon, 1974.

Brook, Peter. *The Empty Space*. New York: Avon Books, 1968.

Brown, Norman O. *Hermes the Thief: An Evolution of a Myth*. Madison: University of Wisconsin Press, 1947.

Brown, Thomas A. *A History of the New York Stage from First Performance in 1732 to 1901*. 3 vols. New York: Benjamin Blom, 1903.

Cassirer, Ernst. *Language and Myth*. Translated by S. K. Langer. New York: Dover, 1946.

Chase, Richard V. *Quest for Myth*. Baton Rouge: Louisiana State University Press, 1949.

Christy, E. P. *Christy's Panorama Songster*. New York: Murphy, 1850.

————. *Christy's Plantation Melodies No. 4*. Philadelphia: Fisher, 1854.

Cole, David. *The Theatrical Event*. Middletown, Conn.: Wesleyan University Press, 1975.

Cornford, Francis M. *The Origin of Attic Comedy*. (Garden City, N.Y.: Doubleday, 1961).

Corrigan, R. W., ed. *Comedy: Meaning and Form*. San Francisco: Chandler, 1965.

————. *Theatre in Search of a Fix*. New York: Dell, 1973.

Crowley, Daniel. *African Folklore in the New World*. Austin: University of Texas Press, 1977.

Curtin, Philip D. *Africa Remembered: Narrative by West Africans from the Era of Slave Trade*. Madison: University of Wisconsin Press, 1967.

————. *The Atlantic Slave Trade: A Census*. Madison: University of Wisconsin Press, 1969.

Davidson, Basil. *The African Genius*. Boston: Little, Brown, 1969.

Davis, D. B. *The Problem of Slavery in Western Culture*. Ithaca, N.Y.: Cornell University Press, 1966.

Delano, I. O. *Atumo Ede Yoruba* (Meaning of Yoruba Words). London: Oxford University Press, 1958.

————. *Owe L'esin Oro* (Yoruba Proverbs). Ibadan, Nigeria: Oxford University Press, 1966.

Deren, Maya. *Divine Horsemen: Voodoo Gods of Haiti.* New York: Dell, 1970.

Dillard, D. L. *Black English.* New York: Vintage Books, 1973.

Dorson, Richard M. *American Negro Folktales.* New York: Fawcett World Library, 1956.

Drewal, Henry J., and Margaret T. Drewal. *Gelede: Art and Female Power Among the Yoruba.* Bloomington: Indiana University Press, 1983.

Elder, J. D. *The Yoruba Ancestor Cult in Gasparillo.* Trinidad: University of West Indies, St. Augustine Branch, Institute of Social and Economic Research, 1969.

Eliade, Mircea. *Mephistopheles and the Androgyne: Studies in Religious Myth and Symbol.* Translated by J. M. Cohen. New York: Sheed and Ward, 1965.

Elkins, Stanley M. *Slavery: A Problem in American Institutional and Intellectual Life.* Chicago: University of Chicago Press, 1959.

Ellis, A. B. *The Yoruba-Speaking Peoples of the Slave Coast of West Africa.* London: Chapman and Hall, 1894.

Ellman, Richard, and C. Feidelson, eds. *The Modern Tradition.* New York: Oxford University Press, 1965.

Epega, D. O. *The Basis of Yoruba Religion.* Lagos, Nigeria: Ijamido Printers, 1932.

Evans-Pritchard, E. E. *The Zande Trickster.* Oxford: Clarendon Press, 1967.

Fadipe, N. A. *The Sociology of the Yoruba.* Ibadan, Nigeria: University of Ibadan Press, 1970.

Fauset, Arthur H. *Black Gods of the Metropolis: Negro Religious Cults in the Urban North.* Philadelphia: University of Pennsylvania Press, 1971.

Faust, Drew G. *The Ideology of Slavery.* Baton Rouge: Louisiana State University Press, 1981.

Feldman, Susan. *African Myths and Tales.* New York: Dell, 1963.

Ferguson, John, ed. *The Yorubas of Nigeria.* Buckinghamshire, England: Open University Press, 1970.

Foner, Eric. *Free Soil, Free Labor, Free Men: The Ideology of the Republican Party Before the Civil War.* New York: Oxford University Press, 1970.

Franklin, John H. *From Slavery to Freedom: A History of Negro Americans.* 3rd ed. New York: Vintage Books, 1969.

Frazer, J. G. *The Golden Bough: A Study in Magic and Religion.* 12 vols. 1911. Reprint. London: Macmillan, 1966.

Frobenius, Leo. *The Voice of Africa.* 2 vols. London: Hutchinson, 1913.

Frye, Northrop. *Anatomy of Criticism: Four Essays.* Princeton, N.J.: Princeton University Press, 1957.

Gassner, John, and Edward Quinn. *The Reader's Encyclopedia of World Drama.* New York: Thomas Y. Crowell, 1969.

Gaster, Theodor H. *Thespis: Ritual, Myth and Drama in the Ancient Near East.* New and revised ed. New York: Harper and Row, 1966.

Genovese, Eugene D. *The World the Slaveholders Made.* New York: Pantheon Books, 1969.

————. *Roll, Jordan, Roll.* New York: Pantheon Books, 1974.

Gibbs, James, ed. *Critical Perspectives on Wole Soyinka.* Washington, D.C.: Three Continents Press, 1980.

Gilman, Richard. *The Making of Modern Drama.* New York: Farrar, Straus and Giroux, 1972.

Gleason, Judith. *Orisha: The Gods of Yorubaland.* New York: Atheneum, 1971.

Gonzalez-Wippler, M. *Santeria: African Magic in Latin America.* New York: Julian Press, 1973.

Grotowski, Jerzy. *Toward a Poor Theatre.* New York: Simon and Schuster, 1968.

Harrison, Jane. *Ancient Art and Ritual.* New York: Holt, 1913.

Hartnoll, Phyllis, ed. *The Oxford Companion to the Theatre.* 2nd ed. London: Oxford University Press, 1957.

Harwood, Ronald, ed. *A Night at the Theatre.* London: Methuen, 1982.

Haskins, James. *Witchcraft, Mysticism and Magic in the Black World.* New York: Doubleday, 1974.

Hastings, James, ed. *Encyclopedia of Religion and Ethics.* 12 vols. New York: Charles Scribner's Sons, 1908–1926.

Herskovits, M. *The New World Negro.* Bloomington: University of Indiana Press, 1966.

——. *Dahomey.* 2 vols. Evanston: Northwestern University Press, 1967.

——. *The Myth of the Negro Past.* Boston: Beacon Press, 1967.

Idowu, Bolaji. *Olodumare: God in Yoruba Belief.* London: Longmans, Green, 1962.

Jahn, Jahnheinz. *Muntu: An Outline of the New African Culture.* Translated by Majoire Grene. New York: Grove Press, 1961.

Jenkins, W. S. *Proslavery Thought in the Old South.* Chapel Hill: University of North Carolina Press, 1935.

Johnson, S. *The History of the Yorubas.* London: Routledge and Kegan Paul, 1921.

Joyner, Charles. *Down by the Riverside: A South Carolina Slave Community.* Urbana and Chicago: University of Illinois Press, 1984.

Kardiner, Abram, and Lionel Ouesey. *The Mark of Oppression: A Psychological Study of the American Negro.* New York: Norton, 1951.

Kern, Edith. *The Absolute Comic.* New York: Columbia University Press, 1980.

Kingsley, Mary. *Travels in West Africa.* London: Cass, 1965.

Kirk-Green, A.H.M. *Crisis and Conflict in Nigeria: A Documentary Sourcebook, 1966–1969.* 2 vols. London: Oxford University Press, 1971.

Kopytoff, J. H. *A Preface to Modern Nigeria.* Madison: University of Wisconsin Press, 1965.

Kott, Jan. *Theatre of Essence.* Evanston: Northwestern University Press, 1984.

Lambo, T. A. *African Traditional Beliefs: A Concept of Health and Medical Practice.* A Philosophical Society Lecture. Ibadan, Nigeria: University of Ibadan Press, 1963.

Lander, R. L. *The Niger Journal of Richard and John Lander.* London: Routledge and Kegan Paul, 1965.

Leach, Maria, ed. *Standard Dictionary of Folklore, Mythology and Legend.* 3rd ed. New York: Funk and Wagnalls, 1972.

Linfors, Bernth, ed. *Forms of Folklore in Africa: Narrative, Poetic, Gnomic, Dramatic.* Austin: University of Texas Press, 1977.

Lloyd, Peter C. *The Political Development of Yoruba Kingdoms in the Eighteenth and Nineteenth Centuries.* London: Royal Anthropological Institute, 1971.

——. *Power and Independence: Urban Africans' Perception of Social Inequality.* London: Routledge and Kegan Paul, 1974.

Loveland, Anne. *Southern Evangelicals and the Social Order, 1800–1860*. Baton Rouge: Louisiana State University Press, 1980.

Lowery-Palmer, Alma. *Yoruba Worldview and Patient Compliance*. Ann Arbor: UMI, 1980. 802–998.

Lucas, J. Olumide. *The Religion of the Yorubas*. Lagos, Nigeria: C.M.S. Bookshop, 1948.

———. *Religions in West Africa and Ancient Egypt*. Lagos, Nigeria: Nigerian National Press, 1970.

Lumley, Frederick E. *Means of Social Control*. New York: Century, 1925.

Mabogunje, A. L. *Urbanization in Nigeria*. London: University of London Press, 1966.

Mbiti, John S. *African Religions and Philosophy*. New York: Praeger, 1969.

McKitrick, E. L. *Slavery Defended: The Views of the Old South*. Englewood Cliffs, N.J.: Prentice-Hall, 1963.

Morgan, Kemi. *The Myth of Yoruba Ancestry*. Ibadan, Nigeria: Sketch Publishing, n.d.

Muecke, D. C. *The Compass of Irony*. London: Methuen, 1969.

Mullin, Michael, ed. *American Negro Slavery: A Documentary History*. New York: Harper and Row, 1976.

Nascimento, Abdias do. *"Racial Democracy" in Brazil: Myth or Reality?* Translated by Elisa Larkin do Nascimento. Ibadan, Nigeria: Sketch Publishing, 1977.

Nathan, Nans. *Dan Emmett and the Rise of Early Minstrelsy*. Norman: University of Oklahoma Press, 1962.

Nietzsche, F. "The Birth of Tragedy." In *The Philosophy of Nietzsche*. Translated by C. P. Fadiman. New York: Random House, 1927.

Oduyoye, Modupe. *The Vocabulary of Yoruba Religious Discourse*. Ibadan, Nigeria: Daystar Press, 1971.

Ojo, G.J.A. *Yoruba Culture: A Geographical Analysis*. Ile-Ife, Nigeria: University of Ife Press; London: University of London Press, 1966.

Osofsky, Gilbert. *Puttin' On Ole Massa: The Slave Narratives of Henry Bibb, William Wells Brown and Solomon Northup*. New York: Harper and Row, 1969.

Oswalt, Sabine. *Concise Encyclopedia of Greek and Roman Mythology*. Chicago: Follett, 1965.

Ottley, Roi, and William Weatherby. *The Negro in New York*. New York: New York Public Library, 1967.

Parrinder, Geoffrey. *Religion in an African City*. London: Oxford University Press, 1953.

———. *Religion in Africa*. London: Penguin, 1969.

———. *African Traditional Religion*. Westport, Conn.: Negro Universities Press, 1970.

Peel, J.D.Y. *Aladura: A Religious Movement*. London: Oxford University Press for International African Institute, 1968.

Ploski, H. A., and J. Williams, eds. *The Negro Almanac: A Reference Work on the Afro-American*. 4th ed. New York: John Wiley and Sons, 1983.

Puckett, Newbell N. *Folk Beliefs of the Southern Negro*. Monclair, N.J.: Patterson Smith, 1968.

Raboteau, Albert. *Slave Religion: The "Invisible Institution" in the Antebellum South*. New York: Oxford University Press, 1978.

Radin, Paul. *The Trickster: A Study in American Indian Mythology*. London: Routledge and Kegan Paul, 1956.

Ray, Benjamin C. *African Religions*. Englewood Cliffs, N.J.: Prentice-Hall, 1976.

Roach, Hildred. *Black American Music: Past and Present*. 2 vols. Melbourne, Fla.: Robert E. Krieger Publishing, 1985.

Roberts, John S. *Black Music of Two Worlds*. New York: Praeger, 1972.

Schechner, Richard, and M. Schumann, eds. *Ritual, Play and Performance: Readings in the Social Sciences/Theatre*. New York: Seabury Press, 1976.

Sedgewick, G. G. *Of Irony, Especially in Drama*. Toronto: University of Toronto Press, 1935.

Sills, David L., ed. *International Encyclopedia of the Social Sciences*. 17 vols. New York: Macmillan and the Free Press, 1968.

Simpson, George E. *Black Religions in the New World*. New York: Columbia University Press, 1978.

Singer, Andre, and Brian V. Street, eds. *Zande Themes: Essays Presented to Sir Edward Evans-Pritchard*. Totowa, N.J.: Rowman and Littlefield, 1972.

Smith, Robert. *Kingdoms of the Yoruba*. London: Methuen, 1969.

Snell, Bruno. *The Discovery of the Mind: The Greek Origins of European Thought*. Translated by T. G. Rosenmeyer. Cambridge, Mass.: Harvard University Press, 1953.

Sobel, Mechal. *Trabelin' On: The Slave Journey to Afro-Baptist Faith*. Westport, Conn.: Greenwood Press, 1979.

Sowande, Fela. *Ifa: Guide, Counselor and Friend of Our Forefathers*. Yaba, Nigeria: Forward Press, 1965.

Soyinka, Wole. *Myth, Literature and the African World*. Cambridge, England: Cambridge University Press, 1976.

Swain, Barbara. *Fools and Folly During the Middle Ages and the Renaissance*. New York: Columbia University Press, 1932.

Tallant, Robert. *Voodoo in New Orleans*. New York: Macmillan-Collier Books, 1962.

Thompson, Robert F. *African Art in Motion*. Los Angeles: University of California Press, 1974.

———. *Flash of the Spirit: African and Afro-American Art and Philosophy*. New York: Random House, 1983.

Tripp, Edward. *Crowell's Handbook of Classical Mythology*. New York: Thomas Y. Crowell, 1970.

Verger, Pierre. *Notes sur le culte des Orisa et Vodun a Bahie de tous les Saints, au Bresil et a l'ancienne Cote des Esclaves en Afrique. Memoires de L'Institut Français D'Afrique Noire*, No. 51. Dakar: IFAN, 1957.

Weatherford, W. D. *The Negro from Africa to America*. New York: George H. Doran, 1924.

Welsford, Enid. *The Fool: His Social and Literary History*. Gloucester, Mass.: P. Smith, 1966.

Williams, Raymond. *Keywords: A Vocabulary of Culture and Society*. New York: Oxford University Press, 1976.

Wood, Peter. *Black Majority: Negroes in Colonial South Carolina, from 1670 through the Stono Rebellion*. New York: Alfred A. Knopf, 1974.

Yonah, Michael A., and Israel Shatzma, eds. *Illustrated Encyclopedia of the Classical World*. New York: Harper and Row, 1975.

Articles

Abimbola, Wande. "Yoruba Traditional Religion." In *Contemplation and Action in World Religions,* edited by Yusuf Ibish and I. Marculescu. Houston: Rothko Chapel Books, 1978.

Abiodun, Rowland. "Identity and the Artistic Process in the Yoruba Aesthetic Concept of Iwa." *Journal of Culture and Ideas* 1, no. 1 (December 1983): 13–27.

———. "Verbal Metaphors: Mythical Allusions in Yoruba Ritualistic Art of Ori." Seminar series, Institute of Cultural Studies, University of Ife, June 1985.

Abrahams, Roger D. "Trickster, the Outrageous Hero." In *Our Living Traditions,* edited by Tristram Potter Coffin. New York: Basic Books, 1968, 170–178.

Akinjogbin, I. A. "The Prelude to the Yoruba Civil Wars of the Nineteenth Century." *Odu* 1, no. 2 (1965).

Apronti, E. O. "The Tyranny of Time: The Theme of Time in the Artistic Consciousness of South African Writers." *African Literature Today* 8 (1976): 106–114.

Bamgbose, Ayo. "The Meaning of Olodumare: An Etymology of the Name of the Yoruba High God." *African Notes* 7, no. 1 (1972–73): 25–32.

Bascon, W. R. "Social Status, Wealth and Individual Differences Among the Yoruba." *Memoirs of the American Anthropological Association* 53 (1951): 490–505.

———. "The Esusu: A Credit Institution Among the Yoruba." *Journal of the Royal Anthropological Institute* 82 (1952): 67–70.

Beier, H. U. "The Historical and Psychological Significance of Yoruba Myths." *Odu* 1 (1955): 17–25.

Biebuyck, D. P. "Textual and Contextual Analysis in African Art Studies." *African Arts* 8, no. 3 (1975).

Biobaku, S. O. "Myths and Oral History." *Odu* 1 (1955): 12–17.

Bishop, Charles C. "The Proslavery Argument Reconsidered: James Henley Thornwell (1812–1862), Millennial Abolitionist." *South Carolina Historical Magazine* 73, no. 1 (1972): 18–26.

Buckley, Anthony D. "The Secret: An Idea in Yoruba Medicinal Thought." In *Social Anthropology and Medicine,* edited by J. B. Loudon. New York: Academic Press, 1976; Association of Social Anthropologists, monograph 13, 1976.

Carroll, K. L. "Religious Influences on the Manumission of Slaves in Caroline, Dorchester and Talbot Counties." *Maryland Historical Magazine* 56, no. 2 (1961): 176–197.

Chappel, T.J.H. "The Yoruba Cult of Twins in Historical Perspective." *Africa* 44, no. 3 (1974): 250–265.

Crowley, Daniel. "The Traditional Masques of Carnival." *Caribbean Quarterly* 4 (1956): 194–223.

Dorson, Richard M. "The African Connection: Comment on African Folklore in the New World." *Research in African Literature* 8 (1977): 260–265.

Drewal, Henry J. "Efe/Gelede: The Educative Role of the Arts in Traditional Yoruba Culture." Ph.D. diss., Columbia University, 1973.

Ellis, A. B. "Evolution in Folklore: Some West African Prototypes of the Uncle Remus Stories." *Popular Science Monthly* 58 (1895): 93–104.

Faust, Drew G. "Evangelism and the Meaning of the Proslavery Argument." *Virginia Magazine of History and Biography* 85, no. 1 (1977): 3–17.

————. "A Southern Stewardship: The Intellectual and the Proslavery Argument." *Virginia Magazine* 85 (1977): 3–17.

Fox, Robert. "Blacking the Zero: Toward a Semiotics of New-Hoodoo." *Black American Literature Forum* 18, no. 3 (Fall 1984): 95–99.

Goines, Leonard. "African Music in the Americas." *Black Books Bulletin* 5, no. 1 (1977): 8–13.

Gordon, Jacob U. "Yoruba Cosmology and Culture in Brazil: A Study of African Survivals in the New World." *Journal of Black Studies* 10, no. 2 (1979): 231–244.

Herskovits, M. "Freudian Mechanism in Primitive Negro Psychology." In *Essays Presented to Seligman,* edited by E. E. Evans-Pritchard, 1934.

————. "African Gods and Catholic Saints in New World Negro Belief." *American Anthropologist* n.s. 39, no. 4 (1968): 635–643.

Horton, Robin. "Ritual Man in Africa." *Africa* 34, no. 2 (1964): 85–103.

————. "African Conversion." *Africa* 41, no. 2 (1971): 85–108.

Houlberg, Marilyn. "Ibeji Images of the Yoruba." *African Arts* 7, no. 1 (1973): 20–27, 91.

————. "Notes on Egungun Masquerades Among the Oyo Yoruba." *African Arts* 11, no. 3 (1978): 56–61, 99.

Ibigbami, R. I. "The Sacred Images of Ogun in Ire Ekiti." *Odu* 16 (1977): 104–110.

————. "Ogun Festival in Ire Ekiti." *Nigeria Magazine* 126–127 (1978): 44–59.

Jung, C. G. "On the Psychology of the Trickster Figure." In Paul Radin, *The Trickster.* London: Routledge and Kegan Paul, 1956, 195–211.

Kerenyi, Karl. "The Trickster in Relation to Greek Mythology." In Paul Radin, *The Trickster.* London: Routledge and Kegan Paul, 1956, 173–191.

Kolchin, Peter. "In Defense of Servitude: American Proslavery and Russian Proserfdom Arguments, 1760–1860." *American Historical Review* 85 (1980): 809–827.

Landes, Ruth. "Fetish Worship in Brazil." *Journal of American Folklore* 53 (1940): 261–270.

La Pin, Deirdre. "Tale and Trickster in Yoruba Verbal Art." *Research in African Literature* 11 (1980): 327–341.

Lawal, B. "The Living Dead: Art and Immortality Among the Yoruba of Nigeria." *Africa* 47, no. 1 (1977): 50–61.

Layard, John. "Note on the Autonomous Psyche and the Ambivalence of the Trickster Concept." *Journal of Analytical Psychology* 3, no. 1 (1958): 21–28.

Leach, Edmund. "Magical Hair." *Journal of the Royal Anthropological Institute* 138, no. 2 (1958): 147–165.

Lloyd, Peter C. "The Yoruba Lineage." *Africa* 25 (1955): 235–251.

————. "Yoruba Myths: A Sociologist's Interpretation." *Odu* 2 (1955): 20–39.

Magel, Emil A. "The Source of Bascom's Wolof Analogue: 'Trickster Seeks Endowments.' " *Research in African Literature* 10 (1979): 350–358.

Metman, Philip. "The Trickster Figure in Schizophrenia." *Journal of Analytical Psychology* 3, no. 1 (1958): 5–20.

Mischel, F. "African Power in Trinidad: The Shango Cult." *Anthropological Quarterly* 30, no. 2 (1957): 45–59.

Moore, Janie G. "Africanisms Among Blacks of the Sea Islands." *Journal of Black Studies* 10 (1980): 467–480.

Morrow, R. F. "The Proslavery Argument Revisited." *Mississippi Valley Historical Review* 47 (1961): 79–94.

Morton-Williams, Peter. "The Yoruba Ogboni Cult in Oyo." *Africa* 30, no. 4 (1960): 362–374.

———. "Yoruba Responses to the Fear of Death." *Africa* 30 (1960): 34–40.

———. "Outline of the Cosmology and Cult Organisation of the Oyo Yoruba." *Africa* 34 (1964): 243–261.

———. et al. "Two Studies of Ifa Divination." *Africa* 36, no. 4 (1966): 406–431.

Ogunba, Oyin, "The Agemo Cult in Ijebuland." *Nigeria Magazine* 86 (1965): 176–186.

———. "Ritual Drama of the Ijebu People: A Study of Indigenous Festivals." Ph.D. diss., University of Ibadan, 1967.

Olajubu, (Chief) O., and J.R.O. Ojo. "Some Aspects of Oyo Yoruba Masqueraders." *Africa* 47, no. 3 (1977): 253–275.

Olaniyan, R. "Element of Yoruba Diplomacy in Oral Tradition." In *Yoruba Oral Tradition*, edited by W. Abimbola. Ile-Ife, Nigeria: University of Ife, 1975.

Olatunji, Olatunde. "Iyere Ifa." *African Notes* 7, no. 2 (1972–73): 69–86.

Oluwole, Sophie. "On the Existences of Witches." *Second Order* 7, no. 1–2 (1978): 2035.

Osoba, Segun. "The Nigerian Power Elite, 1952–65." In *African Social Studies*, edited by P. Gutkind and P. Waterman. New York: Monthly Review Press, 1977, 368–382.

Pollak-Eltz, Angelina. "The Yoruba Religion and Its Decline in the Americas." *International Congress of Americanists* 38 (1968): Part 3.

Prince, Raymond. "The Yoruba Image of the Witch." *Journal of Mental Science* 107, no. 449 (July 1969): 795–805.

Roediger, D. "The Meaning of Africa for the American Slave." *Journal of Ethnic Studies* 4, no. 4 (1977): 1–15.

Shreve, Gregory M., and Ojo Arewa. "Form and Content in African Folklore Classification: A Semiotic Perspective." *Research in African Literature* 11 (1980): 286–296.

Siegel, Fred. "The Paternalist Thesis: Virginia as a Test Case." *Civil War History* 35, no. 1 (1979): 246–261.

Smith, A. Adeyemi. "African Religion in the Americas." *African Mirror* (June–July 1979): 33–40.

Thompson, Robert F. "The Sign of the Divine King." *African Arts* 3, no. 3 (1970): 8–17, 74–80.

———. "Yoruba Artistic Criticism." In *The Traditional Artist in Africa*, edited by Warren L. d'Azevedo. Bloomington: Indiana University Press, 1973.

———. "Icons of the Mind." *African Arts* 8, no. 3 (1975): 52–59, 89.

———. "An Aesthetic of the Cool." *African Arts* 7, no. 3 (1976): 41–43, 62–67, 89.

Trotman, D. V. "The Yoruba and Orisha Worship in Trinidad and British Guiana, 1838–70" *African Studies Review* 19, no. 2 (1976): 1–17.

Usman, Yusufu Bala, et al. "Debate on the Nigerian Economic Crisis." *Studies in Politics and Society* 2 (1984).

Verger, Pierre. "Yoruba Influences in Brazil." *Odu* 1 (1955): 3–11.

———. "The High God." *Odu* 2, no. 2 (1966): 1940.

————. "Iyami Osoronga (My Mother the Witch)." Seminar paper, University of Ife, Nigeria, 1977.

————. "The Status of Yoruba Religion in Brazil." *Kiabara* 2 (1978): 59–79.

Walker, Sheila S. "African Gods in the Americas: The Black Religious Continuum." *Black Scholar* 11, no. 8 (1980): 25–36.

Williams, Denis. "The Iconology of the Yoruba Edan Ogboni." *Africa* 34, no. 2 (1964): 139–165.

Yarbrough, Camille. "Black Dance in America." *Black Collegian* 11, no. 5 (April–May 1981): 10–24.

Plays

Aldridge, Ira. *The Black Doctor.* In *Black Theater U.S.A.: Forty-five Plays by Black Americans, 1847–1974,* edited by James V. Hatch. New York: The Free Press, 1974.

Baldwin, James. *The Amen Corner.* In *Black Theater: A Twentieth Century Collection of the Work of Its Best Playwrights,* edited by L. Patterson. New York: New American Library, 1971.

Baraka, Amiri [Leroi Jones]. *Two Plays by Leroi Jones: Dutchman and The Slave.* New York: Morrow Quill Paperbacks, 1964.

————. *A Black Mass.* In *Four Revolutionary Plays.* Indianapolis: Bobbs-Merrill, 1969.

————. *Jello.* Chicago: Third World Press, 1970.

Carril, Pepe. *Shango de Ima: A Yoruba Mystery Play.* New York: Doubleday, 1970.

Cesaire, Aime. *The Tragedy of King Christophe.* Translated by R. Manheim. New York: Grove Press, 1969.

Fugard, Athol, John Kani, and Winston Nrshona *Sizwe Bansi Is Dead.* In *Sizwe Bansi Is Dead and The Island.* New York: Viking Penguin, 1976.

Garrett, Jimmy. *And We Own the Night.* In *Drama Review* 12, no. 4 (Summer 1968): 62–69.

Glissant, Edouard. *Monsieur Toussaint.* Translated by J. G. Foster and B. A. Franklin. Washington, D.C.: Three Continents Press, 1981.

Hansberry, Lorraine. *A Raisin in the Sun.* New York: Random House/Alfred A. Knopf, 1966.

Harrison, Paul Carter. *The Great MacDaddy.* In *Kuntu Drama,* edited by P. C. Harrison: New York: Grove Press, 1974.

Hughes, Langston. *Tambourines to Glory.* In *Five Plays by Langston Hughes,* edited by W. Smalley. Bloomington: University of Indiana Press, 1968.

Hussein, Ebrahim. *Kinjeketile.* Dar-es-Salaam: Oxford University Press, 1969.

Ijimere, Obotunde. *The Imprisonment of Obatala.* In *The Imprisonment and Other Plays,* edited by Ulli Beier. London: Heinemann Educational Books, 1966.

James, C.L.R. *The Black Jacobins.* In *A Time . . . and a Season: Eight Caribbean Plays,* edited by Errol Hill. Trinidad: University of West Indies Extramural Studies Unit, 1976.

Kalejaiye, Dipo. *The Creator and the Disrupter.* Calabar, Nigeria: Centaur Press, 1982.

Kennedy, Adrienne. *Funny House of a Negro.* In *Contemporary Black Drama,* edited by Clinton C. Oliver. New York: Charles Scribner's Sons, 1971, 187–205.

Ladipo, Duro. *Oba Koso* (The King Did Not Hang). In *Three Yoruba Plays,* translated by Ulli Beier. Ibadan, Nigeria: Mbari Publications, 1964.

Mtwa, Percy, Mbongeni Ngema, and Barney Simon. *Woza Albert.* In *Woza Africa!: An Anthology of South African Plays,* edited by Duma Ndlovu. New York: George Braziller, 1986.

Mukando, Peniah. *Tambueni Haki Zetus.* Translated by L. A. Mbughuni. Dar-es-Salaam: Tanzania Publishing House, 1973.

Nascimento, Abdias do. *Sortilege* (Black Mystery). Translated by Peter Lownds. Chicago: Third World Press, 1978.

Njau, Rebecca. *The Scar.* Nairobi: Kibo Art Gallery, 1965.

Nkosi, Lewis. *The Rhythm of Violence.* In *Plays from Black Africa,* edited by Fredric M. Litto. New York: Hill and Wang, 1968.

Ogunyemi, Wale. *Eshu Elegbara.* Ibadan, Nigeria: Orisun Acting Editions, n.d.

Rotimi, Ola. *The Gods Are Not to Blame.* London: Oxford University Press, 1971.

———. *Ovonramwen Nogbaisi.* Benin, Nigeria: Ethiope Publishing; Ibadan, Nigeria: Oxford University Press, 1974.

Rugyendo, Mukotani. *The Barbed Wire and Other Plays.* London: Heinemann Educational Books, 1977.

Seljam, Zora. *The Story of Oxala: The Feast of Bomfim.* London: Rex Collings, 1978.

Soyinka, Wole. *A Dance of the Forests.* London: Oxford University Press, 1973.

Soyinka, Wole. *Collected Plays.* 2 vols. London: Oxford University Press, 1973.

———. *Death and the King's Horseman.* London: Eyre Methuen, 1975.

———. *A Play of Giants.* London: Methuen, 1984.

Van Peebles, Melvin. *Aint Supposed to Die a Natural Death.* New York: Bantam Books, 1973.

Walcott, Derek. *Dream on Monkey Mountain and Other Plays.* New York: Farrar, Straus and Giroux, 1970.

Ward, Douglas Turner. *Day of Absence.* In *Two Plays.* New York: William Morrow, 1970.

Wa Thiong'o, Ngugi, and Micere Mugo. *The Trial of Dedan Kimathi.* London: Heinemann Educational Books, 1976.

Wilson, August. *Joe Turner's Come and Gone.* New York: New American Library, 1988.

Index

About the Author

FEMI EUBA is Artist-in-Residence in the English and Theatre Departments at Louisiana State University where he teaches modern drama, playwriting and acting. He has also taught and conducted research primarily in the area of comparative black drama. His scholarly articles have appeared in *Black American Literature Forum, Drama and Theatre in Nigeria, African Arts* and various anthologies. Euba is an active director and playwright.